The Disciples' Call

Si quis vult post me venire, abneget semetipsum, et tollat crucem suam quotidie, et sequatur me, luc. 9 . verf. 23 Qui dicit se in ipso manere debet ficut ille ambulauit, et ipso ambulare, 1. Johan. 2 . verse. 6.

Title page illustration from Theobald Stapleton's Latin and Gaelic *Catechism* dated 1639, with priests, religious and lay people following Christ. The two texts below it read:

If any man would come after me, let him deny himself and take up his cross daily and follow me. Luke 9:23

He who says he abides in him ought to walk in the same way in which he walked. 1 John 2:6

Reproduced by kind permission of the Trustees of Downside Abbey.

The Disciples' Call

Theologies of Vocation from Scripture to the Present Day

Edited by
Fr Christopher Jamison, O.S.B

B L O O M S B U R Y
LONDON · NEW DELHI · NEW YORK · SYDNEY

Bloomsbury T&T Clark

An imprint of Bloomsbury Publishing Plc

50 Bedford Square	1385 Broadway
London	New York
WC1B 3DP	NY 10018
UK	USA

www.bloomsbury.com

Bloomsbury is a registered trade mark of Bloomsbury Publishing Plc

First published 2013

British Library Cataloguing-in-Publication Data
A catalogue record for this book is available from the British Library.

ISBN: HB: 978-0-567-31099-6
ePDF: 978-1-472-55838-1
epub: 978-1-472-55837-4

Library of Congress Cataloging-in-Publication Data
Jamison, O.S.B, Christopher
The Disciples' Call/ Christopher Jamison, O.S.B p.cm
Includes bibliographic references and index.
ISBN 978-0-567-31099-6 (hardcover)

Typeset by Newgen Knowledge Works (P) Ltd., Chennai, India
Printed and bound in Great Britain

Contents

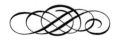

Contributors

Sr Cathy Jones is a Religious of the Assumption and Promoter of Religious Life in the National Office for Vocation of the Bishops' Conference of England and Wales.

Fr Christopher Jamison is a Benedictine monk and Director of the National Office for Vocation of the Bishops' Conference of England and Wales.

Very Rev. David Hoyle is an Anglican priest and Dean of Bristol, United Kingdom.

Sr Gemma Simmonds is a member of the Congregation of Jesus and Lecturer in Theology at Heythrop College, University of London, United Kingdom.

Abbot Geoffrey Scott is the Abbot of Douai and Lecturer in Church History at St John's Seminary, Wonersh and at Blackfriars, Oxford, United Kingdom.

Sr Gill Goulding is a member of the Congregation of Jesus and Associate Professor of Systematic Theology at Regis College, University of Toronto, Canada.

Fr John Hemer is a Mill Hill Missionary and Lecturer in Scripture at Allen Hall Seminary, London, United Kingdom.

Fr Joseph Bolin is a priest of the Archdiocese of Vienna and Lecturer in Theology at the International Theological Institute, Trumau, Austria.

Dr Peter Tyler is Reader in Pastoral Theology and Spirituality at St Mary's University College, Twickenham, London. He is the Director of the Centre for Initiatives in Spirituality and Reconciliation (InSpiRe).

Fr Richard Lennan is a priest of the Diocese of Maitland-Newcastle, Australia and Professor of Systematic Theology in the School of Theology and Ministry at Boston College, United States.

Fr Richard Price is a priest of the archdiocese of Westminster and Professor of the History of Christianity at Heythrop College, University of London, United Kingdom.

Dr Susan O'Brien is a Senior Member of St Edmund's College, University of Cambridge and former Principal of the Margaret Beaufort Institute of Theology, Cambridge, United Kingdom.

Fr Stephen Wang is a priest of the Diocese of Westminster and Senior University Chaplain within the Diocese.

Fr Yuriy Kolasa is a priest of the Ukrainian Greek-Catholic Church, Prefect of Formation at the International Theological Institute, Trumau, Austria and general vicar for the faithful of the Byzantine Rite in Austria.

Introduction

Fr Christopher Jamison

Everybody has a vocation

The simple phrase 'everybody has a vocation' is a common statement in religious conversations today. However, until the middle of the twentieth century, a Catholic man or woman with a vocation was on their way to the seminary or the convent and nowhere else. Even now, to say 'Mary has a vocation' is not met with the question 'who is she marrying?' but rather 'which order is she joining?' The contemporary confusion around the word 'vocation' highlights some of the current theological difficulties that surround the living out of Christian vocation.

This book seeks to clarify the confusion by offering a description of how vocation has been expressed in Christian lives, both in the history of the Church and in the life of the Church today. In technical terms, this book offers a theological anthropology of Christian vocation.

The root of the Christian vocation is Christ calling people to be disciples; from the early church onwards, the response to this call has been expressed through seeking baptism and entering into the life of the Church. This baptismal life leads people into many different paths to holiness, paths that Christians discover in communion with the Church through a process of discernment.

However, Christians and non-Christians alike can also baptize their own instincts, claim a personal attraction to a way of life or simply declare that God has shown them the way. Personal instinct, individual attraction and private revelation can become the guiding principles for declaring something to be 'my' vocation. Modern ideas of autonomy have taken over many people's approach to vocation, with the communal and divine aspects of vocation relegated to the margins.

This self-indulgence is to be distinguished from the search for the authentic self, the self Christ calls to self-giving in imitation of his own love. This self-giving requires knowing, however imperfectly, the self that is to be given away. The authentic self is the person to whom the call is addressed and the one called to be transformed in Christ. To help people hear this call, the Church needs to offer them a clear understanding of the Christian way of discerning vocation. This Christian way is not narcissistic but rather a way of discovery that leads people into a what Newman calls 'some definite service'.

Vocation before vocations

There is no shortage of studies on how to live out particular vocations; for example, priesthood, marriage and even certain jobs such as nurse or teacher. What has been noticeably absent in recent years has been a theology of vocation itself, a lack of reflection on the process by which the call of Christ is heard, the gateway to living out a particular call. Many who work in the field of vocations find that there is currently no shared language of vocation among Catholics in the developed, post-modern world of Europe and North America. This is a major hindrance in carrying out the Church's ministry of helping people to discern their vocation. The decline in practice of the faith and a weakened understanding of Church teaching has led to reduced numbers of people entering into marriage, religious life and priesthood in these continents. This lack of shared language of vocation makes reversing these trends difficult since an understanding of vocation is an essential part of evangelizing the young and deepening catechesis. A poor understanding of the call of Christ, vocation in the singular, can disable people from living out Christ's call to a specific way of life, vocations in the plural. This collection of essays offers a sustained reflection on the Christian understanding of vocation in the singular.

Part one looks at the foundations of vocational theology, leading into a conversation with key elements of the vocational tradition in the second part, and in part three the discernment of specific vocations today is considered.

The conclusion then suggests the practical steps needed to create a culture of vocation today.

Key questions

In reading these essays, the reader may find it helpful to keep in mind some key questions facing the theology of vocation today. In *Part One: The Foundations of Vocational Theology,* the biblical narratives raise the question of the connection between conversion and vocation; are they distinct or the same? The desert fathers and mothers have a vivid sense of vocation but is it the same as the contemporary understanding of a vocation to the consecrated life? This leads into the final essay in this section, which considers the question that underlies all vocational theology: what is the mission of the Church? This in turn raises questions about the shape of ministry, ordained ministry and lay ministry, as well as the relationship between the two within contemporary culture.

In *Part Two: Conversing with the Tradition,* St Thomas Aquinas sees the religious life as the surest way to live out the evangelical counsels of poverty, chastity and obedience. So for Thomas, it is evidently to be preferred to all other Christian ways of life, provided a person has the necessary dispositions to lead this life. How can such an understanding make sense in the contemporary church? The transformation in vocational discernment brought about by St Ignatius Loyola moves the place of discernment from external calculation to the interior world of a person's desires, where the deepest desire is to imitate Christ. How can the Thomist and Ignatian approaches be reconciled? The tension between the two approaches is a reminder of the complexity of God's call and our response.

The Protestant Reformation insisted that vocation belongs to all God's people not just religious and clergy. The call to salvation is the basic vocation but the Reformers located the living out of this shared vocation in work; everybody is called to a certain role in society. How has this understanding coloured all subsequent meanings of vocation? Turning to modern Catholic theology, von Balthasar, describes how every human person is a result of God's loving activity. So the process by which people come to know their vocation is through God's act of unveiling this love to the receptive person. As God's love is unveiled, are there certain common stages in discerning a vocation?

In the Catholic tradition, there are four so-called 'states of life:' priesthood, consecrated life, marriage and the dedicated single life. *Part Three: Discerning Vocation Today* takes this as its starting point with two essays that ask: within the theology of vocation, what is distinctive about the call to the religious life and the priesthood? The vocational processes for the priesthood and the religious life are different but both involve discovering a vocation to celibacy and so this leads into a consideration of the vocation to marriage.

Discovering a vocation to marriage has one very distinctive feature, namely, finding a spouse. Is it possible for somebody to have a vocation to marriage before they have found a marriage partner? The Eastern Catholic tradition has a long established understanding of the holiness of marriage and with that goes an understanding of how it can be compatible with the priesthood. 'Love your wife as Christ did the Church and you will be holier than the holy monks' wrote St John Chrysostom, Patriarch of Constantinople in the fourth century. The Eastern tradition gives a high value to both marriage and to celibacy as a monk, with different processes for discerning whether a married man or a monk should be ordained. How does the Eastern tradition of ordaining married men differ from the Protestant tradition that allows clergy to marry?

In the final essay of this section, the reader is reminded that the discovery of vocation is nothing less than an encounter with the Transcendent Other. The metaphor of the Grail Quest is an apt one and at the heart of the quest lies the ability to ask the right question. Youthful idealism often carries young people into the Grail Castle, the place of transcendent encounter. But this is a place where they need to ask the right question which is: 'whom does the Grail serve?' If we fail to help them ask this question then, like Percival, they will be wounded in their quest and run away. Vocation guides need to enable the questers to ask: 'where is this leading?' 'what is love asking?' 'to where does God call me?' The wrong question to ask is: 'what am I called to?' or 'what is my vocation?' 'I' and 'my' are not the centre of the true vocational quest because the person is not the vocation; the person can only respond to the vocation and continue on the quest.

The final essay, *Conclusion: The Practice of Vocational Discernment*, shows how some of the insights of the previous essays affect pastoral practice. It describes the trajectory of vocational work in England and Wales over the last 60 years. Vocations ministry has now moved from recruitment to discernment, actively going out as part of the New Evangelisation to help people answer the question posed by Pope Benedict XVI to the youth of Britain: 'what kind of person would you really like to be?' Is vocations ministry in the present era aptly described as helping people to answer this papal question?

Editor's note

These essays were first presented to a seminar convened by the National Office for Vocation of the Catholic Bishops' Conference of England and Wales, in collaboration with Boston College, USA and the International Theological Institute, Austria. By drawing on a wide range of theological disciplines across a broad spectrum of views, the seminar aimed to clarify the theology and practice of vocational discernment. The authors presented different aspects of the Catholic tradition (and in one essay the Protestant tradition) but the collection does not claim to be a definitive statement nor is it a teaching document of the Bishops' Conference. Rather, these essays are a contribution to what the authors hope will be a widening circle of reflection about the nature of vocation and discernment.

Part One

Foundations of a Theology of Vocation

1

What theologies of vocation are to be found in the Bible?

Fr John Hemer

This essay will address the above question by examining the calls of various characters in the Bible. Very often in the call narrative God reveals something of himself that neither the person called nor anyone else could have guessed before. So a call is always in some way also a revelation. We might say that one of the ways God reveals himself is by calling individuals to his service. Rarely if ever does the call narrative draw conclusions. The information, the message is in the narrative itself, in other words the truth is in the facts. One thing becomes clear; it is largely in his interaction with individuals together with the record and reflection on those encounters, that God makes himself known. Even when God is revealing himself to the nation as a whole (as at Sinai or in the events of the exile) that revelation is mediated or explained through an individual (Moses or Jeremiah and Ezekiel).

Abraham Gen. 12:1–3

The primeval history in Gen. 1–11 concludes with something of a cliff-hanger. Human beings have made various attempts to get in contact with God. Adam and Eve try to become like him and fail. Cain tries to secure God's favour and fails, and that failure results in murder. The people of Babel try to get to God through their own efforts again resulting in confusion. Everything the human race tries with regard to God fails. One of the things the author(s) is trying to show is that to become like him, to both bear and manifest his image, to 'reach' God is not something that humans seem to be able to manage themselves. After 11 chapters of failure it becomes clear that some other strategy is necessary. That strategy starts to unfold straightaway at the beginning of Ch. 12. *Now the LORD said to Abram, 'Go from your country and your kindred and your father's house to the land that I will show you'* (Gen. 12:1 RSV).

One thing becomes immediately clear; God deals with individuals. Certainly his plan is for all the tribes of the earth (V.3 *and in you all the families of the earth shall be blessed*) but this all-powerful figure who created the universe starts with an individual. As we read on through the Old Testament we see – at Sinai for instance – that the nation as a whole has a vocation, but that means nothing without particular people with whom God, at his own initiative, establishes contact.

This was surprising at the time it was written – the Canaanites had a notion of a supreme god, *El,* but he was too far removed to have anything much to do with mere mortals. There was nothing strange at all for people to have dealings with the gods in their many names and forms. What is strange is that right from the beginning we are shown that the one who speaks to Abram is not just some minor local deity, but the awesome power behind the universe. This is equally a challenge to many modern people who believe that there are forces or a force controlling the universe, who believe that there is 'spiritual energy' available for good, healing, growth, etc. but who would laugh at the idea that this force would want a personal relationship with people. The fact that the story of our salvation begins not with theological propositions about the nature of God, not with philosophical propositions about the nature of man, nor with cosmological propositions about the nature of the universe, but with the bald statement *the Lord spoke to Abram* gives us a huge hint about what we are going to be dealing with for the next 2,000 or so pages.

There is no doubt that there is also an element of challenge here; God does speak in a way that is new. Religion in such nomadic societies was always concerned with maintaining life, stability and fertility and gaining protection from one's enemies. It's about keeping the world safe, keeping the world the way people know it and like it. Here is something quite different, a God who doesn't promise to keep things the way they are, but whose call means that almost everything about Abram's life will change.

But let's not over-spiritualize this either. Abram is not a hermit or a monk. Let's not read this as though it were some sort of religious vocation in the modern sense of the word. *Abram went as The Lord told him.* He obeyed the voice of God, yes. How exactly did God speak to him? We are not told. Somehow he recognized a call to transcend his present circumstances, and probably recognized that something much greater than him, something mysterious was prodding him. But he is not like some low ranking soldier, instantly obeying the orders of his commanding officer without thinking what this will mean for himself. Still less is he the model religious of a previous generation who will instantly stop what he or she is doing at the sound of the bell, who will unquestioningly take up an appointment which he or she finds repugnant when told to by a superior. Abram *wants* to go to Canaan, he sees it is the best thing for him, but it will cost him security and kinship and for someone in that society this cost is very high indeed.

As the Abraham story unfolds, he comes to know God better and to trust him more deeply, the climax being his readiness to obey God all the way to the top of Mount Moriah with his son in tow. When God calls Abraham to make this sacrifice he answers *Here am I* (in Hebrew *hinneni*). This is the first time we hear this response in the Bible, but it will become a characteristic willing response of those whom God calls. He couldn't have made this in chapter 12 because he had no knowledge of God. We find it on the lips of Jacob, Moses, Samuel, Isaiah, Mary and Ananias. The author of Hebrews puts it on the lips of Jesus. It becomes a stereotypical indicator that someone is being called by God to his service and signals that the person is responding generously.

Jacob

In Gen. 28:12–22 Jacob has an encounter with God which might be considered a call narrative. In a dream he sees a ladder linking heaven to earth. In modern terms what's happening is he's having a religious awakening. This clearly gifted but very selfish young man becomes aware that there is a world beyond his immediate concerns and needs. This happens at the moment when he is most wrapped up in himself. It is important to note that Jacob does not ascend the ladder at this stage. The fact that a door has opened between heaven and earth shows that Jacob is invited into the things of heaven, he is invited to go beyond the present world in which he lives, but as yet he is not quite ready for it. Sufficient that he knows it is there.

In 27:20, he is pretending to be Esau, and when his father asks him how he managed to hunt an animal so quickly he replied: *Because the Lord your God made things go well for me.* Note *your God.* At that stage his religion was that of his parents, he had no personal involvement with God. Now, at this first crisis in his life God reveals himself, becomes personal to him, and becomes *his* God. His reaction is pretty crass, he tries to make a bargain with God: *If God remains with me and keeps me safe on this journey I am making, if he gives me food to eat and clothes to wear, and If I come home safe to my father's home, then The Lord shall be my God* (28:20–21). This is nothing like the faith of Abraham, but then he is still young. He has at least acknowledged the fact that there is something bigger than himself which has a part to play in his life (until now, the only 'god' was himself). It's quite clear that here a vocation means a call to transformation, a call to transcend one's self. It may well be that when the individual first becomes aware of this he has no thought of such change.

Often a vocation to the priesthood or religious life goes hand in hand with a religious awakening. It's not unknown for young men to approach vocation directors expressing interest in the priesthood who are not practising Catholics. Jacob, while clearly gifted and now spiritually aware is still far from likeable. He's got a lot of homework to do, a lot of ego to be burned away.

Moses

Moses eventually becomes the agent of Israel's deliverance and the human founder of her religion. But he begins with a liberation project all of his own.

He kills an Egyptian whom he sees ill-treating a Hebrew (Exod. 2:11–15). He has what is in some ways an admirable sense of justice and compassion for the underdog, but he is also hot headed and had he begun some liberation movement at this stage, motivated by (righteous) anger, it would have been crushed by Pharaoh and resulted in even more hardship for the Hebrew slaves. So at this stage, we cannot speak of Moses' vocation. This is Moses' personal project, not God's.

In all, 40 years elapse, Moses leads an ordinary life in Midian and God shows up again. The author wants us to see this call which came from God in contrast to the young Moses' liberationist enthusiasm – which came from him.

God promises a sign in the future: '*But I will be with you; and this shall be the sign for you, that I have sent you: when you have brought forth the people out of Egypt, you shall serve God upon this mountain*' (Exod. 3:12). Note first of *all I will be with you*. This is something we will hear again and again and is one of the signs of an authentic vocation. It's the expression the angel Gabriel uses to reassure a rather frightened Mary in Luke's infancy narrative: *The Lord is with you.*

But the sign itself has puzzled many. Surely a sign should be given before the event rather than after, and surely the sign should be something that God does. Here God says in effect that when the people have done what he told them they will celebrate a liturgy in his honour. Or to put it more simply: the proof of the pudding is in the eating. 'If you take the risk of obeying me, you will, at some later stage when you are free, be able to celebrate a feast to me in freedom, then you will look back and know that I was with you all along, but there are no absolute guarantees beforehand'. It is one of the basic facts of faith that we cannot second-guess God. The only way we know it works is to try it. The only way Moses will know God is with him is to take the risk and obey his voice. He will never be able to know that while living in safety in Midian. Only in striking out on this very risky journey will Moses know God's presence.

Perhaps the biggest question many people discerning a vocation have is: how do I know this is right, how do I know this is really God's call and not my own daft idea? And after much discussion and prayer the only answer left is the one God gives Moses: 'Try it'.

Jephtha – a real vocation gone wrong

Experience makes us aware that sometimes even people who are manifestly called by God can go 'off the rails'. We don't just mean people who leave ministry or religious life, but sometimes people who have had very fruitful lives in God's service seem to take wrong directions. One has to be careful about making comparisons, but the Bible is disarmingly honest about the shortcomings of even Israel's greatest leaders. In Judg. 11:29–40 we find the strange, indeed repulsive story of Jephthah. He is certainly not a great man, the son of a harlot with a chip on his shoulder, but he has leadership qualities. He first gathers a group pretty worthless people round him, but the leaders of Gilead see that he was a valiant warrior so they invite him to help them defeat the Ammonites. Eventually we are told: *Then the Spirit of the LORD came upon Jephthah,* and it is this which guarantees victory. For whatever reason this isn't enough for him of itself, he feels the need to have an absolute guarantee of victory (contrast this with the call of Moses).

> And Jephthah made a vow to the Lord, and said, '*If thou wilt give the Ammonites into my hand, then whoever comes forth from the doors of my house to meet me, when I return victorious from the Ammonites, shall be the Lord's, and I will offer him up for a burnt offering.*' (Judg. 11:30–31)

His vow is redundant, The Lord will give him victory anyway – or not, but The Lord does whatever he wills and his arm cannot be twisted by bribery. Elsewhere God makes it clear enough that he abhors human sacrifice, so Jephthah is working with an understanding of God which is idolatrous. He fails to understand all this, so although he has God's spirit he is too small minded to trust in that. He does have the potential for true greatness, but he is wrapped up in himself, he is insecure and can never really engage in anyone's interests but his own. When his daughter comes out of the house his sympathy is with himself: *Oh my daughter what misery you have brought upon me!* No kind word for the girl who now has to be sacrificed, just a lament about his own plight. In trying to second-guess God, in trying to get, as it were, a written guarantee from him he oversteps the mark and it has tragic consequences.

(It must be stressed that there is no suggestion that the author approves of this, he just reports it without comment.) This says something about Israel's condition, indeed her dilemma. There is the potential for greatness and God is with his people, but so often their own narrow, parochial horizons make them fall short. In our own time, in the selection and formation of candidates one occasionally comes across this, and Judges helps us realize that our struggles are by no means modern phenomena.

Samuel – a vocation which is mediated (1 Sam. 3:1–10)

Samuel grows up as one given to the Lord from his earliest years, and being with God and ministering to him is something very natural to him. Despite this 1 Sam. tells us: *Now Samuel did not yet know the LORD, and the word of the LORD had not yet been revealed to him* (1 Sam. 3:7). So here we have the phenomenon of someone perfectly at home with God and the things of God who nevertheless still lacks what we call in our modern way a relationship with God. Clearly God has plans for him, but because of his immaturity and lack of personal encounter, when God first calls him he mistakes this for the voice of Eli his mentor. He needs Eli to point out to him that it is God calling. In other words Samuel's vocation has to be mediated. He cannot discern or even recognize the voice of God correctly without the help of another. The call narratives we have seen so far have all been accounts of God speaking directly to an individual without the help of another; here we see someone who needs another human to help him know God's call and answer it. Eli tells him what to say.

Sometimes one meets an individual who displays all the signs of being called to the priesthood but doesn't recognize it himself. He needs someone to say: 'have you ever thought of being a priest?' or words to that effect. This is part of what we mean when we say that a vocation comes from the Church.

We should also mention David in this connection. In 1 Sam. 16:1–13 Samuel comes looking for someone to make king in place of Saul, who has turned out to be a dud. God tells him to go to the house of Jesse in Bethlehem where he has chosen a king of his own. Jesse brings out seven of his sons in a scene that for all the world resembles the ugly sisters of Cinderella trying on the glass slipper, to no avail, at the behest of Prince Charming. None of these are right and as an afterthought Samuel asks if there are any more sons. Well there is the youngest, David, but he's out tending sheep, the implication being he is far too young an unsuitable. We know the rest. We know too that although David was a brilliant leader and a man of deep spirituality he had his dark side. Two things come to mind here. The first is that without Samuel asking for him he would never have assumed his role. Once again we have a vocation which is mediated. God has made up his mind who he wants, but it needs some human intervention to make that happen. The second is that David is literally the last person those in charge would have chosen or thought fit for the task in hand. Here is a theme which runs rights through the scriptures, which St Peter picks up, both in Acts 4:11 and in 1 Pet. 2:7 when he quotes Ps. 118:22: *The stone which the builders rejected has become the head of the corner.* We see this principle in operation with Joseph in Genesis, with the nation as a whole, with the suffering servant in Isa. 53, above all with Jesus and St Paul seems to think he fits into that rubric too. *For I am the least of the apostles, unfit to be called an apostle, because I persecuted the church of God. But by the grace of God I am what I am, and his grace toward me was not in vain* (1 Cor. 15:9–10). God often seems to call unexpected, unlikely people to his service and can work in and through circumstances which are far from ideal. Certainly the testimony of many who are now in full time service in the Church suggests that they considered themselves unworthy, unsuitable, sometimes unwilling, but, nevertheless, called.

Isaiah – a call within a call (6:1–13)

The book of Isaiah strangely does not begin with his call; this takes place after five chapters. Some commentators think this is an editorial mistake, but it isn't. For some time Isaiah has been prophesying, calling the nation to account. He's a man passionate about God and seeing the way his fellow Jerusalemites are lukewarm about their faith fills him with dismay and probably a degree of (righteous) anger. In many ways the first five chapters lay out the problem, a nation turned from its God, full of pride on the one hand (Ch. 1) the majesty of God (Ch. 2) and his willingness to bring Israel back and make peace with her (1:18–20). The whole problem is summed up in the song of the vineyard in 5:1–7. *For the vineyard of the LORD of hosts is the house of Israel, and the men of Judah are his pleasant planting; and he looked for justice, but behold, bloodshed; for righteousness, but behold, a cry! (5:7).*

So we have a picture of Isaiah probably at prayer in a darkened temple in the evening, not asking for any vision or deep experience, when suddenly unsolicited comes this blinding light, this realization of the awesome tremendous presence of God. The core of the experience is a realization of the utter majesty and transcendence of God, his wholly other-ness. Obviously God is no stranger to Isaiah, but here his knowledge of him takes a quantum leap and he is left breathless by the experience. His world is shaken to its foundations. He has never known anything like this before. No wonder the door posts shake. The only response the seraphim can make is to shout that word which best describes God (*qadosh,* totally other, totally different, totally transcendent). This holiness is so different that it is frightening, so Isaiah is shattered by the experience. His first response is not praise as modern people might imagine but: *woe is me, I am lost.* He realizes that there is not such a difference between him and the people to whom he is preaching. As a young enthusiastic devotee of the Lord he has been pointing out to people where they are going wrong and calling them to repentance. Compared to them, his life probably was very pure and very good. But now that he has encountered the All Holy he realizes that there is a vast gulf between him and God, and that the side of the gulf on which he lives puts him much closer to his sinful compatriots than to God. Compared with them he is very good. Compared with God he is lost in sin. His response is like that of Peter in Lk. 5:9. When he sees the miraculous catch of fish and realizes that in the presence of Jesus he is with someone altogether in another league, he says: *Leave me Lord, for I am a sinful man.*

In many ways this is a much more mature, a much deeper call than other calls in the OT. Moses objects because he cannot speak very well, Jeremiah because he is too young. Both of these are external circumstances. Here Isaiah has already been ministering for some time, and no doubt is convinced of what he has to do. Suddenly he realizes that he is in truth no better than the people to whom he has been preaching, he has no more right to call them to repentance, than they have to preach to him. He is lost. But then God himself intervenes.

Although we are not told that the seraph acts at God's instruction, that is understood. The coal which comes from the altar is from God's domain, there is nothing human which could adequately purify him. Since as a prophet his mouth is the most important part of his anatomy, the seraph touches and purifies that – it represents his whole body. There is nothing he can do himself to remove his sin or guilt (something which up to now he has not realized, he thought that living a good life was more than enough to justify him in the sight of God). By a completely unmerited act of grace, God makes him able for the task which lies ahead, so when he asks: *Whom shall I send?* Isaiah knows that he can with a clear conscience volunteer. As a sinful man living among sinful people he has no right whatsoever to offer himself, but with this free gift of God's forgiveness he knows that he is the one needed. But from now on he is living from God's strength and not his own. There is an important lesson to learn here about the nature of vocation. Many priests, religious and lay apostles find after a few years of ministry they are not the people they first thought they were. Failure or weakness or disappointment can rob them of their energy and make them wonder if they made the right choice in the first place. If they are fortunate this happens sooner rather than later. If like Isaiah they can recognize all this before God, and then relax into his grace, they can live lives that are very fruitful, but also probably much more at ease, now that they really know who is in charge.

The commission which Isaiah receives is one of the hardest things in the OT to understand. It seems that God actually wants him to preach not to bring people closer to him but in order to lead them away from him. There are various possibilities here.

When people adopt a basically cynical, unresponsive attitude, any effort to get through to them results in rejection rather than acceptance. When a teenager starts to go his own way, his parents often make matters much worse by trying to get him to see things their way. The way to make sure a teenager will *not* attend Mass is often to tell him he *has* to go. People know that if they really listen to Isaiah they will have to change, the one way to avoid that is never to even take the chance of being penetrated by his message. So every time Isaiah appears anew, instead of people saying 'Let's at least give him a chance this time' they say: 'Oh, the old fool is at it again, when is he going to learn that he is wasting his time'. This is the way vast numbers of people today close themselves off to any religious message which might require a change in them. A parallel in the UK might be Lord Longford and Mary Whitehouse who in the 1970s and 1980s vigorously campaigned against the increasing availability of pornography. They were portrayed by the media as out of touch Victorian prudes. Sometimes they may well have been excessive in their judgement of what is right and wrong, but even when they had important, things to say, things which were undeniably true, many people were completely unwilling to hear them, and in fact the more they spoke, the more people scoffed.

Another possibility is that Isaiah wrote down this account some time even some years after the fact and is in fact reflecting on what really happened: 'All I've succeeded in doing is closing people's minds and hearts, God must have known that that was going to happen, so in fact, that is what he was telling me to do'.

We are still left with the possibility that we are meant to read the text as it stands. The concept of The Lord hardening people's hearts is certainly not unknown in the OT. In Exod. 9:16 for example, The Lord says to Pharaoh: *But I have let you live for this; to make you see my power and to have my name published throughout the earth.* The idea is that God can do the strangest things with people in order to let his power be known or manifest. One often hears conversion stories where people seem to follow the most obscure paths to God, where God seems to allow people to do the wildest things, to go in directions opposite to himself in order to bring them back to him. When people remain conventionally religious they never stray far from God. Neither do they ever come to know him as intimately as those who have strayed far from him. When people's lives are ridden with sin they either remain in that sin or they convert with great fervour. One is reminded of St Augustine's long process of conversion.

The fact that Isaiah's message was not heard in his day is not the end of it. His disciples kept the message and repeated it to subsequent generations: *I bind up this testimony, I seal this revelation in the heart of my disciples. I wait for The Lord who hides his face from the house of Jacob, in him I hope* (8:16–17). Jesus seems to see his own ministry in the same terms as Isaiah in Mk. 4:12 where he quotes him verbatim. Ultimately, the hardening of Israel's hearts would lead to the crucifixion, the resurrection and therefore our redemption.

So God's call may well come not just at the beginning but also while someone is engaged in his service. This is a call within a call. A good modern example of this is Mother Teresa of Calcutta, who as a committed, hard-working teaching sister felt a call to do something more radical with the poor. And it may be that rejection and failure is built into that call.

Where are the women?

The reader may well wonder at this stage where are the accounts of women being called. After all, lots of women are involved in the story of Israel. The genealogy at the beginning of Matthew for instance shows how various women played a crucial role in the development of Israel. But call narratives such as we have considered so far in which women receive their vocation are few and far between. Although there is no direct call narrative of Sarah the wife of Abraham, it is clear that she has a huge and obvious part to play in furthering the future of God's people – namely giving birth to Isaac on whom that future will depend. An angel appears to the (unnamed) wife of Manoah in Judg. 13 and announces the birth of Samson. That is in a sense her call narrative. In 1 Sam. 1–2 there is a horrible situation in Israel where the priesthood has become degenerate due to the corruption of the sons of Eli and Hannah prays for children from the Lord who grants her the favour: one of her children, Samuel, is the one who restores the religion of Israel. Various women are commissioned by God to further his project. This commissioning is often tied up with the business of having and nurturing children. Perhaps the reason why there are so few clear 'vocation' narratives is that the way in which women are involved in God's work is often gentler, subtler and less extrovert than their male counterparts. To grossly oversimplify the accounts we have seen so far, God says to a man: 'I need you', the man called hesitates but then overcomes his hesitation and says: 'here I am, tell me what to do and I'll do it'. Or words to that effect. That is the male way of getting things done; direct, outward looking, task oriented. But women's presence in society in general has, at least in traditional societies been more in the background but nevertheless absolutely vital. Perhaps the word would be 'unsung'. Nevertheless we see that while men are busy organizing and fighting battles and taking directions from God, the women are quietly making it possible for all this to happen by giving birth to and nurturing Israel's leaders.

It's no mistake that the first two women with names in Exodus are the Egyptian midwives Shiphrah and Puah (Exod. 1:15) who defy the edict of the (unnamed) Pharaoh. They do this not by direct confrontation the more obvious 'masculine' way, but by subterfuge. The story of the salvation of Israel and therefore of the human race begins at the hands of women. We are told that they *were God-fearing women who did not obey the order of the king of Egypt but allowed the boys to live* (1:17). The story of our salvation begins with an act of civil disobedience. If God's purpose is to be fulfilled, royal edicts will have to be ignored. Once the baby Moses is found and rescued, it's pharaoh's daughter who arranges for his well-being. Hidden, quiet work but absolutely essential.

Matthew begins his gospel with the genealogy of Jesus, a long list of mainly male ancestors of Jesus, many of the most important characters in the Bible. But very surprisingly he also inserts the names of four women, who are not even the four most likely – there is no mention of Sarah, the mother of the nation. Tamar, Rahab, Ruth and Bathsheba all have a degree of scandal clinging to them but they each use their ingenuity, their quick-wittedness and their subtlety to ensure that the chosen people have a future – through offspring. In our modern world where children are no longer safe in the womb, where children are so often regarded as an inconvenience even a curse, the witness, the vocation of all these women in the scriptures is perhaps to remind us that without children none of us have much of a future.

All these various strands come together in the figure of Mary, the Mother of Jesus. In one way, Gabriel's message is like the announcement of a marvellous birth such as that of Isaac or Samson. But at the same time this goes beyond the OT pattern, this is not just an old couple waiting, hoping for a child but something new and unexpected. So this is also the announcement of a vocation, and there are many parallels between this and the call of Moses in Exod. 3:1–14 and the call of Gideon in Judg. 6:11–14. Luke shows Mary standing solidly in the same line as those who did their utmost to work for the deliverance of Israel. In other words, she is not a passive woman of little importance, but someone with a role every bit as big as that of Moses and Gideon.

The Angel doesn't address her as 'Mary' because that is who she is for those who know her. The angel addresses her as *full of grace* or *highly favoured one* since that is who she is for God. She stands in a long line of people who have found favour with God – Noah, Abraham Moses and David. Their favoured status is in one sense a privilege, but it is always for the benefit of others.

The Lord is with you is also an echo of God's words to those whom he calls to liberate or lead Israel; *I am with you* or *I will be with you*. He says it to: Isaac, Jacob, Moses, Joshua, Gideon, Solomon. It features heavily in the second part of Isaiah when God is telling Israel in exile of his desire to bring the people home from exile to save them. So Mary here stands in a long line of the saviours or liberators of Israel.

Mary's reply *I am the servant of the Lord* is a designation applied to Moses, Joshua David, Solomon, Israel and Jacob (as a representative of the whole people in Isa. 26:27). Once again this places her firmly in the line of those who spent themselves in the service of God and his nation.

Mary is seen here as at once continuing the role of the many holy women of Israel and doing the most important thing and actually giving birth to the one in whom God's promises will be fulfilled. At the same time she shares in the role of so many of Israel's great male leaders in that the angel treats her in ways similar to them.

Call of Peter Luke 5:1–11

If we read only the synoptic accounts of the call of the first disciples we get the impression that Jesus comes and calls people he has never met and they without any prior knowledge of him drop their nets and follow him. This is not so. Jesus had already met the four disciples in the company of John the Baptist at Batanaea on the far side of the Jordan. So bear in mind when Jesus calls the first four, he has met them before.

> *The next day again* John was standing with two of his disciples; and he looked at Jesus as he walked, and said, *'Behold, the Lamb of God!'* The two disciples heard him say this, and they followed Jesus. Jesus turned, and saw them following, and said to them, *'What do you seek?'* And they said to him, *'Rabbi'* (which means Teacher), *'where are you staying?'* He said to them, *'Come and see.'* They came and saw where he was staying; and they stayed with him that day, for it was about the tenth hour. One of the two who heard John speak, and followed him, was Andrew, Simon Peter's brother. (Jn 1:35–40)

So probably they went with Jesus to the village of Kochaba where some of his relatives live, and he therefore has a place to stay. They had seen and heard something of him, and on the basis of that they were able, without hesitation, to leave their nets and follow him on the shore of Lake Galillee. So their vocation is not something which comes out of the blue. They are able to follow Jesus because they have some experience of him. Mark and Matthew give very condensed accounts of this call (Mt. 4:18–22; Mk 1:16–20). Luke gives a much fuller account which tells us something about the anthropology of vocation, how Jesus appeals to the human qualities and desires of the people he calls.

Jesus calls Peter first of all by asking for his help, not by offering to do something for him. There is something very manly in this, and what's more he first asks Peter to do what he knows about – managing a boat so that Jesus can speak to the crowd. Without Peter's skill the boat would drift about hopelessly. So Jesus addresses the crowd and Peter 'overhears' what Jesus says.

> He got into one of the boats, the one belonging to Simon, and asked him to put out a little way from the shore. Then he sat down and taught the crowds from the boat.

So far so good but then:

> When he had finished speaking, he said to Simon, *'Put out into the deep water and let down your nets for a catch.'* Simon answered, *'Master, we have*

worked all night long but have caught nothing. Yet if you say so, I will let down the nets.'

The fish mainly come out at night and they mainly concentrate themselves around the shallows, so what Jesus says is daft. What's more he's a carpenter/rabbi from Nazareth and evidently knows nothing about fishing. So Peter's response is something like: 'I know what I'm doing here and we've tried hard all night, so if we have not caught any fish then there are none to be had today. And you rabbis think you know everything, so ok, let's give it a go and then we'll see who knows about fishing!'

When they had done this, they caught so many fish that their nets were beginning to break. So they signaled their partners in the other boat to come and help them. And they came and filled both boats, so that they began to sink.

It may be that Peter sees this catch as miraculous. But it may be that he realizes that here is Jesus, someone who has real access to the ability to make lots of money – through fish, but he seems to have no interest in making money for himself. So we read:

But when Simon Peter saw it, he fell down at Jesus' knees, saying, *'Go away from me, Lord, for I am a sinful man!'* For he and all who were with him were amazed at the catch of fish that they had taken;

His response here is like the response of Isaiah in the presence of the all-holy God. He is out of his league, and so he recognizes who he is in relationship to Jesus – a sinful man. That's part of recognizing God's call but not the end of it. Peter's self-awareness as a sinner does not paralyze him. He allows himself to be drawn on by Jesus. There is an old Catholic adage: 'Grace builds on nature'. We see this happening here. Jesus does not say to the fishermen: 'Follow me and I will make you scholars and teachers like me'. They would have run a mile. He takes the skill they have and the sort of men they are and values it, but the same time re-directs it to a higher purpose. There is continuity with the old life; they will continue fishing, but now in a different way. God doesn't ask the impossible of us, but if we let him he takes our talents and desires and uses them for his own purposes. What's important here is that Peter and the others are open to that. They could have told Jesus, clearly no fisherman, to clear off when he suggested putting the nets into the deep. But they have met him before (we see that in chapter one of John) they know he is no fool so at least they give him a chance. And as the gospel unfolds we see Jesus shaping these unlettered men into apostles and preachers and the pillars of the early church.

Of course if we read this at more than a merely superficial level, Jesus' *Put out into the deep* means much more. Peter and the disciples were just at the beginning of a journey which would take them so much deeper in many different ways; deeper into themselves, deeper into the faith of Israel and deeper into the life of God. The gospels tell us the rest of the story, how that call worked itself out. Mark in particular makes a great deal of the fact the disciples continually misunderstand Jesus, how they willingly responded to Jesus call by literally going with him, but despite this in so many ways they were not with him. So the gospel is the story of how the disciples' call led to a conversion, a slow difficult conversion not really complete until after the resurrection. Each of the call narratives we have seen tell us how that initial call and change of circumstance lead to a much more radical change over time. The gospels tell us that process step by (painful) step.

The call of Paul of Tarsus (Acts 9:1–30)

Scholars argue about this account. Is it a conversion story or a call narrative? Of course it's both and as we have seen a call even of someone as devout and devoted as Isaiah also involves some sort of conversion. With Paul we see how the call to follow Christ and the need to change one's life are inextricably linked. A huge element in Paul's call/conversion is a turning away from a persecuting God.

When Christians today talk about conversion they typically mean the process by which someone who has no faith or weak faith comes to strong personal faith in God. This is not the case with Paul. He had faith and commitment in abundance, as he puts it himself: *I advanced in Judaism beyond many of my own age among my people, so extremely zealous was I for the traditions of my fathers* (Gal. 1:14). He was determined to propagate the whole truth of Judaism. But of course someone else, Jesus the Nazarene had been doing that for a few years and had been killed for it.

One of the deepest truths of the Old Testament is that God takes the side of the victim, of the underdog, of the outcaste. In the Pentateuch there is complex legislation about how to treat the widow, the orphan, the stranger and the poor. The touchstone of Jewish faith is how one treats marginal people, victims. In about 100 of the psalms, God is on the side of the lone victim and against the crowd which is persecuting him. The prophets represent a voice pleading the cause of the victim in a way unparalleled in the ancient world. In the suffering Servant song of Isa. 53, God works through this despised, rejected and persecuted figure of the Suffering Servant, rather than working through the persecuting crowd. Jesus consistently made God available to people in this way, and taking the side of the marginalized was made as marginal as possible through crucifixion. It's not a total surprise then that the only way God can get through to Paul, or the only way he wants to get though, is as The Persecuted One. Paul assumed that his zealotry, his attitudes feelings and opinions were identical to God's. His persecution of Stephen and his fury with the Church had perhaps become the thing dominating his life at that moment. Paul believes he has to do this in order to maintain stability and order, to keep his world safe. Paul has to learn about a new God, or rather the God who was there all the time, the only God the OT makes available. Paul's zeal set him up for being 'tripped' by the voice of God. Jesus doesn't knock him down asking, 'Saul, Saul, why don't you believe in me?' That would be 'ordinary' conversion. Rather, it's 'Saul, Saul, why do you persecute me?' That's Christian conversion.

Faith is always the invitation to step out of the crowd, out of one's culture. When Paul is persecuting, he's just one of his culture defending himself against those who are different. When the *fatwah* was issued on Salaman Rushdie in the late 80's, commentators noted how ironic it was that it was made 'In the name of God, the Merciful, the Compassionate'. People asked how an injunction to kill someone can be made like this. Within a certain understanding of God it makes perfect sense. Some people see God as merciful to the group by defending it against people who are threats, so the killing of a blasphemer or heretic is an illustration of God's mercy. But for instance in the parable of the lost sheep (Lk. 15:4–7) Jesus proclaims a God who behaves in exactly the opposite way and will even put the group at risk for the sake of one wayward person. Paul had thrown all his energy into defending the cause of the God who stands behind *fatwahs*. While he was doing this, the God of Jesus who cherishes even the lost sheep crept up behind him and came as a blinding light, shining in the darkness of sacred violence and knocked him to the ground. So faith became for Paul not that which enabled him to persecute, but that which enabled him to listen to the voice of the persecuted one. This is a perfect example of what Christianity is. Paul's conversion is an archetypal conversion. An essential ingredient of Christianity is learning that God doesn't persecute.

There are many accounts in the OT of God coming to people unexpectedly. What happens here is in line with that. Paul is driven by the very highest of motives, a concern for God's truth. But it leads him to persecute people. Elijah's zeal for God was admirable, but it had led him to kill four hundred false prophets. So he had all his surety taken from him, he was sent to Mount Horeb and there he encountered God in a way that was completely new. Like Elijah, Paul was completely disorientated. Paul's world collapsed, one might say his understanding of God collapsed and the greatest apologist for the Christian message walks out of the ruins. Making this collapse happen so that the true God can be apprehended is part of the Bible's plot from beginning to end.

The fury (sometimes violent) of modern Muslims when they perceive that the Qur'an or Mohammed has been dishonoured is a good illustration of the fury Paul and those like him would have had towards the Church. Perhaps what is significant in all this is that we find in Paul before his conversion echoes of religious attitudes that are becoming increasingly common and increasingly worrying today. His conversion and call consist precisely in realizing how wrong these attitudes are and learning to imitate Christ.

In conclusion

On reflection, we don't have here just one story of a conversion that was also God's call, we have many; many people for whom God's call meant a huge change in their lives. In exploring the complex and varied nature of vocation we do well to reflect how call and conversion always seem to go hand in hand – in the Bible as in our modern world. In helping people to discern their vocation, we are probably also helping them to negotiate their conversion.

2

Did the early monastic tradition have a concept of vocation?

Fr Richard Price

Vocation

Before the question in my title can be answered, a preliminary one must be dealt with. What is a 'vocation', or more specifically a 'religious vocation'? Before I descend into the undergrowth in quest of the little furry beast, I must know what I am looking for.

It may seem too obvious to observe that in popular use the word 'vocation', as when we talk of a vocation to be a teacher or doctor, has no particular baggage; but it may be worth observing that the use of the term in a church context is often as vacuous. When someone asks Sister 'How are you doing for vocations?', all this means is, 'Have you had any recruits?' Many of us will have taken part in discussions in community as to whether a particular postulant should be admitted into the novitiate. The superior, perhaps, reads out his CV, very respectable and very unrevealing, and then a member of the community leans forward and asks with an earnest frown, 'But has he got a vocation?' This doesn't mean, 'Has he heard an inner voice?', still less is it an inquiry about the will of God; it is simply a conventional way of saying, 'Has he got what it takes to be a novice?'

At a higher level of discussion, it was keenly debated in the Catholic Church in the first half of the last century whether a vocation should be defined as 'subjective' or 'objective': was the call an experience of the applicant, or an act performed by those admitting candidates to the priesthood or the religious life? The objectivists went so far as to define a vocation as a call from God that actually takes place as the bishop or abbot utters the magic words. They could cite in their favour the Catechism of the Council of Trent, which had declared, 'Those are said to be called by God who are called by the legitimate ministers of the Church.' According to this view, there is nothing to be said about the candidates in themselves beyond talk of motives and aptitudes. Pius XI declared that a sensible feeling of a vocation on the part of the candidate is unimportant and dispensable.[1]

But the subjectivists, despite the cold wind blowing from the Vatican, did not give up the fight. They insisted that a vocation is something experienced by the applicant, that the little furry beast is alive and kicking before the zoologist picks it up and identifies it as a genuine specimen. But what shape does a vocation take, and how does the candidate recognize it? We are not, of course, talking about an actual voice – like the call of the infant Samuel in the Temple of Shiloh (1 Sam. 3); indeed, if a postulant claimed to have heard an indubitable voice from God, he or she would be rejected on the spot, as certainly arrogant and possibly insane. No, we are talking of something quite normal and therefore somewhat ambiguous. In the words of a judicious article in the *Dictionnaire de Spiritualité*, 'The one who is called recognizes a vocation through desire, inclination, attraction, interior need, and objective aptitude.'[2] The article continues: 'The call is generally sensed as coming from God: the one called has an experience of a personal relation with God and feels his call as a transcendent demand.' But such a 'sense' is, surely, a matter of interpretation: the call is not phenomenally different from a judgement or thought. The following definition in a modern book seems to me helpful:

What we ordinarily name our 'vocation' is in reality a particular way of perceiving God's purpose for us. It designates the divine will as it relates to who the Lord desires us to be, how we are to become that unique person

---

[1] Michael Sauvage, 'Vocation II', *Dictionnaire de Spiritualité* 16 (Paris: Beauchesne, 1994), col. 1092–1158, at 1096–7.
[2] Ibid., col. 1093.

and what we are sent forth do for God and others. Thus, the Lord wills us to be transformed in God, wills us to become our transformed selves through a certain lifestyle and wills us to accomplish some mission.[3]

Notice in this definition the stress on particularity. If the same book proceeds to claim a certain generality in a vocation, it transpires that this means that, to take the case of marriage, the vocation is to the married state in general, not to marrying a particular person. But vocation remains directed to a particular state of life – notably marriage or religion.

A distinguishing feature of a particular vocation, as contrasted to the universal cal address to all believers, is that it is not a command from God that must be obeyed: the obligation is placed upon us to lead a good life, but there is no obligation to adopt a particular state of life. Here a call from God can only be an invitation, which it is pious to accept, rather than a matter of obligation, which it would be impious to ignore.

With these points in mind, let me proceed to my question.

Vocation in monastic rules

Did the monastic writers of the early Church, whether monks or promoters of monasticism, possess the concept of particular vocations? They certainly did not speak of marriage as a 'vocation', though they did not denigrate it. It may also be questioned whether they even thought of priesthood as a vocation in the way we do today. St Jerome, writing to a friend who had abandoned the monastic life, accused him of virtual apostasy, even though he did so in order to become a secular priest.[4] More typical is the discussion in Part One of Gregory the Great's *Book of Pastoral Rule*, which gives as the prime test of whether someone deserves to be made a bishop whether he wants the office. If he does, he is to be excluded; if he would prefer to devote himself to private contemplation, but is ready to take on the heavy burdens of office in response to pastoral need and an earnest request from the faithful, he is your man. The

---

[3]F. K. Nemeck and M. T. Coombs, *Called by God* (Collegeville: Liturgical Press, 1992), p. 20.
[4]Jerome, 'Letter 14', in *Select Letters* (ed. and trans. F. A. Wright; Cambridge, MA: Harvard University Press, 1980), pp. 28–53.

spirit in which Gregory recommends the acceptance of ordination is one of a readiness to serve society out of a sense of duty, inspired by the notion of public service that was strong in the secular world of his time. He does indeed talk of the need for a potential pastor to submit 'to a decision of the divine will' that he takes office,[5] but this is mediated through those who choose him for the office; it has nothing to do with vocation in the subjective sense, that is, with the candidate hearing in his heart a divine call. So, if we follow the Fathers, we should cease to talk of people experiencing a divine call to marriage or the priesthood. The question we have now to ask is, of course: did they have the concept of a religious vocation, of a call to the monastic life?

Where shall we start? An obvious place to look is the great monastic rules, and what they say about the treatment of candidates for the religious life. Take first the Rule of Pachomius (d. 347), probably compiled after the death of this great founder of coenobitism,[6] but still the expression of his system and a hugely influential text. The Rule sets out what new recruits must be taught and what must be expected of them; it says nothing about discernment.[7]

Let us turn on to the Rule of St Basil (in its longer form), a theologically richer text that was hugely influential in Byzantine monasticism. The chapter specifically on admitting novices stresses the need to test them 'by time and laborious exercises'.[8] Again, there is no talk of a call or vocation.

More significant is the preface to the work, a fine piece of exhortation on the purpose of the religious life:[9]

> Let us not remain in idleness and relaxation, always wasting the present moment through idleness, and putting off to the morrow or later still the beginning of our works, lest, being found unequipped with good works by the one who requires our souls, we be cast out from the joy of the bride-chamber, shedding vain and useless tears, and lamenting our ill-spent life.

---

[5]Gregory the Great, *Book of Pastoral Rule* I. 6, Migne, Patrologia Latina 77. 20A.
[6]See Philip Rousseau, *Pachomius* (2nd edn; Berkeley, CA: University of California Press, 1985), pp. 48–53.
[7]*Pachomian Koinonia*, II (trans. A. Veilleux; Kalamazoo: Cistercian Publications, 1981). Section 49–52 (pp. 152–4) covers admitting new members.
[8]Basil of Caesarea, *Regulae fusius tractatae*, *Interrogatio* X, Migne, Patrologia Graeca [PG] 31. 944–8.
[9]Ibid., PG 31. 889B–892A.

Note the phrase 'the one who requires our souls', and the alternative held out to those who ignore God's call – an ill-spent life and eternal damnation. It is clear that even when Basil talks about a call, he is not thinking of religious vocation in particular, but about the call to a good and godly life addressed to all God's people, and which it is sin to ignore. Where, then, does monastic life fit in? As later chapters in the work make clear,[10] the purpose of monastic withdrawal is to make easier the fulfilment of the commandments, which are difficult to follow in the stress of life in the world.

Let us pursue our quest a little further: what do we find in the Rule of St Benedict? Here again, the chapter on taking in new brothers concentrates on the discipline that novices are to be subjected to, as a test of their vocation – worship, labour, orders and rebukes.[11] Nothing is said about vocation.

I could fill up the rest of this lecture in this way, but I remember the story of a candidate for the licence in Rome who wrote his dissertation on how the Fathers treated a certain private but shameful sin. Working methodically through the volumes of the Greek and Latin Patrologies, he solemnly recorded how each Father in turn had failed to mention it.

Vocation in other monastic texts

Do you suspect that I am parading the texts that serve my turn, while keeping others tucked away in the cellar, with the lights switched off? To prove my impartiality, let me put before you the patristic testimonies cited in an article, by L. Sempé, in the *Dictionnaire de Théologie Catholique*,[12] as proof that the Fathers had a notion of religious vocation, and that they stressed the subjective view of vocation, that is, the importance of the motives and feelings of the applicant, prior to any discernment by those in authority.

Sempé cites, as the earliest patristic testimony of the notion of religious vocation, St Athanasius' Life of St Antony. Athanasius relates how one day the

---

[10]*Interrogationes* VI–VII, PG 31. 925–33.
[11]Timothy Frey, ed., *The Rule of St Benedict in Latin and English with Notes* (Collegeville: The Liturgical Press, 1981), ch. 58, pp. 266–71.
[12]L. Sempé, 'Vocation', in *Dictionnaire de Théologie Catholique* 15.2 (Paris: Letouzey et Ané, 1950), col. 3148–81, at 3156–60.

18-year-old Antony on his way to church was thinking of how the apostles left everything to follow Christ and of the reward reserved for them. In this frame of mind, he heard at the liturgy the Gospel words 'If you wish to be perfect, go, sell all you possess, give it to the power, come and follow me, and you will receive a heavenly reward' (Mt. 19:21). The text continues: 'Antony, as if his thinking about the saints came from God and as if the reading had taken place for his sake, immediately left the church and gave his goods away'.[13]

Note particularly the final sentence of this passage. In reading the clause 'as if his thinking about the saints came from God and as if the reading had taken place for his sake', it would be wrong to stress the 'as if' (ὥσπερ, ὡς), which has the force in Greek of making the clause relate to the thoughts in the mind of the subject of the sentence, but without casting doubt on their truth. The meaning, then, is that Antony realized that his reflections on the apostles and the scripture passage he heard were indeed a call, a vocation addressed to him by God. But, we have still to ask, a call to what? Taking the work as a whole, it would be laughable to suppose that Athanasius was saying merely that Antony had a genuine vocation to the monastic life, for he makes a far bigger claim for Antony, namely, that he inaugurated a new pattern of sainthood. The story of his call is meant to put him on the same level as the prophets of the Old Testament and the apostles of the New.

Sempé's next passage is taken from the First Letter of St Antony, an important and influential text, even if its ascription to Antony cannot wholly be relied upon.[14] In this passage Antony distinguishes between three sorts of vocation: (1) that of those 'who, according to the law of nature and freedom given to them from the beginning, accepted whatever came to them through the word of the Gospel, and did so without any delay', like Abraham leaving Haran as soon as God called him (Gen. 12:1–4); (2) that of those who weigh up the Scripture passages that threaten sinners with death and promise a reward to the righteous and (3) that of those who have fallen into sin, but are driven to repentance by afflictions sent by God and enter religious life as a form of

---

[13]Athanasius, *Life of Antony* 2, in Athanase, *Vie d'Antoine*, ed. G. J. M. Bartelink. Sources chrétiennes 400 (Paris: Éditions du Cerf, 1994), pp. 132–5.

[14]Antony, Letter 1, PG 40. 999–1001. See Samuel Rubenson, *The Letters of St. Antony* (Lund: Lund University Press, 1990), who argues for the letters' authenticity.

penance. What is this message that 'came to them through the word of the Gospel'? It appears to be the teaching of Scripture, addressed to all Christians. The distinction being made is not between those who receive a divine call and those who do not, but to different motives and different speeds in responding to the Gospel message. Here again, as we noted above in relation to St Basil, the call is addressed to all Christians, as the common call that everyone needs to heed if they are to be saved. What distinguishes monks and nuns is not that they receive a distinct call, but that they respond to the call by renouncing life in the world.

Sempé proceeds to a passage of John Cassian, manifestly inspired by this letter of Antony's. In one of his *Conferences* Cassian likewise distinguishes three kinds of vocation:[15]

> The first is from God, the second is through human beings, and the third is out of necessity. It is from God, whenever some inspiration is sent into our hearts, at times even when are asleep, which spurs us on to desire eternal life and salvation, and which encourages us to follow God and to adhere to his precepts.

Abraham's call is then again cited, to be followed by mention of St Antony:

> He received this commandment of the Lord with the greatest compunction of heart, as if addressed specially to him, and at once renounced everything and followed Christ, induced by neither human exhortation nor human teaching.

The second kind of vocation is that which 'comes about through human beings, when, spurred by the example or admonition of certain holy persons, we are inflamed with a desire for salvation.' Finally, he continues:

> The third kind of vocation is that which derives from necessity, if we have been addicted to the wealth and pleasures of this world and suddenly encounter trials that threaten us with danger of death or afflict us with the loss and confiscation of property or torment us with the death of loved

---

[15]John Cassian, *Conlationes* III. 4 (ed. M. Petschenig, Corpus Scriptorum Ecclesiasticorum Latinorum 13; Vienna, 1886), pp. 69–71.

ones, and are compelled against our wills to hasten to the God whom we
disdained to follow when things were going well.

This, Cassian continues, may seem an inferior kind, but sometimes produces
just as good vocations as the others. He gives as examples Abba Moses,
who was driven to a life of penance by having committed murder, and also
St Paul, who on the road to Damascus 'was drawn as it were unwillingly to
the path of salvation'.[16] Yet again, we have a passage that certainly treats the
relation between the religious life and a 'vocation' from God, but relates not
to a particular vocation (a way of perfection that is an invitation and not an
obligation), but to the vocation addressed to all Christians and which all have
to follow in order to be saved.

I won't take you through all Sempé's other examples, some of which relate to
a supposed vocation to the priesthood, but I shall take his citation from John
Climacus' *Ladder of Divine Ascent*, since this work has been the text most read
within the monastic world of Eastern Orthodoxy:[17]

> If an earthly king, deciding to go on an expedition, calls us to service in his
> presence, we do not delay or make an excuse, but we leave everything and
> eagerly go before him. When the King of Kings and Lord of Lords and God
> of Gods calls us to this heavenly array, let us so apply ourselves as not in
> any way to decline out of sluggishness or timidity, and be found at the great
> judgement without a defence.

The theme is indeed a call to the 'monastic life' (μοναδικὸς βίος), but in the
broadest possible sense. For Climacus proceeds as follows: 'I have heard some
who are living carelessly in the world say to me, "How can we who are living
with a spouse and burdened with public responsibilities follow the monastic
life?"'[18] And his answer is that they must remain faithful to their spouses, go
to church regularly, help the needy, and, in a word, do all the good they can.
It is clear that he thinks this a second best: it is easier to live the 'monastic' life

---

[16]Ibid. III. 5, p. 72, 26.
[17]John Climacus, *Ladder* I, PG 88. 640AB.
[18]Ibid., PG 88. 640C.

(in this broad sense) within the actual confines of a monastery. But the call is a universal one, and not specifically addressed to monks and nuns.

To do justice to Sempé, he stresses at the same time that the call of religious vocation is not addressed to the few. In this he contrasts it to a vocation to the priesthood, which is indeed a special grace, given to those God has chosen for this office. On religious vocation he writes as follows:[19]

> It is not at all the same with the religious vocation, which has its object a form of life more particularly directed at perfection. Since all human beings are called to perfection, one is aware that no one, in principle, is excluded from this more effective means of attaining it, if he has the supernatural desire and is not kept in the world by obligations independent of him, such as marriage. . . . And so our Lord appears to speak of it as a state accessible to all when he says, 'All who leave their house, their brothers or their sisters, their father or their mother, their wife or their fields for the sake of my name will receive a hundredfold and possess eternal life'. (Mt. 19:29)

This, surely, is confused and confusing. It jumbles together the universal call to perfection addressed to all Christians, for the sake of their salvation, and a call to perfection in a more particular sense that is addressed to those with the required 'supernatural desire', if they happen not to be married.

In fact, the texts I have put before you present the monastic way of life as a particular response to a call addressed to all, and which does not of itself require withdrawal from the world, voluntary poverty, celibacy or any of the special features of the monastic life. The reason given for monasticism is simply that monks and nuns can more easily save their souls, since the discipline of monastic life vastly facilitates obedience to the commandments addressed to us all. The rationale behind this idea is that monastic life, with its fasts and vigils, aided by the quietude of withdrawal, makes possible a conquest of the passions (of acquisitiveness, lust, anger and the like) without which the commandments cannot be fulfilled.

---

[19]Sempé, 'Vocation', col. 3155.

Why be a monk?

The point I have been making is fundamental, but it is not a complete account of the rationale of monasticism in its great period of expansion in late antiquity. The down-to-earth stress on saving one's soul is typical of the realism and humility that characterize the literature about monks written for monks. But it does not exhaust the themes of monastic spirituality.

Take the Syriac writer John of Dalyatha, who writes in the following way of ascension to mystical prayer:[20]

> At the beginning, when grace descends on the monk, it creates in him feelings of tranquillity and consolations hitherto unknown. Then, little by little, it makes the spirit progress through the states of tranquillity, visitations, astounding visions, revelations, until he is established in the cloud of the substantial Light, beyond which one cannot go, and sees the rays of light which, coming from the divine substance, shine upon him, making him shine in his turn.

The scholar to whom I owe this passage adds a note to say that the term 'grace' here refers to a gift of the Holy Spirit that is experienced in the consciousness of the recipient.

Much more common in the literature about monasticism intended for a non-monastic readership are stories about special charisms. Take the following paragraph from Theodoret of Cyrrhus' *Religious History*, written in 440.[21]

> While he wore down his body, he provided his soul unceasingly with spiritual nourishment. . . . And so his familiar access to God increased from day to day, and his requests for what he needed to ask from God were immediately granted. So too he possessed prophetic foreknowledge of the future and received by the grace of the all-holy Spirit power to work miracles.

---

[20]Translation from a Syriac manuscript in Robert Beulay, 'Doit-on, avec les Syro-Orientaux, considerer la vie monastique comme la condition nécessaire de L'éxperience mystique?', in *Le Monachisme Syriaque aux premiers siècles de l'Église IIe – début VIIe siècle. Patrimoine Syriaque, Actes du colloque V* (Antélias, Lebanon: Éditions du CERP, 1998), p. 237.

[21]*Religious History* I. 3, in Theodoret, *A History of the Monks of Syria* (trans. R. Price, Kalamazoo: Cistercian Publications, 1985), p. 13.

Admirers of monastic from a distance (in Syria at least) liked to think of monks and nuns as not just saving their souls, but as living the life of the angels, contemplating God and communicating his graces to their fellow human beings.

But all this did not, however, affect the theology of vocation. We do not read of people embracing the religious life *in order* to attain special charisms of healing, foreknowledge and mystical prayer. Nor was a desire for perfection given as a motive for monastic life, save so far as Christ demanded perfection from everyone. Modern commentators have pointed to a connection between the theme of the angelic life and the monastic goal of attaining *apatheia*, or freedom from the passions;[22] but the prime purpose of *apatheia* was simply to suppress the passions, of anger, lust or resentment, that lead to sin. Thought of higher gifts would only come later, and only to a few, even if the existence of such gifts added to the glamour of the monastic life and its high reputation among the pious laity.

The monastic world of late antiquity was characterized by a fondness for dualistic contrasts – between those who responded to God's call and those who did not, between those who entered a monastery and those who, for tolerable or for dubious motives, remained in the world, but also among monks and nuns themselves, and within a single monastery. If the gifts of foreknowledge and contemplation were the height, the depth was the monk or nun who yielded to sensuality, to resentment, or (worst of all) to despair. Monasteries fostered a healthy self-distrust in their members, and through the severity of their rules endeavoured to protect them from themselves. In this context, of a religious life where the danger of a fall was never forgotten, the key concern was not the discernment of those applying to join religious life, but the proper formation and the appropriate discipline for those who had joined.

What made a monk was not a vocation that could be discerned in advance, but a gradual progress lasting a lifetime. John Climacus describes 30 steps in the progress of those who had already embarked on religious life. An icon from St Catherine's Monastery on Sinai, which won fame in this country through its prominent position in the recent exhibition of Byzantine art at the

---

[22]For example, Hubert Jedin, ed., *History of the Church* (London: Burns & Oates, 1980), vol. 2, p. 340.

Royal Academy, represents Climacus' message in terms of a ladder stretching up into heaven, from which a number of monks are pulled off by lassoes cast by demons.[23] Monks and nuns were not special when they entered religious life, but they became special if and when the discipline of monastic life enabled them to conquer the passions and achieve a pure love of God.

Conclusion

In the context of this conference my conclusion may appear somewhat negative. The monastic writers of the early Church did not, after all, have a concept of religious vocation, in the sense of a special call to the monastic life. I have failed to find the little furry beast with which this paper began; it turns out to be as mythical as the Loch Ness Monster or the Abominable Snowman. Meanwhile, the sifting out of postulants that early monastic writers preached and practised consisted not in discerning whether they had received a call, but in observing how they responded to a first experience of the discipline, the training in humility and perseverance, that awaited them in the noviciate. By their standards I fear that most noviciates today would appear to be holiday camps, or at best health farms, more likely to flatter self-love than mortify it.

What, we should ask, would the Fathers I have cited have said, had they been able to attend our conference? They would have been puzzled by the talk of particular vocations. In answer to the question that is the title of this essay, they would have said that of course they had a concept of vocation, but that vocation is not something special to the religious life, but is the call to repent and follow the Gospel that is addressed by Christ to the whole of mankind. As for the purpose of the religious life they would have said that it is simply to respond to the universal call more fully and more effectively than is possible in the world. If we told them about a crisis of vocations today, they would understand this to mean that the universal call addressed to every man, woman and child is no longer being effectively preached or seriously heeded.

---

[23]Robin Cormack and Maria Vassilaki, *Byzantium 330–1453* (London: Royal Academy of Arts, 2009), pp. 375, 462.

For surely this is where the problem lies, not in some crisis in the religious life, but in a crisis in Christianity as a whole – in the widespread reduction of our faith to a cultural symbol or a vague code of ethics, or at best a man-made, man-centred idealism, where the supreme goal is not the glory of God, but human fulfilment.

What is the message of our faith? That 'God's in his heaven, all's right with the world' – in the words of Robert Browning's play, *Pippa Passes*? Or is it, as one of my students once assured me, that human beings are beautiful? Monasticism flourished in the age of the Fathers because the Gospel was seen as an offer of salvation in the context of a doomed world, as a lifeboat in a stormy sea. If people perceive the faith as a demand and a challenge, a call to redirect their lives, then they will open themselves to receiving a call from God. The message we receive from Christ sets each of us the question, 'How am I to take up my cross and follow you?'

The answer to this question must respect the basic principles of the Christian life, which apply to all of us in all circumstances and are summed up in Christ's great commandment, 'You shall love the Lord your God with all your heart and with all your soul and with all your strength and with all your mind, and your neighbour as yourself' (Lk. 10:27). This commandment is addressed to all; and only those who follow it (with the help of God's grace) have received from Christ an assurance of salvation.[24] A secondary question is the particular state of life that the individual is to choose, as the setting for his endeavours to fulfil this commandment; and here God does not command but invites. This invitation may reach an individual in a variety of ways, including an inner impulse, while not excluding prudential motives, and respecting the free choice of the individual, while not ignoring wise counselling from those able to give it.

Once a particular vocation is embarked upon, the test will be whether it enables progress in the fulfilment of the great commandment. It can only be fulfilled by those who love God more than themselves, and dedicate themselves

---

[24]I have chosen my words carefully. I do not wish to exclude a universalism that appeals to God's 'uncovenanted mercies', but it is the covenanted mercies explicitly revealed in the Gospel that I am referring to.

to him in an act of self-gift, an act that has as its necessary preliminary a genuine self-possession. This applies to all states of life. A particular vocation must be directed towards the fulfilment of the universal call to holiness, the fundamental and common vocation of all mankind. It was the simple desire to achieve holiness, nothing more and nothing less, that was the inspiration of the monastic movement.

3

The Church as mission

Locating vocation in its ecclesial context

Fr Richard Lennan

Presentations of 'vocation', in both secular and religious spheres, tend to focus exclusively on individuals, often portraying them as if they dwelt in splendid isolation. That form of presentation reflects a certain logic: after all, dentists and concert pianists, no less than consecrated religious, do not emerge in 'job lots', but come from particular – individual – backgrounds and journeys. On the other hand, not even the most prodigiously talented individual exists in a vacuum. To be comprehensive, therefore, the story of each vocation must include 'the others', those who helped to nurture a vocation: families and friends; teachers and mentors; benefactors and those who simply encouraged. Such a list reminds us that every vocation has a context, that every vocation expresses something of the connections that make us human. For every Christian vocation, the context is the church.

The vocation of all baptized Christians is, irreducibly, a vocation that is linked to the purpose of the church. Christians, then, can never validly present themselves as solitary virtuosi, as self-made entrepreneurs who have gallantly forged a unique path. No, as Christians we are all part of the one body, all connected, in Christ, to one another. This is not to say that we simply merge into an undifferentiated mass, that we are obliged to renounce our own gifts, or that it is impossible for any one member to be an inspiration for others. On the other hand, our membership of the Christian community does mean that we are not free agents, unfettered by either relationships or tradition. What makes us one is our common sharing in the one mission of the church.

The mission of the church is the topic of this chapter. While other chapters in the book explore specific vocations in the church, this chapter concentrates on the mission that is common to every member of the church, the mission that provides the foundation for each particular vocation.

It is worth noting here that 'mission', not 'vocation' is the term that is best applied to the church as a whole. While 'vocation' highlights the call that builds on an existing identity – thus, one is a woman who becomes a surgeon, an Australian who becomes a chef, and so on – the church exists exclusively for mission. In other words, the church has no identity outside of its mission: 'All those who in faith look towards Jesus, the author of salvation and the principle of unity and peace, God has gathered together and established as the church, that it may be for each and everyone the visible sacrament of this saving unity'.[1] For the church, identity and purpose are indistinguishable: they unite under the caption 'mission'. Bereft of its mission, the church could not remake itself with a new identity, but would be devoid of both identity and purpose.

The church's mission is an unchanging one: to be 'in the nature of a sacrament, a sign and instrument of communion with God and of union among all people'.[2] Nonetheless, different ages in the church's history carry out that mission in different contexts, contexts that affect the church as a whole and the lives – vocations – of individual members of the church as they seek to be faithful to the mission. This chapter, therefore, explores not simply the 'timeless' theological foundations of the church's mission, but also the exigencies that shape that mission in the present-day – more specifically, the chapter's concentration is on issues that relate primarily to the Anglo-American context.

---

[1] *Lumen Gentium* (LG), 'The Dogmatic Constitution on the Church', art. 9; all references to the documents of Vatican II come from Norman Tanner (ed.), *Decrees of the Ecumenical Councils* (Vol. II; Washington, DC: Georgetown University Press, 1990).
[2] LG, art. 1.

This chapter brings into relief the three relationships that frame the church's sacramentality: the relationship with God in Jesus Christ through the Holy Spirit; the relationship with history; the relationship with the world.

The relationship with God is the source and goal of the church. That relationship forms the church as a communion for mission, sustains its mission, and is foundational to the vocation to holiness that is common to all the members of the church, as well as to the particular vocations that serve the mission of the whole communion.[3] The relationship with history and the relationship with the world constitute the environment in which the church is to embody what it means to be a sacrament. The church, therefore, must discern in ever-changing historical and cultural circumstances what expresses faithfulness to its mission.

The three relationships are inextricably linked, but the nuances proper to each mean that they play distinct roles in the church's mission. The three relationships are also dynamic. Accordingly, the church exists, as the Second Vatican Council emphasized, as a 'pilgrim' that 'will reach its completion only in the glory of heaven'.[4]

Before analysing the three relationships, there is a matter of definition to address: to specify whom the paper includes when it refers to 'the church', which is a term that can be endowed with a greater or lesser richness, a broader or more narrow band-width. Joseph Komonchak nominates a series of questions that give focus to the need for clarification: 'Of whom is one speaking when one speaks of the Church? To whom does the word refer? Of whom is it true? *In* whom is it true?'[5] More incisively, Komonchak asks of the terms 'People of God', 'Body of Christ', and 'Temple of the Spirit': 'What must be true of you if these terms are true of the Church? If these terms are not true of you, are they true of anyone else in the Church? After all, if they are not true of anyone in the Church, what can it mean to say that they are true of the Church?'[6]

---

[3]For the universal vocation to holiness, see LG arts 39–42.
[4]LG, art. 48.
[5]Joseph Komonchak, *Who Are the Church?* (Milwaukee, WI: Marquette University Press, 2008), p. 10; original emphasis.
[6]Ibid.

At first glance, it may seem that members of the church would be less likely to consider themselves represented by 'the church as sacrament' than by the terms on Komonchak's list. Underpinning this paper, however, is the conviction that all the baptized participate in the three relationships identified above, the three relationships inseparable from the church's identity as a sacrament. Consequently, the contribution of every member of the church, working in communion with every other member, is needed if the church is to fulfil its mission as sacrament. As the chapter will illustrate, achieving that level of participation is no small challenge, perhaps especially in the contemporary church, but it remains a challenge that a church proclaiming itself to be 'catholic' must continue to embrace.[7]

The church's relationship with God

The church's relationship with God is a product of God's self-revelation, which is at once historical and symbolic. Reference to God's self-revelation as 'symbolic', which can serve as a synonym for 'sacramental', indicates that it describes something that is more than – indeed, other than – the conveying of information about God. In fact, an effective symbol 'imparts its meaning not by explicit denotation but by suggestion and evocation. Working on the imagination, emotions, and will, and through them upon the intelligence, the symbol changes the point of view, the perspectives, the outlook of the addressee.'[8] In order to illustrate the dynamics of God's symbolic or sacramental revelation, thereby laying the foundations for a theology of the church and its mission, the most helpful route goes via the paradigm of God's self-communication: Jesus Christ, 'the mediator and the fullness of Revelation.'[9]

In Jesus, God, from the depths of divine love, becomes a part of human history – 'as we are, yet without sin' (Heb. 4:15; NRSV). In Jesus, through the

---

[7]For discussion of 'catholicity' as an element the 'inner' life of the church, see Richard Lennan, 'Catholicity: Its Challenge to the Church', *New Theology Review* 24 (2011), pp. 36–48.

[8]Avery Dulles, *A Church To Believe In: Discipleship and the Dynamics of Freedom* (New York, NY: Crossroad, 1982), p. 47.

[9]*Dei Verbum* (DV), 'The Dogmatic Constitution on Divine Revelation', art. 2.

Holy Spirit, God 'in his great love speaks to humankind as friends and enters into their life, so as to invite and receive them into relationship with himself'.[10] In Jesus, God inaugurates the kingdom – 'a gracious gift from God, who comes with unconditional love to seek out humankind and to offer ultimate salvation to all . . . God is coming toward us as unconditional love, seeking communion and intimacy. Since it is a gift of love, the only concrete description of it can be in terms of symbols and images'.[11] In Jesus, through words and actions that heal, reconcile, and establish possibility where none was taken to exist, God not only challenges existing ideas of how God should act, but calls people to new forms of relationship, new ways of living.

That this kingdom embodied in Jesus is God's kingdom, that it is a gift vulnerable to neither the vicissitudes of history nor the inconsistencies of human faithfulness, is evident in the death of Jesus. That death does not rupture God's solidarity with humanity, does not become the death of the kingdom, but, as Walter Kasper expresses it, 'this death is the form in which the Kingdom of God exists under the conditions of this age, the Kingdom of God in human powerlessness, wealth in poverty, love in desolation, abundance in emptiness, and life in death'.[12]

Most particularly, the fact that the death of Jesus is not the final word about that kingdom makes clear that it is God's kingdom. In the resurrection, Jesus, who lives and dies with trust in God, is raised from death: an unequivocal revelation of God's creative love and faithfulness that give life even when all human potentiality collapses. God's faithfulness to Jesus is not only the climax of God's faithful care for creation and Israel, but it also signals God's commitment to bring the whole of creation, in Jesus the Christ, to fulfilment in the kingdom.

The mission of leading humanity in Christ to the fullness of the kingdom, to the fullness of communion with God and reconciliation with one another, is the particular mission of the Holy Spirit. The Spirit completes

---

[10]Ibid.

[11]John Fuellenbach, *The Kingdom of God: The Message of Jesus Today* (Maryknoll, NY: Orbis, 2002), p. 97.

[12]Walter Kasper, *Jesus the Christ* (trans. V. Green; New York: Paulist Press, 1985), pp. 118–19.

the revelation of God as trinity and ensures that the new life of the risen Christ remains available for all times.[13] The Spirit, however, does not become incarnate in history. Rather, the Spirit builds on what was begun through the preaching and action of Jesus: the Spirit forms the church as the body of Christ, the communion of faith. The church, therefore, 'is the sign of what God has done in Christ, is continuing to do in those who serve him, and wills to do for all humanity. It is the sign of God's abiding presence, and of his eternal faithfulness to his promises, for in it Christ is ever present and active through the Spirit. It is the community where the redemptive work of Jesus Christ has been recognized and received, and is therefore being made known to the world'.[14]

As the product of Christ and the Spirit, the church symbolizes the universality of grace, the presence of the risen Christ. Through the church, 'the *Absent One* is present in his "sacrament" which is the Church: the Church rereading the Scriptures with him in mind, the Church repeating his gestures in memory of him, the Church living the sharing between brothers and sisters in his name. It is in these forms of witness by the Church that Jesus takes on a body and allows himself to be encountered'.[15] As sacrament, then, the church 'receives the mission of announcing the kingdom of Christ and of God and of inaugurating it among all peoples, it has formed the seed and beginning of that kingdom on earth'.[16]

The church's existence as sacrament establishes it as a theological reality, one that can be fully apprehended only in faith. This is not to suggest that the church can claim immunity from sociological analysis – after all, the church can only be sacrament if it is both a fully human reality, as well as fully the product of Christ and the Spirit – but it does underscore that God's self-communication is the key to the church's identity. There are three specific consequences of that identity that shape the mission of the church.

---

[13] US Catholic Church, *Catechism of the Catholic Church* (New York, NY: Catholic Book Publishing Company, 1994), 732.

[14] Anglican-Roman Catholic International Commission, *Church as Communion* (London: Catholic Truth Society, 1991), art.18.

[15] Louis-Marie Chauvet, *Symbol and Sacrament: A Sacramental Reinterpretation of Christian Existence* (trans. P. Madigan and M. Beaumont; Collegeville, MN: Pueblo, 1995), p. 163.

[16] LG, art. 5.

First, the fulfilment of the church is eschatological and is directed to the future. Since the gifts of the Spirit come from the future, drawing the church forward, the church can never graduate from its pilgrim status, but must remain engaged with history, seeking to respond to God's Spirit who calls the church to service of God's kingdom.[17] The implications of this pilgrim status emerge starkly in Vitor Westhelle's definition of the church:

> The church, as the space of grace, as the conduit of the Spirit that is at the eschata, the place of risk, of condemnation, but so also the place of healing and salvation, is the community of those who in the margin barely hanging on to life are sustained as a body by their faith and by one another, and are there in the midst of the unutterable turmoil able to name and be named by their relationship to God and to one another.[18]

Secondly, the need for conversion is a permanent characteristic of the church. Since we resist, in both our individual and communal lives, the pilgrimage to the fullness of God's kingdom, since we succumb at times to the preference for an 'earthly tent' (2 Cor. 5:1; NRSV), rather than being willing to live 'stretched between heaven and earth', we need to acknowledge that, as church and not simply as individuals, we can fail to be the sacrament that we are constituted to be.[19] Indeed, we need to acknowledge that our lives as church can 'constitute a countertestimony to Christianity … and that our sin has impeded the Spirit's working in the hearts of many people'.[20] The notion of 'the church as sacrament', therefore, no less than of a 'holy church', is not a declaration of perfection, but a profession of faith in the permanence of God's commitment to the church.[21] Our ultimate trust, then, is in God, not the church.

---

[17] For the notion of the Spirit's gifts coming from the future, see John Zizioulas, *Communion and Otherness: Further Studies in Personhood and the Church* (New York, NY: T&T Clark, 2006), p. 296.

[18] Vitor Westhelle, *The Church Event: Call and Challenge of a Church Protestant* (Minneapolis, MN: Fortress, 2010), p. 119.

[19] Karl Rahner, 'Utopia and Reality: Christian Existence Caught between the Ideal and the Real', *Theological Investigations* (vol. 22; trans. J. Donceel; New York, NY: Crossroad, 1991), pp. 32–33.

[20] John Paul II, 'Mysterium Incarnationis', *Origins* 28 (1998), p. 450.

[21] For Vatican II's understanding of God as the source of the church's holiness, see LG arts. 39–41.

In order that the church might not lose sight of its own limitations, or fail to acknowledge God as the source of its holiness, the church must always remain, argues Karl Rahner, a 'self-critical' church.[22] The need for self-criticism arises because of the ineradicable gap between the church and the God whom it symbolizes. Accordingly, the church must remember that it is the sacrament of Christ, not a new incarnation. The church, then, in all its expressions, can always become more authentically what it professes to be.

Thirdly, human initiative alone cannot determine the church, which is God's work. As the product of God's action, the church is not fully at our disposal. Indeed, this God-given identity of the church means that the church constructs us, we do not construct the church: 'Christianity is the religion of a demanding God who summons my subjectivity out of itself only if it confronts me in a church which is authoritative . . . a church which confronts me in a mission, a mandate and a proclamation which really make the reality of salvation present for me'.[23]

As noted in recent Protestant ecclesiology, this 'givenness' of the church, the fact that we are not the source of the word that calls us to faith, is especially confronting today. This is so as the contemporary western emphasis on freedom prefers to envisage the church as a loose amalgamation of independent contractors: 'According to this model, rather than constituting its members, the church is constituted by believers, who are deemed to be complete "spiritual selves" prior to, and apart from their membership in the church. The church, in turn, is an aggregate of the individual Christians who "contract" with each other to form a spiritual society'.[24]

---

[22]For an example of Rahner's emphasis on the need for a self-critical church, see Karl Rahner, 'The Function of the Church as a Critic of Society', *Theological Investigations* (vol. 12; trans. D. Bourke; New York, NY: Seabury, 1974), pp. 229–49.

[23]Karl Rahner, *Foundations of Christian Faith: An Introduction to the Idea of Christianity* (trans W. Dych; New York, NY: Seabury, 1978), p. 344.

[24]Stanley Grenz, 'Ecclesiology', in *The Cambridge Companion to Postmodern Theology* (ed. Kevin Vanhoozer; Cambridge: Cambridge University Press, 2003), p. 257; Grenz's critique of contemporary practices finds an echo in Gary Badcock, *The House Where God Lives: Renewing the Doctrine of the Church Today* (Grand Rapids, MI: Eerdmans, 2009), p. 337. For a Catholic perspective on the issue, see Walter Kasper, 'Ecclesiological and Ecumenical Implications of Baptism', *The Ecumenical Review* 52 (2000), pp. 530–31.

The 'givenness', however, does not mean that the church is a hermetically sealed unit, one that presents us with a choice between unquestioning acceptance and outright rejection. Rather, the 'givenness' of the church is a reminder that the authenticity of the community of faith, the possibility of its being a truly efficacious sacrament, depends on the community remaining 'a community of reception', which involves openness to God's self-giving in Christ, especially as mediated through the normative witness of the Spirit-inspired scriptures.[25]

The church's relationship with history

The church, as a community of reception, receives and transmits, through the Spirit, all that God has revealed in Christ. As discussed above, that revelation, witnessed to by the first generation of disciples and given its authoritative expression in scripture, forms the church, which 'in its teaching, life and worship, perpetuates and hands on to every generation all that it is and all that it believes'.[26] Although the designation of the church as a community of reception identifies it as a community grounded in history, the church has had a vexed relationship with history – 'to a neophyte or neurotic in religion, history seems the great enemy, for it challenges the rituals and forms of religion'.[27]

The particular challenge of history for the church arises from the experience of change which can seem incompatible with the apostolic faith that the church professes. Properly understood, however, the apostolic faith is not a bulwark against change. It is certainly true that apostolic faith 'means being continuously and vitally the same Church as the Church of the apostles, led through history by the same Holy Spirit to proclaim the same Good News and to bring the same salvation'.[28] To achieve this, the church cannot simply

---

[25]For the notion of the church as a community of reception, see Ormond Rush, *The Eyes of Faith: The Sense of the Faithful and the Church's Reception of Revelation* (Washington, DC: The Catholic University of America Press, 2009), pp. 42–46.

[26]DV art. 8.

[27]Thomas O'Meara, *Theology of Ministry* (Mahwah, NJ: Paulist, 1999) (rev. edn), p. 83.

[28]John Wright, 'The Meaning and Structure of Catholic Faith', *Theological Studies* 39 (1978), p. 709.

repeat the past, but must discern how to be 'the community in its eschatological experience of being on the front, where there is no *safety*, but the bursting out of *salvation*'.[29]

At the heart of the apostolic faith is what Joseph Ratzinger refers to as the church's 'base memory'.[30] In order to be the church of Christ, the church must remain faithful to that 'base memory', centred as it is on God's self-communication in Jesus. The memory, however, is, like all other aspects of the church, eschatological in its orientation: it constitutes a living tradition, one animated by the Spirit and directed to a future fulfilment. The base memory anchors the church on the witness of the apostles, a witness shaped by the same Spirit who guides the church in the present, and who will lead it into the future. As such, the memory functions to help the church in every age determine what constitutes a faithful response to the Spirit. Paradoxically, then, through its tradition, 'the Church with the help of the past liberates the future from the unconscious limitations and illusions of the present'.[31]

The continuity of the Spirit's presence ensures that the church ought not to anticipate an irresolvable opposition between the base memory and contemporary needs and questions. Nonetheless, it is important to clarify the operation of that memory in the life of the church. That requirement becomes apparent when we ask two questions: Who is 'the keeper' of the base memory? How does that memory operate to help the church address new questions in ways that are faithful to the Spirit of the church's past, present, and future, in ways that build up the unity of the church for the fulfilment of its mission?

Vatican II gives a twofold answer when ascribing responsibility for the church's memory: on the one hand, the answer is 'all the members of the church' – 'the universal body of the faithful who have received the anointing of the holy one cannot be mistaken in belief [*in credendo*]'.[32] On the other hand,

---

[29]Westhelle, *The Church Event*, p. 123; original emphasis.

[30]Joseph Ratzinger, *Called to Communion: Understanding the Church Today* (trans. A. Walker; San Francisco, CA: Ignatius Press, 1991), p. 20.

[31]Maurice Blondel, 'History and Dogma [original publication: 1904]', in *The Letter on Apologetics* and *History and Dogma* (trans. A. Dru and I. Trethowan; New York, NY: Holt, Rinehart and Winston, 1964), pp. 281–82.

[32]LG, art. 12.

the answer is 'the bishops' – 'the faithful ought to concur with their bishop's judgment concerning faith and morals which he delivers in the name of Christ, and they are to adhere to this with a religious assent of the mind'.[33]

Clearly, the council did not intend its answer to be recast as an 'either/or' or imagine divisions within the *sensus fidelium*. In practice, however, there has been, and continues to be, a radical disparity in outcome between the two affirmations: the exercise of episcopal, and particularly papal, authority has expanded, while participation by all the baptized in discerning the church's faith and action has diminished, often as a direct consequence of the expansion of episcopal authority. Consequently, the '*pastorum et fidelium conspiratio*', which John Henry Newman advocated, has become increasingly rare.[34]

In *Novo Millennio Ineunte* (2001), Pope John Paul II described the church as 'the home and school of communion'.[35] If the church is to reveal itself as the sacrament of Christ and the Spirit, that communion needs to become more evident today. This does not mean merely that we need greater civility in the church, but a recovery of a shared responsibility for the church's faithfulness to its mission, and its memory. In particular, 'those who exercise *episcope* must not be separated from the "symphony" of the whole people of God in which they have their part to play'.[36] In order to achieve that outcome, dialogue in the church, a dialogue characterized by both listening well and speaking well, is necessary.[37]

The willingness to promote and engage in dialogue can indicate trust in the Spirit's capacity to be a source of reconciliation. That trust in the Spirit also counters any tendency to stigmatize criticism in the church as 'disloyal' or 'disobedient'. The church in our time could benefit from a collective appreciation of the fact that, as Yves Congar recognized, 'Catholic self-criticism is

---

[33]LG, art. 25.

[34]John Henry Newman, *On Consulting the Faithful in Matters of Doctrine* [original publication: 1871] (London: Collins, 2001), pp. 103–04.

[35]John Paul II, *Novo Millennio Ineunte*, art. 43; the document can be found in *Origins* 30 (2001), pp. 489–508.

[36]Anglican-Roman Catholic International Commission, *The Gift of Authority* (London: Catholic Truth Society, 1999), art. 30.

[37]Bradford Hinze, *Practices of Dialogue in the Roman Catholic Church: Aims and Obstacles, Lessons and Laments* (New York, NY: Continuum, 2006), pp. 253–54.

frank, sometimes even harsh. It does not arise from a lack of confidence or from a lack of love for the church but, on the contrary, from a deep attachment and from a desire to be able to trust, despite the disappointment of someone who loves and who expects a great deal from the church'.[38] Dissatisfaction with the current life of the church, with the style of its governance and its pastoral priorities, can express itself in laments that are not necessarily indicative of either a loss of faith or a lack of respect for those in authority. Those laments 'can serve a diagnostic purpose in surfacing and analyzing potentially with great precision what problems need to be addressed, what desires and intentions need to be purified, and what new habits of mind and heart need to be learned'.[39]

In the church today, there is a particular need to pay attention to what Tom Beaudoin calls 'secular Catholics', those at risk of 'deconversion' out of the church – 'those with a Catholic heritage, however nominal, who cannot find Catholicism central to the everyday project of their lives and are in varying degrees of distance from what they take to be normative or prescribed Catholicism'.[40] Such Catholics, he argues, are not simply 'lapsed' or 'non-practising' – 'this is too convenient a story for "us" to tell about "them"' – but people for whom 'the apocalypses of their lives, whether dramatic or gradual, were not able to be located on the map of faith they had been taught'.[41] Similarly, Rahner argues that we ought not to presume that 'border-line' Catholics are 'centrifugal'; they might well be 'centripetal', people who have yet to acquire more than half their faith, rather than those who have only half of their faith left.[42]

It is important to note that dialogue on all matters that generate tension in the church is not the denial of faith in revelation. Rather, 'in such a dialogue,

---

[38]Yves Congar, *True and False Reform in the Church* (trans P. Philibert; Collegeville, MN: Michael Glazier, 2011), p. 36.

[39]Bradford Hinze, 'Ecclesial Impasse: What Can We Learn from our Laments?', *Theological Studies* 72 (2011), p. 494.

[40]Tom Beaudoin, 'Secular Catholicism and Practical Theology', *International Journal of Practical Theology* 15 (2011), p. 24.

[41]Beaudoin, 'Secular Catholicism', p. 26.

[42]Karl Rahner, 'On the Structure of the People of the Church Today', *Theological Investigations* (vol. 12; trans. D. Bourke; New York, NY: Seabury, 1974), pp. 224–25.

without prejudice to the divine truth, the Church can and must also be she who learns as well, she who is capable of being led into still deeper levels of her own truth and her understanding of that truth. In such a dialogue she can be purified from misunderstandings and distorted interpretations . . . and she can herself become more believing'.[43] Dialogue is rarely neat, particularly when it focuses on topics that are divisive, but it can manifest that the church is other than 'a power structure that hides rather than illuminates the face of God (and the sex scandal did not help)'.[44] Dialogue embodies the recognition that the gifts of the Spirit flow through the entire church; it also embodies surrender to that Spirit:

> The partners in such a dialogue can thereby express that eschatological modesty most becoming of a pilgrim Church, a Church that believes that it abides in the truth but does not possess it in its entirety. This pilgrim Church will be most faithful to its truest identity when all the baptized acknowledge the wisdom of listening before speaking, of learning before teaching, of praying before pronouncing.[45]

In the contemporary church, 'ministry' is an apt subject for such dialogue. Indeed, there is an urgent need for the church to discern communally what the Spirit might be saying to our time about the structure and practice of ministry. In order to appreciate why this is so, it is important to review the evolution of ministry in the recent history of the church.

The focus on ministry is a post-Vatican II phenomenon: the council itself neither provided a detailed treatment of the topic nor applied the term to the activities of the laity in any thoroughgoing way.[46] Still, the emergence of 'ministry' as a significant area in the life of the church expresses the reception of the Second Vatican Council's emphasis on the fact that all the baptized share in

---

[43]Karl Rahner, 'Dialogue in the Church', *Theological Investigations* (vol. 10; trans. D. Bourke; New York, NY: Seabury, 1977), p. 105.

[44]Pierre Hegy, *Wake Up Lazarus!:On Catholic Renewal* (Bloomington, IN: iUniverse, 2011), p. 173.

[45]Richard Gaillardetz, *By What Authority? A Primer on Scripture, the Magisterium and the Sense of the Faithful* (Collegeville, MN: Liturgical Press, 2003), p. 118.

[46]For a detailed analysis of the context and implications of all the usages of 'ministry' in the council's documents, see Elissa Rinere, 'Conciliar and Canonical Applications of "Ministry" to the Laity', *The Jurist* 47 (1987), pp. 204–27.

the priestly, prophetic and royal offices of Christ.[47] The council's teaching over-turned that state of affairs in which 'the laity were erroneously regarded as not "having a vocation" in the sense of a state of life that was specifically directed towards holiness or some special form of Christian service'.[48]

While Vatican II taught that the members of the laity, no less than the ordained, were called to participate fully in the mission of the church, it envisaged 'the world' as the proper sphere for the action of the laity.[49] That emphasis, which continues to be prominent in official documents, reinforced the perception that 'the church' was the proper sphere of the ordained.[50] The expansion of ministry among the laity in the last generation, no less than the sharp decline in the number of ordained ministers, has meant that the neat separation into two different theatres of operation has collapsed. How ought we to assess that change?

Not surprisingly perhaps, that question evokes different answers. The response of official documents tends to be suspicious of the current trends in ministry. Thus, the documents emphasize the difference between the laity and the ordained, both in terms of their respective representation of Christ and their respective roles in the church and the world. More specifically, the documents highlight the danger of 'clericalizing' the laity, turning the gaze of the laity inward to the church and away from the world.[51] Beyond the documents, but with related concerns, other sources warn that lay ministers might fall victim to an elitism that fails to reflect the equality of all the members of the church.[52]

---

[47]See particularly LG arts. 9–12.

[48]Aurelie Hagstrom, *The Emerging Laity: Vocation, Mission, and Spirituality* (Mahwah, NJ: Paulist, 2010), p. 29.

[49]For a review of the council's teaching on the laity's role in the world, see Rinere, 'Conciliar and Canonical Applications', pp. 206–07.

[50]For an example of the stress on 'the world' as the province of the laity, see John Paul II, *Novo Millennio Ineunte*, art. 46.

[51]The most complete statement of the suspicions common to many documents can be found in *Ecclesiae de Mysterio*, 'On Certain Questions Regarding the Collaboration of the Lay Faithful in the Sacred Ministry of Priests', issued by nine curial dicastries in 1997, *Origins* 27 (1997), pp. 397–410; see also Robert Connor, 'Why the Laity are not Ministers: A Metaphysical Probe', *Communio* 29 (2002), pp. 258–85.

[52]For the fear of 'elitism', see Teresa Pirola, 'Church Professionalism – When Does It Become "Lay Elitism"?' in *Redefining the Church: Vision and Practice* (ed. Richard Lennan; Alexandria, NSW: E.J. Dwyer, 1995), pp. 71–85.

On the other hand, the burgeoning theological reflection on ministry, particularly in the United States, stresses that far from being a refuge for those lay people unwilling to engage with the world, ministry is 'the vocation of leading disciples in the life of discipleship for the sake of God's mission in the world'.[53] Indeed, Avery Dulles claims that lay ministers can even offset the impact of secularism on the church as 'they can form a Catholic people sufficiently united to Christ in prayer and sufficiently firm and well instructed in their faith to carry out the kinds of apostolate that Vatican II envisaged'.[54]

Similarly, theologians stress that ministry is other than a 'zero-sum game' between ordained and lay ministers. Thus, Edward Hahnenberg marks a shift from 'a linear model putting clergy over against laity to a model of two concentric circles, where various ministries are seen within the whole church community and its mission in the world'.[55] In a related vein, Richard Gaillardetz proposes the use of 'ordered church ministry' as a category that could include both forms of ministry. By that designation, Gaillardetz seeks to highlight 'a reality broader than the ministry of the ordained (though inclusive of it) and narrower than Christian discipleship'. All ordered ministries would involve 'a new ecclesial relationship', would involve being 'ecclesially re-positioned'.[56]

The complexity and challenge, no less than the possibility, of our present moment in regard to 'ministry' is well captured by Bernard Sesboüé:

We are now encountering a phenomenon that cannot but be authentically and officially ecclesial, a reality of the Church in the fullest sense: male and female Christians are putting themselves forward to help the Church in its properly pastoral role and are doing this on the strength of an official mandate from the bishop. They are offering themselves for this task out of

---

[53]Kathleen Cahalan, *Introducing the Practice of Ministry* (Collegeville, MN: Liturgical Press, 2010), p. 50.

[54]Avery Dulles, 'Can Laity Properly Be Called "Ministers"?', *Origins* 35 (2006), p. 730.

[55]Edward Hahnenberg, 'Lay? Ministry?: Christian Mission in a Pluralistic World' in *Catholic Identity and the Laity* (ed. Tim Muldoon; Maryknoll, NY: Orbis, 2009), p. 209.

[56]Richard Gaillardetz, 'The Ecclesiological Foundations of Ministry within an Ordered Community' in *Ordering the Baptismal Priesthood: Theologies of Lay and Ordained Ministry* (ed. Susan Wood; Collegeville, MN: Liturgical Press, 2010), p. 36.

Christian conviction, out of a desire to serve the Church and to give it a new ministerial form.[57]

It is evident that the current shape of ministry raises questions for which answers cannot be found solely by reference to the past – this is particularly so for issues related to the ministry of women in the church. The church, however, must answer those questions in ways that accord with its apostolic identity, as well as its need for unity. The resolution of this conundrum must centre on the church's attentiveness to the Holy Spirit, expressed in the discernment of the whole community of faith, the *sensus fidei fidelium*, to seek what is the most appropriate expression of the pilgrim church in the present.

Just as history presents new challenges that have implications for the *ad intra* life of the church, so do changes in the broader social and cultural milieu have implications for the church's life *ad extra*. In the latter as in the former, what is at stake is the church's capacity not only to discern where the Spirit might be at work in the new circumstances, but also to fashion responses that reveal the church as a sacrament of that Spirit.

The church's relationship with the world

The caption under which it is usual to assemble reflections on the church's relationship with the world is the one that is the integrating principle of this paper: 'mission'. As the paper has argued, mission is not simply a sub-set of ecclesiology, but constitutive of the identity and purpose of the church understood as 'sacrament': 'the church is the community of people called by God, who through the Holy Spirit, are united with Jesus Christ and sent as disciples to bear witness to God's reconciliation, healing and transformation of creation'.[58] Consequently, the relationship with 'the world' is not merely an option, but a necessary element of the church self-realization. That relationship is also

---

[57]Bernard Sesboüé, 'Lay Ecclesial Ministers: A Theological Look into the Future', *The Way* 42 (2003), p. 69.

[58]World Council of Churches, 'The Nature and Mission of the Church: A Stage on the Way to a Common Statement' in *Receiving 'The Nature and Mission of the Church': Ecclesial Reality and Ecumenical Horizons for the Twenty-First Century* (ed. Paul Collins and Michael Fahey; London: T & T Clark, 2008), p. 141.

irreducibly complex with a complexity that reflects the complexity of its two constituent partners.

For much of the church's history, however, that complexity was scarcely acknowledged, perhaps scarcely imaginable. This was largely so because members of the church saw 'the world' as a reality separate from themselves, as an alien place characterized by the absence of God. Vitor Westhelle attributes much of this perception to Augustine's analysis of the 'two cities', which left the world as 'the space of aimless wanderings', a place of decay and annihilation, with no role in salvation history.[59] When the church views the world in this way '[the church] can become locked in its own world, possessed of an essentially self-referential hermeneutic that at worst is triumphalist and at best a sort of paternalistic vision in which the wisdom and the folly of the world alike are both subsumed in the totalizing explanation of faith'.[60]

Vatican II's *Gaudium et Spes*, particularly that document's opening equation of the concerns of the followers of Christ and of all people, opened a different window on to the world. Fifty years on from Vatican II, some in the church have a less positive view of the world than the one prevailing in 1965.[61] It could be that this burgeoning suspicion of 'the world' is simply a by-product of the contemporary debate about the most appropriate hermeneutic for viewing Vatican II: continuity, rupture or reform?[62] It is more likely, however, that it expresses a reaction to new forms of complexity emerging in the church-world relationship. At the heart of the new situation is the fact that members of the church, as citizens of the world, are more likely to be influenced by the culture in which they live than by the church's liturgy or doctrine. In addition, in the age of social media, globalization, religious pluralism and other dramatic

---

[59]Westhelle, *The Church Event*, p. 114.

[60]Paul Lakeland, "'I Want to Be in That Number": Desire, Inclusivity and the Church' in *CTSA Proceedings* 66 (2011), p. 22.

[61]For an assessment of the contemporary critiques of *Gaudium et Spes*, see James McEvoy, 'Church and World at the Second Vatican Council: The Significance of *Gaudium et Spes*', *Pacifica* 19 (2006), pp. 37–57.

[62]For discussion of the controversy about the interpretation of Vatican II, see John O'Malley, *What Happened at Vatican II* (Cambridge, MA: Belknap Press, 2008); for the issue of 'continuity, rupture, or reform', see Joseph Komonchak, 'Benedict XVI and the Interpretation of Vatican II' in *The Crisis of Authority in Catholic Modernity* (ed. Michael Lacey and Francis Oakley; New York, NY: Oxford University Press, 2011), pp. 93–110.

social forces, it has become increasingly difficult for 'the church' to influence 'the world'.

How, then, ought the church to respond to this new situation? It is important to begin with the recognition, reinforced by Pope Benedict XVI, that the church maintains a fundamental 'yes' to the world.[63] The challenge comes in trying to determine what to do when we recognize, again in Pope Benedict's terms, that the relationship with the world cannot be one of 'pure harmony' and that the church cannot abolish the gospel's opposition to 'human dangers and errors'.[64]

For the 'official church' at least, 'new evangelization' is a central aspect of the contemporary response to the world. At the heart of this emphasis is a desire for renewal in the church, in order that the members of the church might live their faith in the world more courageously. There is a need to ensure, however, that such renewal avoids a defensive outlook on the modern world, that it does not aim at 'reconquering' the world for Christendom.[65] In order to defuse such dangers, a self-critical dimension ought to be characteristic of proposals for new evangelization so that we remember that the church undertaking this new evangelization is a church in need of reform, not simply renewal. If this dimension is absent, it is difficult to see how such a process might speak to the 'secular Catholics' described in the previous section, let alone alleviate the profound scepticism towards the church's authorities that is a legacy of the sexual abuse tragedy.

Viewed through the lens of the church as sacrament, mission becomes not conquest, but dialogue. Indeed, as expressed by John Zizioulas, the church, having received from both God and the world, offers itself to the world for reception, rather than imposing itself on the world.[66] Such an approach builds

---

[63]Pope Benedict XVI, 'A Proper Hermeneutic for the Second Vatican Council' in *Vatican II: Renewal Within Tradition* (ed. Matthew Lamb and Matthew Levering; New York, NY: Oxford University Press, 2008), p. xiv.

[64]Ibid.

[65]For a critique of trends in Catholic 'new ecclesial movements', see Enzo Pace, 'Increase and Multiply: From Organicism to a Plurality of Models in Contemporary Catholicism' in *'Movements' in the Church* (ed. Alberto Melloni; London: SCM, 2003) [*Concilium*, 2003/3], pp. 67–79 and Luca Diotallevi, '"Catholicism by way of Sectrarianism?" An Old Hypothesis for New Problems' in *'Movements' in the Church* (ed. Alberto Melloni; London: SCM, 2003) [*Concilium*, 2003/3], pp. 107–21.

[66]John Zizioulas, 'The Theological Problem of "Reception"', *One in Christ* 21 (1985), p. 189.

on the church's sacramentality: the church out of its own grounding in grace can help people to become aware of the grace of God already at work in the world; the church, because it does not yet enjoy the fullness of God's kingdom, can itself continue to grow in grace through its encounters with the Spirit at work in the world. In its engagement with the world, then, the church is both benefactor and beneficiary: the church hears its own good news more fully in proclaiming it and learns the implications of its own preaching by listening to the world.[67] In order to do this, the church, in the wonderful phrase of John Fuellenbach, needs to be attentive to 'sniffing out' the presence of God's kingdom in the world and to 'feast' on that presence wherever it finds it, just as it feasts on the presence of God in the eucharist.[68]

This notion of the sacramental church engaging in dialogue with a graced world neither presumes harmony with that world nor excludes the church's proclamation of God's word and its prophetic challenges to the world. In terms of proclamation, the focus can be on the gospel as dialogue. Dialogue with the world requires, in the paradoxical formulation of Stephen Bevans and Roger Schroeder, 'a bolder humility and a humbler boldness'.[69] In short, as formulated by Pope Paul VI, 'the spirit of dialogue is friendship and, even more, is service'.[70] Those qualities are manifest in listening to one's dialogue partner with patience and respect – 'listening equates to "leaving" one's homeland'.[71] The need for those qualities applies urgently in today's complex social and religious environment:

> It will be important that those entrusted with the task of proclamation engage intelligently with their interlocutors' frameworks of meaning. Failing to engage with these would mean a failure in the task of proclamation;

[67]Michael Himes, 'The Church and the World in Conversation: The City of God and "Interurban" Dialogue', *New Theology Review* 18 (2005), p. 32.

[68]John Fuellenbach, 'The Church in the Context of the Kingdom of God' in *The Convergence of Theology: A Festschrift Honoring Gerald O'Collins S.J.* (ed. Daniel Kendall and Stephen Davis; Mahwah, NJ: Paulist, 2001), pp. 236–37.

[69]Stephen Bevans and Roger Schroeder, *Constants in Context: A Theology of Mission for Today* (Maryknoll, NY: Orbis, 2004), pp. 379–80.

[70]Pope Paul VI, *Ecclesiam Suam* [1964] (Boston: St Paul Book & Media, n.d.), p. 88.

[71]Stephen Bevans and Roger Schroeder, *Prophetic Dialogue: Reflections on Christian Mission Today* (Maryknoll, NY: Orbis, 2011), p. 59.

condemning the culture as intrinsically subjectivist would deny interlocutors the opportunity to hear the gospel in words that make sense to them.[72]

Similarly, the church's prophetic engagement with the contemporary world needs nuance – 'the missionary nature of the church in a secular society need not be reduced to laying religious siege to the secular structure of a modern society'.[73] If the church is to claim a prophetic role in society, if it is to speak for those without voice and help them to find a voice, then it needs to be self-critical and to avoid temptations such as 'Caesaropapism and papal theocracy'.[74] Even more, those who represent the church officially in the public arena must do so in ways that speak to the breadth of vision and compassion revelatory of God's kingdom. The latter is an urgent requirement since:

> a secularist mode of governance is facilitated when Catholic interventions in the public domain can be marginalised as special interests, rather than listened to – not necessarily heeded – as the expression of a wider claim to be a universal religion and a moral teacher . . . Bishops as the shop stewards of Catholicism are doomed to lose their moral authority and become one more negotiator with government.[75]

Although constructive and imaginative action by bishops is clearly important, the church's prophetic activity does not begin and end with the bishops, but is the responsibility of all the faithful.[76] Since love of neighbour takes place in concrete circumstances, its shape cannot be determined independently of those who must enact it in their particular circumstances.[77] The church's doctrine can promote 'orthodox practice', but it requires the individual members

---

[72]James Gerard McEvoy, 'Proclamation as Dialogue: Transition in the Church-World Relationship', *Theological Studies* 70 (2009), p. 894.

[73]Thomas Hughson, 'Missional Churches in Secular Societies: Theology Consults Sociology', *Ecclesiology* 7 (2011), p. 194.

[74]John Rist, *What is Truth?: From the Academy to the Vatican* (Cambridge: Cambridge University Press, 2008), p. 338.

[75]Ian Linden, *Global Catholicism: Diversity and Change Since Vatican II* (New York, NY: Columbia University Press, 2009), p. 263.

[76]Rahner, 'The Function of the Church as Critic of Society', p. 243.

[77]Karl Rahner, 'The Church's Commission to Bring Salvation and the Humanization of the World', *Theological Investigations* (vol. 14; trans. D. Bourke; New York, NY: Crossroad, 1976), p. 312.

of the church to translate it into action.[78] Rahner's argument reinforces a key dimension of this paper's thesis: that the realization of the church as sacrament depends on all its members.

The complexity of the church's relationship with the modern world can serve as a reminder of the implications of the church's pilgrim existence. Faithfulness to that pilgrimage requires that we engage, in faith, with what we cannot control, seeking outcomes that we cannot be sure that we will accomplish. The Christian vocation to discipleship, then, can never separate itself, as Johann Baptist Metz reminds us, from the sense of danger that is inextricably linked with faithfulness to the crucified Jesus.[79] That danger not withstanding, there can be no substitute for faithfulness to the crucified Jesus if the church is to fulfil its mission. In its faithfulness, the church witnesses to the hope that we have in the risen Jesus, 'and hope does not disappoint, because God's love has been poured into our hearts through the Holy Spirit that has been given to us' (Rom. 5:5; NRSV).[80]

The focus on the mission of the church, on the church's relation to God, history, and the wider world, saves all discussion of vocation from declining into a narcissistic 'God and me' framework. The fact that the church as a whole exists for mission, not for self-interest, reinforces that all vocations in the Christian community must also be other-directed, must seek to be sacramental of the God who, in Christ through the Holy Spirit, comes to meet us in our time and place in order both to nurture us where we are and lead us beyond the limits of where we are. In being willing to be formed as sacraments of the Spirit, therefore, all who live out their vocation as members of the church are also sacraments of the church whose mission they share.

---

[78]Rahner, 'The Function of the Church as Critic of Society', pp. 243–44.

[79]Johann Baptist Metz, *A Passion for God: The Mystical-Political Dimension of Christianity* (trans. J. M. Ashley; Mahwah, NJ: Paulist, 1998), pp. 46–48.

[80]For the relationship between the church and 'hope', see Richard Lennan, 'The Church as a Sacrament of Hope', *Theological Studies* 72 (2011), pp. 247–74.

Part Two

Conversing with the Tradition

4

'The will to enter religious life does not need to be tested to see whether it is from God' (ST II–II 189:10): Can Aquinas' understanding of vocation still work?

Fr Joseph Bolin

Thomas Aquinas argues that one may and should heartily invite all persons to consider religious life and insists that someone wanting to pursue religious life to grow in holiness and love need not deliberate for a long time and seek much advice in order to determine whether this is God's will. This paper aims, firstly, to root Aquinas's understanding of vocation to religious life in the whole of his theology and understanding of christian vocation,[1] and, secondly, to examine whether, and to what extent his view of religious vocation can work today.[2]

---

[1] Richard Butler, a staunch defender of Aquinas's view, notes that a correct theology of religious vocation can only be recovered by locating the individual elements pertinent to religious vocation in the whole context of theology. *Religious Vocation: An Unnecessary Mystery*, pp. 33–34.

[2] Though many of Thomas's considerations on religious life may be equally applied to other forms of consecrated life, I will retain the term 'religious life' in expounding Thomas's view, not only because it is the language he uses, but also because many of the other forms of consecrated life known to us today did not exist in his time.

Aquinas argues for his position in the following manner:[3] first, Christ invited us to this way of life, indicating it as a better way to grow in charity, and so it is unnecessary or even wrong to doubt that it is in itself the better path. Secondly he notes that the ability to live religious life is not some special faculty to be found within ourselves, but is a gift of God, given to those who ask for it; consequently, he concludes, there is no need to carefully scrutinize ourselves to determine if we have this faculty, but need to ask God for this gift if we undertake this way of life. As in general, however, Aquinas holds that grace builds on and completes natural gifts, so here he recognizes that some degree of deliberation and consultation may be necessary in the event that particular obstacles to religious life are present, such as physical weakness or large debts that must be paid. Again, some deliberation and consultation may be necessary to decide which religious community to enter, to determine the appropriate way to prepare oneself to enter, and such things. But in general, when someone knows he wants to enter religious life to serve God, he need not hesitate on the grounds of making sure it is the 'right thing' or 'God's will' or his vocation.

Though Aquinas does not employ the term 'vocation' in this article, he considers his position to be faithful to the presentation of religious vocation in Sacred Scripture and in the patristic tradition.[4] He sees the position that long deliberation is unnecessary illustrated by the scriptural record of the disciples Peter and Andrew, who immediately left their nets to follow the Lord when he *called* them, and as being in complete harmony with Augustine, who decries the one who, when 'The morning star', that is, Christ, 'calls him', seeks advice from human beings who are frail and prone to error.

While Aquinas does not frequently use the term 'call' or 'vocation' in his works, a solid understanding of vocation is woven throughout his writing, an understanding that also underlies his treatment of entering religious life. I shall begin with this underlying view of vocation in order to properly understand Aquinas's view of religious vocation.

---

[3]*Summa Theologiae* II–II 189:10.

[4]The patristic tradition indeed saw religious life as open to all christians, and principally as a choice made in order to more surely and more fully realize the call to holiness in Christ, rather than a distinct calling.

Vocation within God's plan

Even where Aquinas does not use the term vocation at all, his christian anthropology reveals the role of vocation in christian life. One can roughly define vocation in the primary sense, the vocation to holiness, as the divine action by which God enters a person's life, makes himself known to that person, and directs and moves that person to himself. These elements are present throughout Aquinas's vision of the human person's journey to God. His teaching on grace as a precondition and cause of the human movement towards God shows the divine *initiative and action* in an individual human life. His teaching on the response of faith and charity shows how the person drawn to God under the impulse of grace comes to God as one whom he or she *encounters*. His teaching on the guiding role of the Holy Spirit shows the individual, *personal* manner in which God meets and moves the human person.

When Aquinas speaks explicitly about the place of God's call in his plan of salvation, he describes it in varying ways, but always in a pattern consistent with the foregoing: first comes God's plan and decision to bring a man to faith and salvation (election, foreknowledge, predestination), then God produces a movement (an interior light and movement of the will, as well as in some cases an exterior call) drawing a man to holiness/faith/justification, so as ultimately to bring him to the glory of heaven.

Predestination/Foreknowledge/Election > call > sanctification/
justification > glorification

Aquinas does not limit the means by which God accomplishes his election and call to special charisms or mystical experiences. To lead a person to himself, God may use direct external causes, the natural inclinations of the particular human person, providential circumstances that come together to influence that person in a certain way, an internal inspiration, or the connatural inclination of charity, which inclines a person to act in a manner befitting God's will. All of these are included in God's plan and are all suitable means for achieving his salvific will.

God does not merely plan in a generic fashion to bring a person to salvation; his plan includes the various details – the particular way of life, profession, etc., – by which a person realizes and lives the grace of baptism and holiness. The call to religious life is thus included in or is a concretization of the principal vocation to faith and to holiness.

Vocation in human experience

Such is vocation from the theological point of view; how does it appear from the point of view of the one called? How does he experience a vocation? Aquinas's treatment of the choice of a state of life moves between two different perspectives the person called may have. The person may be looking to the goal: the perfection of charity, which is the ultimate goal of every human vocation, and to a particular way of life, as the means to realize that goal. Or he may be looking to the moving principle within him: charity and the working of the Holy Spirit.

Both perspectives are legitimate and are really two sides of the same thing. On the one hand, we cannot will or do something good without God's acting within us to bring about this will, so a genuine pursuit of charity always presupposes God's action already at work within the soul.[5] And on the other hand, God's action within the soul, the inclination of charity cannot fail to be directed towards our true good.[6]

But though these two aspects of a vocation are always united in reality, a person may be more conscious of one or the other. One may perceive that one's genuine love for God and neighbour inclines one more to a particular choice, without being able to explain exactly why that choice is preferable to the alternative; or one may judge a particular choice to be better and more conducive to love, without having any feeling or *experience* that charity is inclining one to that act.

---

[5]Aquinas, *Commentary On the Lord's Prayer*, Article 5.

[6]'Frequently we do not know what we should do or desire. But charity teaches all things necessary for salvation. . . . For, where charity is, there is the Holy Spirit, who knows everything, and leads us in the way of righteousness'. Aquinas, *Commentary on the Two Precepts of Charity*. 'With the Holy Spirit directing and inspiring our heart, our desires cannot but be beneficial for us'. Aquinas, *Commentary on the Letter to the Romans*, ch. 8, lec. 5.

One of these two things implies the other, and therefore it is sufficient for one element to be present. If someone is really and reasonably sure that it is divine charity which inclines him to make a particular choice, he can be confident that it is a good choice. And conversely, if a person who loves God is really and reasonably sure that a particular choice is the better choice, he can be confident that it is in accordance with charity, and that his readiness or will to make the choice is from God. Accordingly, Aquinas concludes, a person who is intent on living religious life, on living and growing in love in this way of life, may be confident that 'the will to enter religious life that has arisen in his heart is from the Spirit of God, who leads men and women into the right land'.[7] Aquinas does not hesitate to say, even if someone were to come upon the idea of entering religious life through the devil's intervention, if he honestly wants to enter this way of life to serve God, this desire can only be from God's interior movement in his soul.[8]

Aquinas concludes, when a person is called to religious life, whether by an interior movement of his heart, or by Christ calling him sensibly, or through the words of the Scripture, for example, 'If you would be perfect, go, sell everything you have, give to the poor, and come follow me', it is not right to insist on seeking advice as though it were uncertain whether one should pursue religious life.[9]

What if these two approaches are in conflict, or appear to be in conflict? Suppose someone in his deliberation thinks to himself, 'I see no obstacle to my living religious life, and I believe that it is a surer and better way to grow in charity', yet at the same time, through experience of discernment of spirits, comes to the conclusion that his inclination to witness Christ in the world by marrying and raising a holy christian family is from the Holy Spirit, in the sense of a particular, connatural movement of charity? Since Aquinas attributes the greatest importance to the internal calling, it seems one has to say that in such a situation one should follow the interior inspiration rather than the reasoning

---

[7]*Summa Theologiae* II-II, q. 189, a. 10, ad 1.

[8]*Contra Doctrinam Retrahentium*, ch. 10.

[9]'It is not praiseworthy, but blameworthy, after an internal or external calling, made either in words or in the Scriptures, to put off following it, and to seek counsel as though the matter were doubtful'. *Contra Doctrinam Retrahentium*, ch. 9.

process based on what is generally better objectively. However, caution would be indicated in such a case to be sure that the inclination to a life in the world rather than religious life is really from the Holy Spirit.[10]

Variety of vocations

In this paper I am focusing on Aquinas's view of vocation to religious life. Nonetheless I wish to add a few words here on the question of vocations to particular states of life and professions: to marriage, to teaching, to medicine, etc. Aquinas holds that the diversity of states within the Church is not an accident or a side effect of human freedom, but is willed by God. There is a deep christological reason for this: no one person can manifest the fullness of Christ's grace; each person has a particular, partial share in this grace. So that the Church as a whole may more fully share in Christ's grace, there must be different persons in different states, with different graces and charisms. Furthermore, the mutual relationships and the complementarity of the states of life contribute to the dignity and beauty of the Church. The distinction of states within the Church is thus not due to the accidents of history or merely human choices; it arises from the divine ordination.[11] Still, this ordination is to a great extent accomplished by *means* of the diverse inclinations of human beings: some are inclined more to one way of life, some more to another, and consequently also some choose one way of life, some another. 'The distribution of tasks, so that different persons be occupied with different tasks, happens principally by divine providence, but secondarily by natural causes, through which a man

---

[10]Aquinas himself does not seem to foresee such a conflict scenario arising at all. According to the ignatian tradition, which foresees the possibility of a conflict here, caution would need to be exercised in such a case, and indeed, the objective or rational way (the 'third time') is generally considered surer than the way of discernment of spirits. Ignatius himself says that greater signs from God are needed to discern a call to lay life (life according to the commandments without the evangelical counsels) than to religious life (life following the evangelical counsels) (*Directoria Ignatiana Autographa*, n. 9), and suggests that sometimes the 'third time' for making a choice should be recommended by the director of the Exercises, when the choice arrived at through discernment of spirits is in his judgment not a good choice. Early Jesuit notes on the Spiritual Exercises likewise indicate that the third time is the surer and safer way of choosing.

[11]*Summa Theologiae*, II-II, q. 183, a. 2.

is more inclined to one action than to another'.[12] Since God accomplishes his plan for diversity within the Church and mankind through human inclinations, man is in general not obliged to any particular profession or way of life, but only when there is no other legitimate way to survive or ensure essential human goods.[13] Man is free to choose what to do with his life, and God carries out his plan through man's free choice.

Accordingly, when a person makes a prudent choice of a way of life as a means and way of holiness, this choice and way of life is embedded within the original divine call to holiness: the person intends to pursue this way of life in order to realize the call to holiness and charity, and this way of life and intention is included in God's providence, which arranges that different persons choose different ways of life for the perfection of the Church. In this sense marriage, professions of service, and finally all good and christian ways of life can legitimately be called vocations, inasmuch as they flow from and are embedded in the original vocation to charity.

Summary of Aquinas's approach to religious vocation

Let us briefly sum up Aquinas's view of religious vocation. In choosing a particular way or state of life as a way to fulfil the fundamental call to holiness and love, one may orient oneself by the *impulse* of charity and of the Holy Spirit – what does charity impel me to do? or one may orient oneself by the *goal* of charity – what is more beneficial for the growth and promotion of the life of charity? When deliberating about religious life, one may be sure that religious life per se is a better means to promote the growth of charity. Consequently, in the absence of positive impediments or reasons to the contrary, one who wishes to enter religious life may intend to do so with confidence that this is in accordance with God's will, though certainly entering with an openness to finding otherwise, if an unexpected obstacle is found, for example, during the novitiate.[14]

---

[12] *Contra Impugnantes* II, ch. 4, ad 1; see *In IV Sent.* d. 26, q. 1, a. 2, ad 4; *Summa Contra Gentiles* III, 134.
[13] Ibid.
[14] See *Summa Theologiae*, II-II, q. 189, a. 4, ad 2.

Promotion of religious vocations

What does this mean for vocational practice and discernment? The practical conclusion would seem to be, don't present a religious vocation to persons deliberating about and discerning their way in life as something that maybe, just possibly is somehow the right way for you, but present it as an invitation. Richard Butler summarizes this practical conclusion in his work *Religious Vocation: An Unnecessary Mystery*.

> The writer or speaker discussing religious life, therefore, should make his appeal general and objective. His approach should not be: 'Is God calling you – look into your heart of hearts, etc.' Rather, the approach should be the Christlike challenge to all, appealing to personal courage and generosity to effect a response: 'God *is* calling you, daring you to follow Him. Are you generous enough, etc.?'[15]

This approach was not infrequent in the first half of the twentieth century, at least in theory. But a trend may be seen, at least from the 1950s on, to place greater emphasis on the ecclesial and charismatic nature of religious life,[16] as well as on the importance of semi-conscious and unconscious factors influencing the will to enter or to live religious life. Accordingly, the traditional approach, where religious life was presented as the better means for attaining perfection in charity, open to all those ready and willing to commit themselves to it and live it faithfully, dropped gradually out of favour.[17]

---

[15]Butler, *Religious Vocation*, p.154.

[16]Agnes Patrice Sheehan, *The Charismatic Character of Consecrated Virginity: A Study of the Status of the Question Since 1945*, Catholic University of America, 1967. The increasing use of the term 'charism' in relation to the choice of consecrated life since the 1940s reveals a greater emphasis on the value to the whole Church of the election and vocation of the few to this state of life, in comparison with the traditional principal emphasis on the value to the individual who chose it – a better and surer means to attaining salvation and to perfection in love – with the value to the Church understood principally as a consequence of the growth in charity of the individual.

[17]Alongside the general decline in thomism around the time of Vatican II, the number of works presenting the thomistic or traditional view of religious vocation sharply declined after the council.

The viability of Aquinas's approach

Is Aquinas's approach still valid? Can it work today? In the second part of this paper I examine the value of Aquinas's approach for today, aiming to shed light on its strengths and possible weaknesses for the promotion of vocations.

Let us first be clear what we mean when we ask whether an approach to religious vocation 'works'. The basic criteria for judging an approach to discernment are: how accurate is it? And how beneficial is it? A good approach to religious vocations will (1) maximize the number of people who correctly determine that they do have a religious vocation and follow it, and (2) minimize the number of people who suffer loss by incorrectly determining that they have a religious vocation or by leaving off the pursuit of a religious vocation. Furthermore, a sound approach to religious vocation (3) should not detract from other vocations, but should fit into a comprehensive approach to vocation that also encourages the vocation to the priesthood, to holy and good marriages, to works of charity, professions of service, lay witness, etc.

Some comments on these criteria. The first criterion is: does this approach function well to 'identify' a vocation when present? Or are there many persons who in fact are called to religious life, but whom this approach would not identify as having a vocation? A strict approach to vocation, which insisted that the one pursuing religious life be so sure about the call that he is utterly unable to doubt that he is called to religious life[18] would exclude many genuine vocations. St Thérèse of Lisieux, who was strongly assailed by doubt about the genuineness of her vocation just before taking vows,[19] could by such an approach have been identified as not having a vocation. A sound approach to vocations will as far as possible correctly identify all true vocations to consecrated life.

---

[18]This is the kind of surety indicated in Ignatius's 'first time' of making a choice. Of course, Ignatius recognizes two other times of making a choice as well.

[19]The saint describes her feelings at that moment: 'The devil – for it was he – made me feel sure that I was wholly unsuited for life in the Carmel, and that I was deceiving my superiors by entering on a way to which I was not called. The darkness was so bewildering that I understood but one thing – I had no religious vocation, and must return to the world'.

Again, a good approach to vocations will minimize the incorrect identification of religious vocation where there is none, or at least will minimize the cases where this identification is harmful to the person in question, or is a burden to the religious community. For, sometimes it may do no harm, but even be beneficial that someone thinks he has a religious vocation, and prepares himself for such a way of life. If in such cases one can speak about an 'inaccurate' identification of a religious vocation, it still redounds in such a case to the benefit of the one discerning. Such a case could perhaps more accurately be described as God calling a person to pursue religious life for a time, without calling him or her to enter or to make a definitive commitment through final vows. In other cases, however, the incorrect discernment of a religious vocation could be harmful; a person breaks off studies, relationships, etc., to pursue religious life, without the prerequisite qualities and so without a true vocation, and after giving up the pursuit of religious life feels abandoned and lost and is worse off than before. A good approach to vocations should minimize such tragic cases.

The third criterion for a well-functioning approach to vocations is: does it integrate well into christian life as whole, to the promotion of virtuous and christian life in all areas of society and the Church? Or does it, for example, detract from the promotion of holy married life, by giving the impression that anyone who is serious about holiness is a religious, and married persons don't have a chance of being holy anyway, so why try?

First criterion: Maximize the number of correctly discerned vocations

The thomistic approach should work very well according to the first criterion. For this approach says that *it does not matter* what the original occasion or motivation was that gets someone interested in religious life; it could be admiration for a religious brother or sister, it could be the faith that shines in the life of the community, the feeling that the interested candidate 'fits in' here, the experience that this form of life is an inspiration and help to prayer and charity, a feeling of inner peace when visiting the community and living their way of life. This approach to vocations will not turn anyone away from religious life on the grounds that they discerned their vocation to religious life by another way, as long as the person, at the latest within the novitiate, manifests a firm will to live the religious life as a path of growth in charity, to take the means necessary to live it well, to make the sacrifices involved, etc.

Since the will to live the consecrated life as a way of charity is in any case a canonical requirement for acceptance into this state of life,[20] in principle the thomistic approach should not exclude any genuine vocations.

Second criterion: Minimize the number of 'false positives', and persons somehow hurt in following a perceived religious vocation

The second criterion is that a sound approach to religious vocations should minimize the number of 'false positives', the number of people who think they have a vocation when they do not. This criterion discloses the most plausible weaknesses of the thomistic approach.

Religious life is not a free choice, but requires a call

First, it may be objected that religious life is never simply an option which a person is free to choose or not.[21] One must be called by God, and so the reasoning 'this way of life is a better way (to grow in charity, or to serve the

---

[20]CIC 597 requires a 'right intention' to be admitted to consecrated life; this right intention consists fundamentally in the will to embrace and live out the way of life in accordance with its specific goals and character, the perfection in charity through the exercise of the evangelical counsels in the fashion peculiar to the specific institute. See Edward Farrell, *The Theology of Religious Vocation*, p. 48 and Charles Schleck, *The Theology of Vocations*, pp. 188–95.

[21]Emphasis on the role of charism in religious vocation is one factor underlying or supporting this objection.

Church, etc.) and therefore I will choose it' is inappropriate. One must always wait for God's call.[22]

This objection to the thomistic approach has roots in Ignatian spirituality, but is somewhat one-sided. From a thomistic perspective, one may make two responses to this objection: first, God's will is manifested in a general way in the invitation to follow him in celibacy and poverty and the preferential favour given to this way of life;[23] secondly, and more importantly, God's will is concretely manifested in the will to live religious life as the better and surer way of growing in and realizing love of God and neighbour, a will that springs from the charity placed by God within his heart.

The 'Firm will' may be deceptive

A second objection to the thomistic approach is that the presence of the requisite 'firm will' is sometimes difficult to determine, contrary to Aquinas's claim that for the person willing to enter religious life, there can be no doubt that this will is from the Holy Spirit.[24]

One might be mistaken about the real motivation of the will. Someone's real motives might be hidden, even from herself. A young woman might think she wants to remain a virgin for God's sake, but might really want to embrace this way of life due to a repulsion for sexual intercourse, out of a feeling of shame rather than from the virtue of chastity. A desire to embrace the evangelical counsel of obedience might derive from an unwillingness to take responsibility for her actions. Consequently, a reliance on the conscious motive and will

---

[22]Ignatius of Loyola's advice tends somewhat in this direction; he says that though in general one may encourage persons who seem suitable candidates for religious life to choose 'continence, virginity, the religious life, and all manner of evangelical perfection', the director of spiritual exercises should refrain from any such encouragement to a particular state of life, because it is better for God to direct and incline the person to choose a way and state of life (*Spiritual Exercises*, n. 15). Hans Urs von Balthasar, drawing on Ignatius, speaks even more strongly against the idea that one can simply choose to embrace the evangelical counsels, arguing that one must always wait for God's individual election to the state of the counsels (*Christlicher Stand*, 42, 130–31).

[23]As noted above, Ignatius says that greater signs are necessary to choose marriage than religious life, because Christ recommended the evangelical counsels and warned of the difficulties wealth brings with it.

[24] *Summa Theologiae*, II-II, q. 189, a. 10, ad 1.

of the one discerning a vocation will result in false positives, in the identification of a religious vocation where there is none.

Similarly, a mere 'will' to live religious life may not be as firm as it seems, if the person as a whole is not fitted for religious life. Addressing the challenge to faithful and enthusiastic young persons 'God is calling you, daring you to follow Him. Are you generous enough, etc.',[25] will result in people, particularly young people, forcing themselves into a way of life that in the end is unpleasant to them, in which they do not fit well, does not make them happy, etc. It is true that in general 'forcing' oneself to do something for greater love is neither strange nor uncommon. Husbands, wives, celibates, and others have many occasions to show their love through overcoming their inclinations to do something for love of another.[26] The problem here is that these young persons get trapped in a situation where they remain under the obligation to live this way of life, and yet live it only reluctantly and half-heartedly. It is far better to be, for example, a loving and devoted wife and mother who puts her heart and love into her family, than a consecrated religious who only lives half-heartedly the 'complete dedication to the Lord' that she professed.

These concerns are surely real concerns today, where many young persons experience great difficulty in knowing what they really want to do, in making up their mind and committing to it. However, the difficulty does not seem to be peculiar to the thomistic approach. Regardless whether or not one takes a vocational approach that sees a firm will to live a way of life as the principal indicator of a vocation to that way of life, one ought to do all one can to ensure that there is such a firm will. However someone comes to the decision to marry, the pastor should do what he can to ensure that there is a real and strong will to live marriage according to God's plan, in good times and in hard times. Similarly, however someone comes to the decision to enter religious life, the vocations director and superiors should do all they can to ensure that the will to enter religious life is neither superficial nor fragile, but deeply rooted

---

[25]Butler, *Religious Vocation*, p. 154.
[26]Exactly in regard to the choice of religious life, the Carmelite saints Teresa of Avila and St Thérèse of Lisieux see a special grace and blessing at work in the one who chooses religious life without feeling attracted to it, and in this sense 'forcing' themselves to it. St Thérèse of Lisieux, LT 169, August 19, 1894; *Œuvres Complètes*, 507. St Teresa of Avila, *Libro de la Vida*, Ch. 3–4, in *Obras Completas*, 14, 16.

in the person.[27] The helps offered by modern psychology can and should be employed for this purpose at a suitable time. We must, however, avoid 'naturalizing' the divine call, reducing the divine election to a matter of human fitness. Though grace presupposes and *perfects* nature, it is not derived from nature. The divine call to religious life presupposes (apart from more or less miraculous gifts) a certain natural basis in the human person, but cannot be deduced from this basis.[28]

This approach is harmful to aspirants

A third objection to the thomistic approach is that it will cause people who consider religious life, perhaps enter for a time, and then cease pursuing this vocation to have a negative self-image, perhaps to give up christian life altogether, or at any rate to be satisfied with mediocrity in living the christian vocation. For, if the will to embrace and follow the religious life as a way to love God is all that is necessary for a vocation, then leaving the religious life would seem to indicate a lack of love, an unreadiness to serve God without reservation. This lends itself to the practical conclusion that if one is not capable of attaining holiness in the easier and better way, there is really no hope of becoming holy in the lay state.[29]

This danger also seems to be a real one. However, I think it is possible to avoid this danger adequately by presenting the truth of consecrated life and consecrated persons accurately. We should avoid giving the impression that consecrated persons are always better, holier, and love God more than lay persons, since this is untrue, tends to induce pride in consecrated persons, and,

---

[27]The strength of will one should expect will vary according to the stage of discernment. One can expect and require much more firmness of will from one about to take final vows than from one in the first stage of serious interest in religious life.

[28]Pius XI in *Divini illius Magistri*, n. 64, sharply condemns the attempt to do so.

[29]Indeed, many texts in the spiritual and ascetical tradition rather lend themselves to this conclusion. Thomas Aquinas says that if someone who is not already preeminent in virtue 'strives to attain perfection while retaining possessions and entering into marriage', his mistake in thinking little of the Lord's advice to give up everything to follow him will soon be manifest, suggesting that he will surely not attain perfection (*De Perfectione Spiritualis Vitae*, Ch. 9). Alphonsus Liguori says that holy married women are very rare, and they are always in sorrow that they did not consecrate themselves to Jesus Christ when they had the chance, suggesting that married life never turns out to be a good and happy way to holiness.

as indicated in the objection, tends to make lay persons settle for something less than complete holiness. Again, we should emphatically avoid giving the impression that a person not in consecrated life can only reach a certain limited degree of holiness in comparison with consecrated persons. Such a lay person is also called to holiness and love without limit, and there is no limit to the degree of holiness and love he or she can attain through fidelity to God's grace in his or her state of life.

Similarly we should note that the difference between those entering consecrated life and those who do not is not a difference in the degree of their love, but a difference in the ways they choose to grow in love. Granted that the most fundamental motivation for a person to enter religious life is love for God, and granted that Christians are generally invited to religious life, it does not follow that those entering religious life are always, or even on average, better, holier, or love God more than those who do not enter religious life. One does not embrace the evangelical counsels because one is already perfect, but in order to strive to grow towards perfect love. It seems that in most cases it is in fact not principally the *degree* of a person's love for God that leads someone to the decision for religious life, but a host of other factors.[30] These factors include both natural inclinations, interior graces and external influences; taken together, they constitute the seed of a call to consecrated life.

Third criterion: Harmonize with a comprehensive approach to vocations

The third criterion for a healthy approach to religious vocation is that it fit in well with a comprehensive approach to vocations. In particular, it should be in

---

[30]I am unaware of particular studies that attempt to assess the average degree of generosity, selflishness, piety, etc., of those entering the consecrated state. Postulants and novices might in fact be above average in many virtues, if for no other reason than that those who manifest extreme problems in these areas would frequently be excluded by the community's screening process. In any case, it would be difficult to match up in any sure way any average superiority in particular virtues such as piety or generosity with charity.

harmony with Vatican II's emphasis on the universal vocation to holiness[31] and the promotion of marriage as a call to holiness.[32]

In the thomistic approach, the religious vocation is principally a determination or realization of the common vocation to faith and to holiness, and so fits in very well with the emphasis on the universal vocation to holiness, and is consistent with the promotion of other ways to live a life of faith, love and holiness, that is, with comprehensive vocational promotion. Still, one element is unique to the religious vocation, namely that religious life is 'better in itself' and therefore considering the way of life as making space for the growth of charity, in the absence of strong evidence to the contrary the presumption can be made that this way of life would be better for a given individual if he or she has no major impediments and undertakes it wholeheartedly.

One objection that could still be raised, however, is that we need outstanding examples of Christian love in each state of life. If all persons with their heart set on serving God devoutly and loving him as much as possible become religious, this will leave only lukewarm and mediocre Christians as married persons, with the result that married persons are let without holy role models.[33]

Two responses can be made to this objection from a thomistic perspective. First, as noted above, people do not enter religious life because they are particularly good followers of Christ, but in order to help them follow Christ better. Thus it is unjustified to conclude that those entering religious life will be overall better and holier than those who do not. Secondly, even if we grant that the prerequisite qualities necessary for someone to firmly choose religious life set him or her apart in some way, manifest some particular christian virtues, virtues that it would be helpful to have present to a greater degree in other states of life, it belongs to those with care for the common good to regulate this, rather than the individual choosing his or her way of life. It is not, for

---

[31]Pope Paul VI and Bl. Pope John Paul II describe the council's exhortation to holiness as the most characteristic element of the council's teaching. Paul VI, *Sanctitatis Clarior*, 19 March 1969, AAS 61 (1969), pp. 149–50; John Paul II, *Christifideles Laici*, n. 16, and homily of 9 May 1988.

[32]John Paul II frequently calls for christian formation that shows marriage as a vocation and mission, and a place where holiness can be attained. (*Familaris consortio*, n. 66, *Tertio millenio adveniente*, n. 37, General audience, 23 July 1988).

[33]Pius XII in *Sacra Virginitas*, nn. 41–42 seems to take up, and reject, this kind of argumentation when it is used to dissuade anyone from choosing the virginal way of life.

example, the responsibility of the person discerning his vocation to determine whether the Church's need for good examples of married life should outweigh other considerations, and lead *him* to choose marriage, even if he were otherwise convinced that he could become holier in religious life.[34]

Empirical testing

In this work, I have presented Aquinas's view of religious vocation and considered its suitability for present day vocational ministry in light of recent theological and ecclesial developments. Following these more general considerations, I would like to close with a proposal to study more closely in an empirical manner the actual effect of this approach to religious vocation. Such a study would require, first, gathering or compiling statistical data on the way vocation was presented and discerned or chosen (e.g. was religious life presented as a challenge offered to all, or as a special way offered to a limited few, was much emphasis given to objective considerations, in particular to an objective superiority of religious life?), and the vocational outcomes: (1) the degree of 'success' in the case of a perceived and followed religious vocation (could be measured by the percentage who persevere and by personal happiness or satisfaction with one's life as a way of holiness); (2) the number of vocations (could be measured by the percentage of persons from a given stage of discernment of religious life who choose religious life) and (3) the degree of 'success' in the case of a negative discernment of religious vocation (could be measured negatively by the percentage of persons who at a later point in their life choose religious life after all, and positively by happiness and satisfaction in their other way of life as a way of holiness). Then one would have to examine this data for patterns. Can the presentation of religious life as a means to more

---

[34]The Church neads good examples of all states of life. Hence, for the individual deciding on a way of life, the need for good examples is just as much a motive to choose religious life as to choose marriage, unless those responsibility for the governance of the Church determine that there is a *greater* need for the christian witness of holy married persons than the christian witness of holy religious. At least till now, the Church's approach seems to have been quite to emphasize the goodness of marriage as a way to holiness, without emphasizing the need for holy married persons *more* than the need for holy religious.

readily attain love and holiness, as a challenge offered to all, be seen in fact to promote good vocations to religious life? Does it result in relatively more frequent dissatisfaction with the spiritual progress of those persons who do not pursue religious life? Does it lead to the other dangers feared by the other objections proposed above to the thomistic approach?

Such a study is fraught with many difficulties: most of the factors to be measured are not black and white, but vary in many degrees; apart from the purely quantitative aspect of how many persons enter religious life, and how long they remain in religious life, the study would depend almost entirely on questionnaires, often filled out years after the deliberation and discernment, and thus potentially subject to remembering the decision differently than one actually made it at the time.

Nonetheless, I believe such a study, using the methods of modern statistical analysis, is feasible, and would be helpful to evaluate and compare the outcomes of various vocational approaches, including the thomistic approach, and to identify their respective strengths and weaknesses, helping vocational directors and others to refine and improve the approach.

Bibliography

Bandera, Armando, 'Recent Church Teaching on Religious Profession: Temporary or Perpetual?', *The Thomist* 34 (1970), pp. 584–635.

Balthasar, Hans Urs Von, *Christlicher Stand* (Einsiedeln: Johannes Verlag, 1977).

Butler, Richard, *Religious Vocation: An Unnecessary Mystery* (Chicago, IL: Henry Regnery Company, 1961).

Davis, Fr. Henry, S. J., *Moral and Pastoral Theology* (London: Sheed and Ward, 1936).

Farrell, Edward P., *The Theology of Religious Vocation* (St. Louis: Herder, 1952).

Haughey, John C., S. J. (ed.), *Revisiting the Idea of Vocation: Theological Explorations* (Washington, DC; Catholic University of America Press, 2004).

Libano-Monteiro, Jose Pedro Rosas, *La vocación en Santu Tomás de Aquino* (Universidad de Navarra (Spain), 1987).

Schleck, Charles A., CSC, *The Theology of Vocations* (Milwaukee: Bruce Publishing Company, 1963).

Sheehan, Agnes Patrice, *The Charismatic Character of Consecrated Virginity: A Study of the Status of the Question Since 1945* (Washington, DC: Catholic University of America, 1967).

Vermeersch, A., SJ, *De religiosis institutis & personis: tractatus canonico-moralis* (Heverlee-Louvain: Editions de la Bibliotheque S.J., 1962).

5

The Spiritual Exercises *of Ignatius of Loyola and their contribution to a theology of vocation*

Sr Gemma Simmonds

'*To fall in love with God is the greatest of romances, to seek God the greatest adventure, to find God the greatest human achievement.*'

ST AUGUSTINE

As a starting point for a theology of vocation there can be few better places than Ignatius of Loyola's *Spiritual Exercises*. The text maps out an experience of call, desire, response, confusion and, eventually, clarity. In his own experience, Ignatius found an insight and a method that, down the centuries, would become crucial in the personal journeys of people seeking and finding a direction for lives given over to God. This essay begins with an overview of the dynamics of the *Spiritual Exercises* and then looks at how they contribute to the mapping out of a theology of vocation. In much of what I write I am indebted to the work of the late Joseph Veale SJ.[1]

---

[1]Joseph Veale, 'The Dynamic of the Exercises', *The Way Supplement* 3 (1985), pp. 18–52.

The *Spiritual Exercises* presuppose God's desire for us. They also presuppose, and articulate clearly at the beginning, that the purpose of our creating is the knowledge, love and service of God, in which we find our truest selves in a free response to the gifts that God has given us. Thus our greatest act of freedom is to assent to become who God created and calls us to be, that is our most complete self. This requires a degree of self knowledge through the gift of discernment. One of the most remarkable things about the Principle and Foundation, the 'manifesto' at the beginning of the *Spiritual Exercises* that encapsulates its underlying theology of vocation, is that it places no premium on any particular way of life. There is no spiritual hierarchy of value here, so that God may be best served by riches or poverty, a long life or a short one, health or sickness, so long as God's will for us, manifested in our deepest sense of our life's orientation, is found and embraced.

> We are created to praise, reverence and serve God our Lord, and by this means save our soul. All the other things on the face of the earth are created for us, that they may help us in pursuing the end for which we are created. From this it follows that we are to use them as much as they help us on to our end, and ought to rid ourselves of them so far as they hinder us in that aim.
>
> For this it is necessary to make ourselves indifferent to all created things in all that is allowed to the choice of our free will and is not prohibited to it; so that, on our part, we want not health rather than sickness, riches rather than poverty, honour rather than dishonour, long rather than short life, and so in all the rest; desiring and choosing only what is more conducive for us to the end for which we are created. [23][2]

The *Spiritual Exercises* also presuppose our desire for God, but make clear that in order to find our personal vocation and act upon it we must be free. The *Spiritual Exercises* are divided into four 'weeks' or sections. Not a formal division of time, these weeks have both an individual character in themselves and follow one from one another in a clear dynamic flow. A major aspect of the first week, which also runs throughout the later weeks, is the unfolding process of recognition of and liberation from any illusions or disordered desires

---

[2]References to the *Spiritual Exercises* throughout are to paragraph number, as is customary.

that are operative within us. In his own memoir, Ignatius refers to himself as 'the Pilgrim', and there is a very real sense of profound personal journey or pilgrimage in the exercises. Those involved in accompanying them often speak of retreatants or directees as pilgrims and themselves as companions. Many pilgrims begin the exercises or the process of spiritual direction by naming a deep but sometimes inarticulate longing for their life to have meaning and purpose. That longing in time becomes expressly a desire to be in relationship with God or to offer their life in God's service in some way. For this to happen effectively, and for the relationship and its consequences to clarify, the pilgrim has to discover the desire beneath the desire, the true inclinations that disclose to us what we most deeply want and therefore who we are most deeply created to be. This requires a radical openness to God, a readiness to receive the gift that God desires to give us, namely the gift of our own truest identity. The companion's task is to enable pilgrims to trust their own deep desires, to recognize that they contain truth about who they are created to be and to respond to the God who is revealed in those desires in a personal way. This may require, at least initially, engaging in the frightening and costly exercise of peeling away layers of self-delusion or negative thinking or false images of self or of God in order to get at the truth that sets us free. What is clear here is the fact that our very understanding of who God is and how God operates can itself be a source of confusion and unfreedom. In contemporary giving of the exercises, the companion would always at an initial stage check this out in terms of how a pilgrim prays and speaks of God, how a pilgrim relates the different aspects of their religious and secular life to one another. Any compartmentalization of life or projection of false images onto God would suggest potential difficulties in being free enough to imagine a God who is truly revealed in human reality. This would also have adverse effects on notions of personal vocation.

Much of this is discussed in Edward P. Hahnenberg's *Awakening Vocation: a Theology of Christian Call*.[3] Hahnenberg claims that 'the question of vocation taps into our deepest assumptions about God, ourselves, church, and moral commitment'. For Ignatius, God's action is discernible in a person's interior life

---

[3]Edward P. Hahnenberg's, *Awakening Vocation: a Theology of Christian Call* (Collegeville: Liturgical Press, 2010).

as well as in the external events of that life. Hahnenberg points to a period in Catholic thought when vocation 'became some thing *in* an individual that was separate *from* that individual', a thing, as it were, imposed by God on a possibly unwilling subject from on high. A more modern interpretation, more akin to Ignatius, can be found in Karl Rahner, whose theology of grace Hahnenberg describes as holding 'a vision of vocation that takes seriously the concrete particularity and freedom of the human subject'. A person's vocation is understood 'in the harmony between the path that is before me and the mystery that is me'.[4]

It becomes clear, looking at all this, how the *Spiritual Exercises* can contribute to a theology of vocation. Ignatius learned theology in the University of Paris, where the theologies of Augustine and Aquinas dominated. Augustine, whose honest prayer, 'Lord, give me chastity, but not yet' renders him a suitable patron saint of desire, gave a strong articulation of the dynamic interplay between desire itself and our capacity to receive its ultimate object,

> The whole life of a good Christian is holy desire. What you desire you cannot see yet. But the desire gives you the capacity, so that when it does happen that you see, you may be fulfilled . . . this is our life, to be exercised by desire.[5]

This desire is at the heart of any deeply committed search for God. Although Emmanuel Levinas denied the role of the divine in all this, he nevertheless spoke powerfully of the formative role of desire in a way that parallels what we find in Ignatius. Understood in the *Spiritual Exercises* as the desire for God, it is 'a distance more precious than contact, a non-possession more precious than possession, a hunger that nourishes itself not with bread but with hunger itself'.[6]

A gift of God in itself, desire in some way prepares and opens the pilgrim to receive the one who is desired. Ignatius urges the pilgrim to approach the *Spiritual Exercises* with open-hearted generosity [15] but lays down markers

---

[4]Hahnenberg, *Awakening Vocation*, pp. xi, 89, 156.
[5]St Augustine, *Homily on the First Letter of John*, pp. 4, 6, 2.
[6]Emmanuel Levinas, *Totality and Infinity*, p. 179.

in the Principle and Foundation that God does not work to a rigid blueprint, favouring only one way of mapping out one's life. It may prove better for an individual to exercise power and wealth responsibly and be satisfyingly married than to opt for a life of poverty, chastity and obedience out of misguided motives. The *Spiritual Exercises* urge pilgrims to trust their own instincts and deep desires as and when these are held up to the mirror of Christ himself. Simultaneously they disclose the ambiguity of many of our desires and the unfreedoms that make us inclined to addictive or idolatrous patterns of self-delusion. The first week encourages pilgrims to explore these unfreedoms and to develop the courage to name the fears that lie beneath them. The deep desire at this stage becomes a prayer for light: to see ourselves as God sees us, as loved and forgiven sinners, to know our gifts and the ways in which we habitually thwart the desire of the giver and, by knowing ourselves unconditionally loved, to allow God to strip away our idols and masks. The desire expressed at the outset of the *Spiritual Exercises* is, in a sense, an articulation of having fallen blindly in love with God. The prayer of the first week is for God to open our eyes.

In some senses this is a process most fit for a religious novitiate, but it is also, at least in embryo, an essential process in the discovery of one's personal vocation. Ignatius sees the desire to be free that emanates from the grace of true selfknowledge as the precondition for a desire for growth. In the text of the *Exercises* this desire is articulated as, 'What have I done for Christ, what am I doing for Christ, what am I to do for Christ?' [53]. For one whose desire for God has clarified and become focused this is experienced as a longing to be identified with Christ and to respond to his call. This is not self-generated, but is a gift of God worked out in the poverty of contemplative prayer and expressed through our imagination. Imagination played a pivotal role in the working out of Ignatius' own vocation, and he understood the positive role that imagination can play in moving our hearts towards a loving response to God. His own early imaginings were projections of a naïve and self-centred nature, but for all that he was able to recognize the generosity and longing for intimate union with Christ that lay beneath them. His vocation was effectively sparked off by the novels that were the sixteenth-century equivalent of adventure movies or cyber-games in which exhilaratingly heroic deeds are done for some great cause. Ignatius was able to take these crudely shallow and naively romantic beginnings and detect within them not only the delusions of the emotionally adolescent ego but the embryonic promptings of a generous heart fit for discipleship.

At all times we are made aware in the *Spiritual Exercises* of the importance of dialogue with God, especially the articulating of *id quod volo* – what I want. It is an aspect of contemporary consumer culture that, faced with so many choices, we find it particularly difficult to know what we really, really want. So the repeated prayer to know this is in itself an experience of grace as our desires are sifted to relieve them of ego and self-seeking and we become more aware of desires that are in themselves a response to a divine initiative. This tells us something about the premium Ignatius places on desire as the way in which the Spirit communicates God's will to us. Within the instructions about prayer he also emphasizes a review of each session of prayer in order to get a clearer idea of what is attracting and drawing us. He speaks of what, in praying with scripture and imagination, our heart relishes and enjoys and reminds us that it is in that consolation that we are most likely to find the Spirit at work [2]. He urges a holistic view of prayer in which our bodily senses and our imaginative use of them as agents of response help to clarify and solidify what our mind and heart have fleetingly captured. In this attraction we begin to determine where God's power is at work in us and what choice it prompts us to.

Many of us who work in vocations discernment know that candidates will often present themselves for engagement in a discernment process with a fear of the decision to be made, especially that it will in some sense be a decision imposed from outside by a God, or a church or a sense of duty that works against their own desires. There can be a fear of decision itself, since any choice made naturally implies other choices rejected. The theological and psychological assumption inherent in the *Spiritual Exercises* is that God does not act in a way that contradicts our own nature and natural orientation. In instructions to the companion, Ignatius frequently emphasizes the freedom of God and the sacredness of the freedom of the pilgrim, beyond any possible religious or ideological agenda to which the companion may be consciously or unconsciously working [15]. The significance of the Rules for Discerning Spirits and the whole teaching on consolation and desolation are crucial here. Consolation will manifest itself as whatever inclines us towards God in greater faith, hope and love, even if that is experienced as dark, challenging and painful. Like the disciples in John's Gospel we may be left with nothing else to say but 'Lord, to whom shall we go?', but even within that statement is a declaration of commitment.

Ignatius is always conscious of the possibility of illusion and warns of the dangers of false consolation, of the 'angel of darkness disguised as an angel of light', but also of desolation, the cynicism that can lead to our losing hope in a welter of bitter resentment. But above all the *Spiritual Exercises* teach us to encounter God in the experience of daily reality, to 'greet him the days I meet him, and bless when I understand'.[7] That sense of embracing fully the incarnate God who makes of all creation a sacramental reality lies at the heart of this theology of vocation. It means that at best any vocation process is a deeper embracing of reality and of the God who is to be found within it. Once this is established it's not only a case of what shall I do, but how shall I do it? In the contemplation of *The Call of the King* and the second week that follows it lies an invitation to work with Christ at reconciling the world back to God with whatever skills and gifts I have. That is the what. During the second week the pilgrim learns to follow not only the what but the how of Jesus. The pattern of his way is always kenotic, though this is a self-giving that is neither constrained nor coercive, and we see it as a developing pattern of stepping away from the unfree use of power, wealth and status. As we pray the way of Jesus so our desire is to become more and more like the one whom we contemplate.[8]

In some of the great set piece meditations of the second week such as *The Two Standards* and the *Three Classes of People*, there is a gradual illumination of the pilgrim's judgement and will, and a purifying of anything that might remain illusory in the desire to serve and follow Christ. The pitfalls of vocation discernment are laid bare with the constant postponing of decisions or in wanting to make a

---

[7]Gerard Manley Hopkins, *The Wreck of the Deutschland*.
[8]George Aschenbrenner, 'Becoming Whom We Contemplate', *The Way Supplement* 30 (1985), pp. 42–52.
[9]Notes [153–54].

'free' decision so long as it goes my way.[9] This is contrasted with the embodiment of that 'indifference' or fine balance of freedom referred to in the Principle and Foundation where the pilgrim is willing to hold on to a choice or let it go, depending on what is understood to be God's will.[10] There is no denial of one's own deepest desires but a move to accepting that my deepest, truest self lies in what God desires for me. This acceptance is tested most fully in the third week as we follow Christ in his passion and death. There is an understanding that the acceptance of one's vocation entails an acceptance of the reality of oneself with all the struggle that may entail, and an acceptance of the reality of the incarnation of God into human reality beyond any fantasy or projection or escapism of our own. The third week is the ultimate embracing of the real as my life's project.

The fourth week of the *Spiritual Exercises* takes us, rather like Eliot's poem, to where we started in order to know the place for the first time. In the *Contemplation for Attaining Love* there is a repetition of much of the prayer on one's life history that goes on in the early stages of the *Spiritual Exercises*. Here it is experienced as an opening up to the recognition of my life and history as graced. In the first week we travel in faith and hope, in the fourth we travel in the knowledge of Jesus crucified and risen, who brings to new life all that is within us. There are two 'prayers of St. Ignatius' common in spiritual resource

The first runs:

Lord, teach me to be generous;

Teach me to serve you as you deserve;
To give and not to count the cost;

To fight and not to heed the wounds;

To toil, and not to seek for rest;
To labour, and not to ask for any reward –
save that of knowing that I do your holy will.

The second, the *Suscipe* runs:

Take Lord, and receive all my liberty,
my memory, my understanding, and my
entire will, all that I have and possess.
You have given all to me. To you, O Lord, I return it
All is yours, dispose of it wholly according to your will. Give me your love
and your grace, for this is sufficient for me.

---

[10]Note [155].

collections, but the only one fully authenticated is the *Suscipe* found in the fourth week [234]. It bears contrasting with the other.

The first is the prayer of the beginning of a vocation process, full of eager passion, generosity and not a little self-delusion. The subject of the verbs is mostly me, the great I Am. There is a touch of heroic fantasy, the super-hero wading into battle, tireless, invincible and heedless of wounds. The pilgrim praying the *Suscipe* has come a long way and understood whose kingdom it really is. The subject of most of the verbs is God, by whose power alone we can hope to do great things for the kingdom. The pilgrim has learned to acknowledge both gift and Giver, to 'greet him the days I meet him, and bless when I understand'. This may mean taking up a way of life hitherto unknown and untried, or it may mean continuing to do the same thing differently. Some years ago, a pilgrim I accompanied went into a 30 day retreat faced with a vocation question. Should she give up the successful but very stressful practice of family law for something more 'spiritual', like becoming a spiritual director, or should she stay as she was? Her branch of law was, after all, problematic, as it deals with divorce, family breakdown and numerous relationship permutations outside the strict law of the church. She had a great gift of prayer and a longing to make better use of it for God's people. Yet what more fertile field could there be than this very painful arena of fragmented human relationships in which to serve the Christ of the beatitudes as a peace maker and justice broker? In the end her prayer led her to the conclusion that she was called to continue the practice of law with a renewed sense of vocation and according to the principles of discernment found in the *Spiritual Exercises*. The conclusion brought consolation and a confirmation of a sense of herself as loved and graced.[11]

The *Spiritual Exercises* contain a powerful theology of grace building on human nature while also challenging the unfreedoms that lead us to inordinate attachments. Insofar as they present a person's vocation as 'the harmony between the path that is before me and the mystery that is me', they contain a rich resource for a theology of vocation.

---

[11]This story is told with permission of the pilgrim.

6

How did the Reformation develop the theology of vocation?

The Very Revd David Hoyle

Attend evensong in Bristol Cathedral and look under your seat, as the last, careful cadence fades, and you could find yourself, disturbingly, face to face with a naked priest. On the eve of the Reformation, somewhere between 1515 and 1525, Abbot Robert Elyot set up new choir stalls in, what was then, the Augustinian abbey church in Bristol. Confident of his legacy, he had his initials carved in the wood-work and was, probably, fortunate to have died before he had to acknowledge that the confidence was misplaced. His scheme included a wonderfully robust set of carved misericords: a mermaid, a hunted stag, two nude wrestlers and a sequence of scenes from the fable of Reynard the fox. It is there we meet our alarming cler-gyman. The story goes that Reynard persuaded Tybert, the cat, to go mousing in a priest's barn. Tybert was reluctant at first, 'these prestes ben so wyly and shrewyssh'. Still, tempted by tales of more mice than he could carry away in a cart, he gave in and was promptly caught in a trap set for Reynard himself. The enraged priest leapt from his bed and started belabouring the poor cat, convinced that he had caught the hated fox. Tybert retaliated and, there they are, frozen forever on the misericord, a cat with his claws in the priest's back and Dame Julock, rushing to the rescue, grabbing Tybert by the tail.[1]

---

[1]M. D. Anderson, *The Medieval Wood Carver* (Cambridge: The University Press, 1935), pp. 111–12; Juanita Wood, *Wooden Images: Misericords and Medieval England* (London: Fairleigh Dickinson University Press, 1999), pp. 122–23.

This is a complicated image and full of confusions and mistaken identities. The whole story of Reynard examines the way we live up to the roles we have as well as begging questions about justice, power and the church. To top it all there is the naked priest, a ludicrous thing, a figure of fun and the presence of his 'wife', Dame Julock, only makes it more problematic. On the face of it, what we have here is an outbreak of sixteenth century anticlericalism, a bit of evidence eagerly sought out by a certain kind of historian. Yet, it is all contained in a scheme that the Abbot of St Augustine's commissioned for his own abbey church and to which he added his initials. If it really was anticlericalism, it did not much disturb Abbot Elyot. He, or someone near him, clearly had a playful interest in questions of order and expectation. Histories of reformation that tidy things like this into boxes marked 'anti-clericalism', or 'social unrest' make the categories too simple. In all the fun and frolic around Reynard we need to see a passionate concern that we should find our place in the order of things and inhabit it fully.

When the carpenters were at work in Bristol there was a lively debate about expectations and it was focussed on the clergy. In February 1512, John Colet preached to Convocation and launched into a passionate assault on the greed and secular preoccupations of his own kind,

> those whose duty it is to draw men from this world, teach men to love this world by their own devotion to worldly things, and by their own love of this world are themselves carried down headlong into hell . . . mixed up and confused with the laity, they lead, under a priestly exterior, the mere life of a layman

Not very long ago, some historians took those stinging criticisms, salted them with the *Supplication of Beggars* by Simon Fish, with its 'greedy sort of sturdy idle holy thieves' and served them up with more besides and tried to persuade us that everyone knew what was wrong with the clergy in the early sixteenth century.[2] For a generation we were told that anti-clericalism was a fact of late

---

[2]For Colet's sermon, *English Historical Documents V 1485–1588* (ed. C. H. Williams; London: Routledge, 1967), pp. 652–60 reprinted from J. H. Lupton, *Life of John Colet* (London: George Bell and Son, 1887); Part of *A Supplication for Beggars* is reprinted in *The Reformation in England* (ed. A. G. Dickens & Dorothy Carr; London, 1967), pp. 16–19; see also A. G. Dickens, *The English Reformation* (London: Pennsylvania State University Press, 1964), p. 112.

medieval life. The truth turns out to be much more complicated.[3] Notice, for example, that Colet was peculiarly annoyed about confusion, about priests who look like laymen, 'if the priests and bishops, the very lights, run in the dark ways of the world, how dark must the lay people be'. Colet had high aspirations for the clergy and much more confidence in his own priestly ministry than he was, at least at first, letting on,

> priests are 'soldiers of God'. Their warfare truly is not carnal, but spiritual: for our warfare is to pray, to read, and to meditate upon the Scriptures; to minister the word of God, to administer the sacraments of salvation, to make sacrifice for the people, and to offer masses for their souls

This was a sermon about differences of kind and degree, Colet was not merely wagging a finger, he was asking questions about what the ministry is and what priests do. This was a sermon about callings.

Soldiers of God or mumbling mass hunters?

Again and again, we are told that late medieval clergy were defined by their role in the mass and that their key role was in the performance of worship.[4] There was one way for a priest to be devout, and another for the laity

> Priests with matins and with mass
>
> And lewd men with righteousness[5]

---

[3]Richard Rex *Henry VIII and the English Reformation* (London: Macmillan, 1993), pp. 50–56; Christopher Haigh, *English Reformations: Religion, Politics, and Society under the Tudors* (Oxford: Clarendon Press, 1993), pp. 9, 44–51; R. N. Swanson, 'Before the Protestant Clergy: The Construction and Deconstruction of Medieval Priesthood', in *The Protestant Clergy of Early Modern Europe* (ed. C. Scott Dixon & Luise Schorn-Schütte; Basingstoke: Palgrave Macmillan, 2003), pp. 50–55.

[4]Swanson, 'Before the Protestant Clergy' pp. 39–41; R. Emmet McLaughlin, 'The Making of the Protestant Pastor: The Theological Foundations of a Clerical Estate', in Scott Dixon, Protestant Clergy, p. 6; Rosemary O'Day, 'The Reformation of the Ministry 1558–1642', in ed. Rosemary O'Day and Felicity Heal, p. 55. It was a commonplace of protestant polemic that the catholic clergy were defined by the mass, hence Thomas Becon's 'popish massmongers' and 'mumbling mass-hunters' Thomas Becon, *a New Catechisme sette forth Dialogewise . . . The Catechism of Thomas Becon* (ed. John Ayre; Cambridge: The University Press, 1844), p. 448.

[5]J. Small (ed.) *English Metrical Homilies from Manuscripts of the Fourteenth Century* (Edinburgh: W. Paterson, 1862), p. 2.

Understood like this the clergy were an 'estate', set apart by dress, by their ton-
sure, but above all by the distinctiveness of what they did at the altar with
bread and wine.[6] There is some truth in this, Colet, notice, spoke of the clergy
as those who, 'make sacrifice for the people, and to offer masses for their souls'.
Nonetheless, it is clumsy and too simple to confine priestly ministry like this.
In truth, the late medieval clergy knew very well that they must tread a fine
line between being set apart and being in relationship.[7] From the thirteenth
century onwards, in manuals designed to help priests administer the sacrament of penance, it was commonplace to exhort the clergy to be attentive to
their people, but to know themselves distinct.

> There are many priests and there are few priests. For there are many in
> name, but few in deed.[8]

When John Myrc wrote a manual for the clergy he concentrated on certain
tasks, but insisted priestly ministry was complex,

> A preste owe to be holy, deperted or disseuerede fro synnes, a gouernour
> and not a rauenour, a true stuard or dispensour and not a wastour, piteous
> in doome, rightful in consel, true in worde, meke in company, paciente in
> aduersite, benynge and mylde in prosperite, rych in virtues, a knight stronge
> in gu dedes, soubre in quere, chaste in herte, wyse in confession, sekyr in
> prechynge.[9]

Priestly identity was not just a matter of sacraments. Eamon Duffy's account
of the life of the Devon parish, Morebath, does not leave the priest, Sir
Christopher Trychay, isolated at the altar, but has him utterly engaged, in the
rhythms of parish life.[10] Priests were members of the community who had to

---

[6]Rosemary O'Day, *The Professions in Early Modern England 1450-1800* (Harlow: Longman, 2000),
pp. 50–54.

[7]Joseph Martos, *Doors to the Sacred* (London: SCM, 1981), pp. 496–99.

[8]William of Pagula, 'Oculus Sacerdotis', in *The English Church in the Fourteenth Century* (ed. W. A.
Pantin; Cambridge: The University Press, 1955), p. 198

[9]John Myrc, *Speculum Christiani* (ed. G. Holmstedt Early English Texts Society Old Series 182; London,
1933), p. 230.

[10]Eamon Duffy, *The Voices of Morebath* (Yale: University Press, 2001), the whole book is a catalogue of
the parish priest's engagement, but for particular examples see pp. 48, 55–58, 80.

build community and then they were something else besides.[11] There was no one single task that unlocked this mystery, the mass was indeed the glass that refracted everything to a burning focus, but penance was a crucial social ministry, Colet insisted that priests must also 'minister the word of God' and everyone knew that priests must both belong and be apart. Ministry was rather more than the mass.

All alike are consecrated priests

However, you define the role of the priest; the Reformation did bring a sea change. It was not just that function and action changed, there was a new debate about vocation, identity and that crucial and difficult business of being set apart. In 1520 Martin Luther was condemned for heresy, 'For me the die is cast'. It was the year he published a series of short and explosive manifestoes. *The Address to the Christian Nobility of the German Nation* was a brutal attack on the spiritual estate in general and the papacy in particular.[12] Here Luther swept away any difference of degree conferred by ordination and set out instead a vision of a Christian society built on the shared sacrament of baptism

> all Christians are truly of the Spiritual Estate, and there is no difference among them, save of office alone. As St. Paul says we are all one body, though each member does its own work, to serve the others. This is because we have one baptism, one gospel, one faith, and are all Christians alike; for baptism, gospel and faith, these alone make Spiritual and Christian

Relying heavily on I Peter and 'You are a royal priesthood', Luther believed that we have a common dignity that ordination can never eclipse.

> A cobbler, a smith, a peasant, every man has the office and function of his calling, and yet all alike are consecrated priests and bishops, and every man in his office must be useful and beneficial to the rest,

---

[11]John Bossy, *Christianity in the West 1400–1700* (Oxford: University Press, 1985), p. 64.
[12]The text is available online in the Christian Classics Ethereal Library www.ccel.org; it is reprinted in Luther's *Works* (vol. 44; ed. Franklin Sherman; Philadelphia, 1971) and in Henry Bettenson, *Documents of the Christian Church* (Oxford University Press, 1963) pp. 192–96.

Ministry then became a function that, for convenience, the church would delegate to individuals.

> For, since we are all priests alike, no man may put himself forward, or take
> upon himself, without our consent and election, to do that which we have
> all alike power to do

In a second publication, *The Babylonian Captivity*, Luther made a yet more radical assault on catholic teaching, bristling with anger and claiming what has been called a 'clerical confidence trick'.[13] No priest, only faith given by God, could assist us to encounter Christ who is, in fact, the only priest. Ordination was not to be regarded as a sacrament at all.[14]

In principle, Luther had demolished the distinctiveness of ordained ministry which so many had defended for so long. A further pamphlet, *Of the Abrogation of Private Masses,* took issue with the idea that on each and every occasion Christ's sacrifice was being offered again to God and moved on to challenge assumptions about any peculiarly priestly practice. It prompted an impassioned reply from Bishop John Fisher, *The Defence of the Priesthood*. Taking issue with the idea that Christ is the only priest we need, Fisher set out to show that priesthood was indeed necessary. Because the faithful will always fall away from the faith they need pastors and guides. Because they have dull minds they need teachers. Because they slip into sin they need monitors to keep an eye on them. Because they are sluggish they need someone to stir them up, and because the devil and false teachers get to work on them they need priests to defend them.

> How many, alas, are lukewarm in these days of which our Lord foretold
> that as iniquity would abound so would the charity of many grow cold!
> How blind then, is he who would deny that, to stir up the people from their
> lethargy, pastors and teachers are necessary![15]

Something had been lost. Colet had argued simply that secular and spiritual must be set apart; Luther however, had prompted Fisher into arguing about precisely what *job* it was that needed doing.

---

[13]Diarmaid MacCulloch, *Reformation* (London: Penguin, 2003), p. 129.

[14]Luther reduced the number of sacraments to three and later to two.

[15]John Fisher, *The Defence of the Priesthood* (trans. P. E. Hallett; London: Burns, Oates, Washbourne, 1935), p. 26.

There was a further consequence. Urging the idea that the cobbler, the smith and the peasant had their calling, Luther prompted a new, broader conversation about callings. Suddenly there was a theological legitimacy to the idea that vocation belongs to all God's people. So, by 1550, Thomas Becon could pray,

> O heauenlye father . . . thou hast appoynted in thy blessed law certayne honest & godly states and degrees, wherein thy people shoulde lyue, and haste streyghtelye commaunded that so manye as professe the and thy holye worde, shoulde continue in the same, eueri one accordyng to hys vocacion and calling[16]

Becon's theology was rooted in a staggeringly pessimistic reading of human nature which left humankind utterly dependent on God for any action and his understanding of vocation was clearly that it too was God's gift and not in any way something inherent in us,

> make vs newe creatures, trade vs in ye pathes of thy holye lawe, and geue vs grace to walke accordinge to our vocacion in thy feare, & in the obedience of thy godly wyll[17]

That said, Becon was confident that vocation was sufficiently personal for him to suggest that it might issue out in husbands who loved their wives, wives who would be subject to their husbands (there were limits even for a radical), servants obedient to masters and, perhaps most improbably of all, young men made sober minded.

This was a theology of vocation that became increasingly familiar. The evangelical printer Robert Crowley produced a volume of verse urging the 'right path of the vocation' that easily made up for its brevity by its density and urged even beggars to accept the dignity of their vocation.

> Fyrste walke in they vocation,
> And do not seke thy lotte to change:

---

[16]Thomas Becon, *The Flour of Godly Praiers Most Worthy to be Vsed in These our Daies for the Sauegard, Health, and Comforte of all Degrees, and Estates Newlie Made by Thomas Becon*, reprinted in *Prayers and Other pieces* (ed. John Ayre; Cambridge: The University Press, 1844), p. 36.

[17]Becon, *The Flour of Godly Praiers*, p. 36.

For through wicked ambition
Mani mens fortune hath bene strange[18]

Crowley larded the text with biblical examples reminding servants that Jacob had shared their station once, warning all and sundry of the perils of ambition and reminding the learned of the temptations of hypocrisy. Interestingly, Crowley's protestant fervour led him to explore the idea of a vocation that had failed, denouncing the lewde or unlearned priest, 'Desire no moe masses to say, But get thy fode with labours sore.'[19]

There is, without doubt, a real enthusiasm for the idea that we all have callings, in texts like these, but there was evidence of mounting anxiety too. There was fear of envy and ambition that might upset the order of things. In a late sixteenth century dialogue, urging a fruitful and necessary vocation, the cheerfully naïve country boy, Puer, meets the almost unbearably smug Civis as he walks to London, hoping to make his fortune. Civis wants to send him home again and dismisses his ambitions as foolish and dangerous. Puer is made to sound merely lazy as he longs for a different future and explains why he cannot bear to stay a day longer working the land

> Mary syr there is such moyling and toyling, and taking of great paynes, with harde fare, that I must needes to London to be a Townseman, thereto liue more at ease[20]

In another, much later work, by the non-conformist George Swinnock, the emphasis falls on the fact that too much enthusiasm for your calling might deflect you from a greater calling

---

[18]Robert Crowley, *Apocalips Callynge Al the Estates of Menne to the Right Path of their Vocation, Wherin are Contayned xii. Lessons to Twelue Seueral Estates of Menne, Whych if They Learne and Folowe, Al Shal be Well and Nothynge Amise* (London: Robert Crowley, 1549), fol. A ii.

[19]Crowley, *Apocalips Callynge*, fol. B ii.

[20]John Fit John, *A Diamonde Most Precious, Worthy to be Marked Instructing All Maysters and Seruauntes, How They Ought to Leade Their Lyues, in that Uocation which is Fruitfull, and Necessary, as Well for the Maysters, as also for the Seruants, Agreeable Vnto the Holy Scriptures. Reade Me Ouer, and then Iudge, if I be not Well, then Grudge: Thinke Well of Him that Mee Made, for Gods Worde Shall Neuer Fade* (London: Hugh Jackson, 1577), fol. B iii v.

Godliness must be the key to open the shop; Godliness must be the whip to drive the Cart; Godliness must be the Cock to call thee to work; Godliness must be the clock to call thee off from thy work; Godliness must be the principle, the rule[21]

Called and elected

Luther's confidence in our shared baptismal vocation was, by now, heavily re-worked by a different and less optimistic protestant tradition. By the early seventeenth century it was Calvinist assumptions that governed in the English theological academy. Calvin, of course, was clear that ministry included deacons and elders, working alongside pastors and teachers, and was more insistent than Luther had been on particular ministerial roles. That did not inhibit him, however, from embracing a generous approach to other callings. As he worked out his theology of election he expressed his conviction that God calls us all. It was then but a short step to suggest that all human beings might have a vocation and that some forms of work are approved by God. So, he could write about those in civil authority

> Their functions were expressly approved by the Lord. Wherefore no man can doubt that civil authority is, in the sight of God, not only sacred and lawful, but the most sacred, and by far the most honourable, of all stations in mortal life.[22]

In the hands of those who came after him these ideas grew into a fully fledged doctrine of callings. William Perkins was clear that God deliberately differentiated one person from another

> For if all men had the same gifts, and all were in the same degree and order, then should all have one and the same calling ; but inasmuch as God giveth

---

[21]George Swinnock, *The Christian-Man's Calling: or, A Treatise of Making Religion Ones Business. Wherein the Nature and Necessity of it is Discovered. : As also the Christian Directed How He May Perform it in [brace] Religious Duties, Natural Actions, his Particular Vocation, his Family Directions, and his Own Recreations* (London: Printed by J.B. for Tho. Parkhurst, 1662), p. 466.

[22]John Calvin, *Institutes of the Christian Religion* (ed. John T McNeill; Philadelphia: The Westminster Press 1960), 20.4, p. 1490.

diversities of gifts inwardly, and distinction of order outwardly, hence proceed diversity of personal callings.[23]

Similarly, Laurence Chaderton, first master of that godly 'seminary' Emmanuel, could write

> Above all things, it behoveth you that be the Lord's servants in magistracy to establish everyone within his charge and jurisdiction, this general law providing that every man have wherein to occupy himself and his gifts according to the tenor of this law in his own standing, place and vocation; and that he do discharge it according to the measure and proportion of his gifts which he hath received for that purpose.[24]

It needs to be noted, however, that this was a theology of vocation developed within an abiding acknowledgement of human sinfulness and with a determination to impose social control. Chaderton was urging others to accept their lot, 'being fully contented and satisfied therewith.'[25] There was no enthusiasm here for personal choice and parents were urged to help children learn their place. We would be mistaken if we tried to read back into this period the language of vocation that is familiar now.[26] Chaderton, like Calvin, was convinced that the only really interesting question about calling turned on whether or not we would be saved. Convinced that the fundamental reality about humanity is that it is sinful and under judgement he had no interest in the conversation about personal development that features in vocations work today.

Nonetheless, the reformation had shattered one set of assumptions about ministry and fashioned a new language of vocation that, even in the hands of conservatives, changed the way men and women thought about themselves and the dignity of their work.

---

[23]William Perkins, *A Treatise of Vocations or Callings of Men*, p. 759, quoted O'Day, *Professions*, p. 35.

[24]Laurence Chaderton, *A Fruitful Sermon, upon the 3, 4, 5, 6, 7, and 8 Verse of the 12 Chapter of the Epistle of St Paule to the Romanes* (London: Printed by Robert Walde-graue, 1584), pp. 28–9, quoted in Peter Lake, *Moderate Puritans and the Elizabethan Church* (Cambridge: The University Press, 1982), p. 29.

[25]Chaderton, *Fruitful Sermon*, p. 12; contemporaries like Perkins and Abdias Ashton made very similar and equally conservative points, Lake, *Moderate Puritans*, p. 139.

[26]O'Day, *Professions*, pp. 36, 37.

The ministry of the word

Meanwhile, the clergy were working hard to adapt to new realities. Our prevailing assumption has been that it was the medieval priesthood that was dominated by its function, and narrowly defined by the mass. It could be argued that, in fact, it was Luther and the reformation that prompted an endless argument about what it is that priests actually *do*. Luther himself was certainly clear that some tasks were critical. First among them were reading God's word and then explaining it; an assumption that made ministry into a business of scripture and sermons. Those ideas quickly surfaced in this country in Bishop Hooper's belief that the only qualification needed for ministry was a deep knowledge of scripture and in Latimer's scathing assault on the failures of prelates to provide a preaching ministry,

> Ye that be prelates loke well to your office, for right prelatynge is busye labourynge and not lording. Therefore preche and teach and let your ploughe be doynge.[27]

The sound of preaching was everywhere.[28] Parishes sought to supplement what was already a rich diet, pulpits were lifted higher, and galleries were added for those who came to listen where once they had come to rehearse the rituals of community.[29] The cry went up for a learned ministry, good preachers it was thought were fashioned by study. In the short term, the aspiration was impossible to meet.[30] The ambition though was there, in 1562 John Moore urged a congregation of Norwich gentry

---

[27]Neal Enssle, 'Patterns of Godly Life: The Ideal Parish Minister in Sixteenth- and Seventeenth- Century English Thought', in *Sixteenth Century Journal* XXVIII/1 (1997), p. 14; From Latimer's 'Sermon of the Plough', see Selected Sermons of Hugh Latimer (ed. Allan G Chester; University Press Virginia, 1968), p.35 and online at http://anglicanhistory.org/reformation/latimer/sermons/plough.html

[28]Andrew Pettegree, *Reformation and the Culture of Persuasion* (Cambridge, 2005), pp. 10–11.

[29]Patrick Collinson, *The Religion of Protestants: The Church in English Society 1559–1625* (Oxford: University Press, 1982), pp. 172–6; Anthea Jones, *A Thousand years of the English Parish Church* (Windrush, 2000) p. 142; on church furnishings see for example the church in Burntisland described by Pettegree, *Reformation*, p. 38, or Great St Mary's in Cambridge, see Patrick Collinson, 'Reformation or deformation? The reformed church and the university', in (ed. John Binns and Peter Meadows; Great St Mary's: Cambridge's University Church, Cambridge, 2000), pp. 38–39.

[30]O'Day, *Reformation*, p. 57.

> If you will be saved get you preachers in your parishes, . . . bestow your
> labour, cost and travail to get them. Ride for them, run for them, stretch your
> purses to maintain them. We shall begin to be rich in the Lord Jesus.[31]

Gradually the situation changed. Between 1600 and 1606 there were 109
ordinations to the diaconate in London and 82 of them were graduates. The
Universities were growing fast to meet the need and colleges like Sidney Sussex
and Emmanuel, in Cambridge, explicitly understood their purpose to be the
business of equipping a learned clergy.

> In establishing this College we have set before us this one aim, of rendering
> as many persons as possible fit for the sacred ministry of the Word and
> Sacraments; so that from this seminary the Church of England might have
> men whom it may call forth to instruct the people and undertake the duty
> of pastors (a matter of all things most necessary).[32]

Little by little it became the prevailing assumption that the ordained ministry
was for graduates. Richard Baxter was consequently almost deterred by his
own want of a formal education which 'was like to make me contemptible
with the most, and consequently hinder the success of my endeavours'.[33] A
Reformation launched by a particular kind of biblical scholarship was issuing
out in an ordained ministry that was bookish and literate and, all over again,
the clergy were being set apart.[34]

Good shepherds

Alongside the learning and in the wake of all those conversations about salvation, there was evidence of a revised pastoral practice. For those committed to
the principles of reformation there were new models of parochial commitment
to admire. Arthur Hildersham, for example, for nearly 40 years minister in

---

[31]Patrick Collinson, 'The Foundation and Beginnings', in *A History of Emmanuel College, Cambridge*
(ed. Sarah Bendall, Christopher Brooke, Patrick Collinson; Woodbridge: Boydell, 1999), p. 20.
[32]Collinson, 'Foundation and Beginnings', p. 24.
[33]Quoted O'Day, 'Reformation', p. 73.
[34]R. Emmet McLaughlin 'Protestant Pastor', p. 75.

Ashby de la Zouch, setting out 'to instruct the ignorant, to satisfie the doubt-full, to settle the wavering, to comfort the dejected and to encourage all sorts in the exercises of Religion'.[35] This was doctrine, ministered through preaching, teaching, and counsel and it gave the Christian community a different char-acter. George Downame, published a sermon, in 1608, in which he set out the essential duties of a minister. At first glance, he seemed to be offering a fairly wide-ranging account of what a minister might do, 'to instruct the ignorant, to reduce the erroneous, to heal the diseased, to seek the lost . . .'. In truth, he was most interested in what the minister might *say*, he was after all, 'the mouth of God to his people [and] the mouth of the people unto God . . .'.[36] The work was urgent because the world was beset by sin. So, Samuel Hieron could argue,

> it is strongly thought by many, that it were no danger to men's souls, though there were no minister at all to instruct them . . . [yet] ordinarily there is no more hope of a man's salvation without an able and industrious minister, than there is that the fish in the sea will of itself come ashore.[37]

Ideas about christian vocation and ministerial practice were now controlled by the presiding assumption that, whether or not we have confidence in our elec-tion, we need to hear the words about sin and salvation. It was for this reason that so many of the apostles of further reformation worked themselves into a fury in their denunciation of priests who failed their parishes or who, worst still, could not preach. In 1587 one of the first fellows of Emmanuel used the pulpit of the University Church to announce:

Thousands of souls were murdered by the non-residents of the university.[38]

---

[35]William Haller, *The Rise of Puritanism* (University of Pennsylvania, 1972), pp. 55–56.

[36]Enssle, 'Patterns of Godly Life', p. 4; Downame was quoting Perkins (William Perkins, *Of the Calling of the Ministerie A Treatise of The Duties and Dignities of the Ministerie* (London: Thomas Creede, for William Welby, 1606), p. 4.

[37]Samuel Hieron, *The Spiritual Fishing: A Sermon Preached at Cambridge* (London: Printed by I. Beale for widow Helme, 1618), quoted in Enssle, 'Patterns of Godly Life' p. 5.

[38]David Hoyle, *Reformation and Religious Identity, in Cambridge, 1590–1644* (Woodbridge: Boydell, 2007), p. 61, see also pp. 62, 63.

Reformacon of the mynistrye

There has been a tide of print running to tell us what happened to ministry at the reformation and, latterly, a growing interest in ideas about vocation and identity. We have been told about the godly preachers of the 'puritan movement', about the emergence of a learned ministry and, in a series of magisterial works by Rosemary O'Day, about the 'professionalization' of the clergy in early modern England.[39] We can identify new forms of clergy collegiality in the classis movement, in shared lectures and in the extraordinary network of marriage and relationship that created godly dynasties. There is a glimpse of new forms of training in the communities that gathered around Richard Greenham and John Cotton. There was a renewed emphasis on the parish and we know, for example, that the Archdeacon of Coventry, Thomas Lever composing 'notes for some reformacon of the *mynistrye and mynisters' in the* 1570s, took preaching very seriously, but insisted that clergy must have a cure.[40] We hear routine denunciations of the pride of the Catholic clergy, but can then watch as a self-consciously learned protestant clergy learnt to sit in judgement on those committed to their care. Richard Bernard argued that when the minister entered the church it should be plain that parishioners were in the presence of

> all reverence, and such and inward feeling of the business, as it may frame him outwardly in countenance, in behavior, in his attire, and in all outward appearance . . . the well disposed should love him, the indifferent should stand in awe, and the worst should bee kept more in than perhaps they would.[41]

The protestant clergy set themselves apart. Perkins encouraged them to think of themselves as unusual, 'No common or ordinary man but thin sowne . . . on

---

[39]Haller, *Rise of Puritanism*; Irvonwy Morgan, *The Godly Preacher of the Elizabethan Church* (Aylesbury: Epworth, 1965); John Morgan, *Godly Learning*, pp. 95–120; Emmet McLaughlin 'Protestant Pastor'; Rosemary O'Day, The English Clergy: *The Emergence and Consolidation of a Profession 1558–1642* (Leicester, 1979); O'Day *Professions*; O'Day 'Reformation'.

[40]Enssle, 'Patterns of Godly Life', p. 66.

[41]Richard Bernard, *The Faithfull Shepherd: Wholly in a Manner Transposed and Made Anew, and Very Much Inlarged Both With Precepts and Examples, to Further Young Divines in the Studie of Divinite: With the Shepherds Practice in the End* (London, 1621), pp. 77, 130, quoted in Enssle, 'Patterns of Godly Life' p. 13.

of a thousand'.[42] It is here perhaps that we begin to see how far we have come from Morebath with its network of relationships and associations. There have always been turbulent priests, but where Sir Christopher Trychay would have seen his role as in terms of sanctifying the bonds of charity in a parish, many of the reformed would have felt they needed to begin by destroying what they found, assuming it must be corrupt.

The reformation made the Christian community into a cockpit in which sin and salvation were at war, a conviction expressed in a new language and with an extraordinary fervour. The ordination service in *The Book of Common Prayer* insisted that it was good doctrine, and then the capacity to live up to it, that made ministry.

> Mercifully behold these thy servants now called to the office of Priesthood; and replenish them so with the truth of thy doctrine, and adorn them with innocency of life, that, both by word and good example, they may faithfully serve thee in this office

George Herbert was hardly the most reformed of parish priests, but we can trace in his work the evidence of a long engagement with the challenges of sin and salvation. His hope was sure, but he still worked a treadmill and thought himself a *wretch*, a *crumme of dust, a brittle crazy glass.*

> Sorrie I am, my God, sorrie I am,
>
> That my offences course it in a ring.[43]

George Herbert tells again the story of human sinfulness, Christ's death and passion and he makes it into a story about him and his parish.

> The Countrey Parson is generally sad, because hee knows nothing but the Crosse of Christ, his minde being defixed on it with those nailes wherewith his Master was.[44]

---

[42]William Perkins, *Of the Calling of the Ministerie*, p. 4.

[43]George Herbert, *Sinnes Round*, p. 122.

[44]*The Countrey Parson* XXVII; see also *The Author's Prayer Before Sermon*

The effect of this single-minded determination to tell, and tell again, the drama of redemption was striking. It could be argued that, with some very honourable exceptions, there had been a tendency before the reformation to turn priest-hood into a craft. The manuals of instruction produced by men like John Myrc knew all about holiness and its importance, but did dwell on rather practical advice. After the reformation there was a recovery of the assumptions that had once been familiar, a return to a vocabulary that stressed that ordained minis-try was challenging because it required a near impossible public holiness.

Herbert wrote, 'The greatest and hardest preparation is within.'[45]

William Perkins acknowledged the same difficulty in contemplating what it is

> to enter into the holy of holiest, to goe betwixt God and his people, to bee god's mouth to the people and the peoples to God . . . to stand in the roome and beare the office of Christ himself, to take the care and charge of soules[46]

with one hand he had developed a theology of callings and lifted all the faithful to a new dignity, with the other he had re-imposed the peculiar dignity of the clergy. The reformation had liberated vocation and ensnared it again. Within a century of being created the choir stalls in Bristol, where a priest and a cat were still locked in combat, were a distant memory of different, but perhaps more playful times.

---

[45]Herbert, *Countrey Parson*, Chapter 2.
[46]William, *Of the Calling of the Ministerie A Treatise of The Duties and Dignities of the Ministerie* (London, 1606), p. 4.

A *note on the* Imitation of Christ *and vocation in the* post-Reformation Church

Abbot Geoffrey Scott

David Hoyle has introduced us to the changing world of Christian vocation in the reformed Churches, especially in the Church of England. This is a world 'full of confusion and mistaken identities' where we are shown the balancing act of the medieval clergy 'set apart' yet 'in relationship' with their congregations. Luther attempted to abolish elitism and segregation in favour of the priestly vocation of all believers, while Calvin maintained that vocation was God's gift to an individual. In England, a learned, preaching professional ministry evolved which, Hoyle argues, set the clergy apart again, but this time without the earlier medieval engagement in the rhythms of parish life.

The articulation of vocation in post-Reformation Catholicism was heavily reliant on the determination of the Council of Trent (1545–63) to revitalize the Church. Catholic renewal was heavily dependent on Trent's reform of the religious orders, institutions not present in English Protestantism and on the Council's appreciation of the necessity of a universal Church at a time when some national churches were separating from Rome. Modern commentators have been struck by Trent's apparent lack of interest in legislating for the period's expanding missionary activity and by its silence in regard to another contemporary phenomenon, the growing popularity of apostolic religious

life among women. Nevertheless, Trent had a clear vision of the vocation of
the Church itself and elaborated a distinctive ecclesiology which has survived
until the present. The impact of its teaching on authority, on clearly defined
institutions and structures, on the supreme importance of the priesthood, on
the necessity of the sacraments, all developed in the centuries which followed
the form of an individual Christian's vocation as a microcosm of the vocation
of the Church itself.[1]

What follows is a brief examination of the post-Reformation Catholic view
of the nature of the Christian vocation in the Reformation period by some
reflections on the classic vocational text, *The Imitation of Christ*, whose author
is now definitely thought to have been the Augustinian canon, Thomas à
Kempis who died in 1471. The Christian vocation as portrayed in this work
and later sharply defined by Tridentine ecclesiology is most strikingly depicted
in a series of identical frontispiece engravings in editions of *The Imitation*
which achieved enormous popularity as they spread and were copied from
one press to another across Catholic Europe.[2] Their popularity was largely
thanks to their adoption by the Plantin Press in Antwerp, the most prestig-
ious and influential Catholic publishing house in northern Europe of the time.
Their design is simple: Christ on his way to Calvary stumbles as he carries his
cross. Behind him is a motley crowd of individuals who make up the Church
and who represent the various orders of Christian society. These carry their
own crosses as they follow Christ.[3] In these popular devotional prints, monks,
friars, priests, nuns, women, merchants, layfolk and cripples all jostle along
behind Christ with little hint of precedence, as in a twentieth-century resurrection scene from a Stanley Spencer painting. Has one ever seen the vocation
of the universal church depicted so clearly in this corporate way in medieval
art? To what extent does this image reflect Tridentine ecclesiology as outlined
above? *The Imitation* universalizes the Christian vocation in a Church whose
hierarchical structure had been defined by Trent.[4]

---

[1]Gabriel Flynn and Paul D. Murray, *Ressourcement. A Movement for Renewal in Twentieth-Century
Catholic Theology* (Oxford, 2012), pp. 190, 192.

[2]See frontispiece of this book for one example.

[3]Thomas à Kempis, *De imitatione Christi* (Antwerp: Plantin Press, 1601 and 1652), t.p.

[4]The presence in the crowd of nuns outside their cloisters in copies of the engraving dating from the
1580s, despite Trent's insistence on female papal enclosure, suggests a more flexible attitude to female
religious life 'in the world' had developed twenty years after the Council.

What is doubly significant about this image of the Christian vocation in its varied forms is its widespread circulation in works other than *The Imitation*, particularly among those persecuted English Catholics surviving in England or among members of English religious orders in exile abroad. For this image is to be found in books by English Jesuits from Saint-Omer and by Irish Franciscans at Louvain and Brussels. A pocket missal carried by secular priests onto the English mission has this image prefacing the rite of baptism. It is also found in works published by secret presses in London for the laity in England, one being by Thomas Hide, the exiled ex-headmaster of Winchester College, and, as far as I can see, a layman.[5]

The Imitation of Christ not only had a widespread circulation, but its specific imagery of the Christian vocation seeped into many other popular books. It is difficult to exaggerate *The Imitations of Christ's* importance for helping to configure the Christian vocation throughout Europe during the time of the Reformation. Between 1500 and 1650 no other work, except for the Bible itself, was so frequently reproduced or translated.[6] To appreciate its popularity, we must understand its context. It represented the late medieval flowering of *devotio moderna* spirituality (the first published edition appeared in 1472, and the first published English translation in 1503). Although its origins lie with the school of *devotio moderna* as practised by the Augustinian canons and canonesses, the book actually reflects the earlier charism of the medieval Brethren and Sisters of the Common Life who did not take vows. The Latin text was soon translated and vernacular editions were eagerly sought among devout laity and among members of the new burgeoning confraternities. *The Imitation* was popular and definitely not elitist. Furthermore, during the iconoclasm of the Reformation, this medieval classic not only survived but increased its dominance, in that it was adopted by Protestants and promoted by the

---

[5]Richard Hopkins S. J., trans., *Of Prayer and Meditation* (Paris, 1582), t.p. and *A Memorial of a Christian Life* (Rouen: London secret press, 1586 and 1599), pp. 287, 684. Florence Conry's translation into Irish of Miguel de Comalada's *Tratado llamado el Desseoso* (Louvain: Irish Franciscan Press, 1616), t.p. Theobald Stapleton, *Catechismus seu doctrina Christiana* (Brussels: Irish Franciscan Press, 1639), t.p. Thomas Hide, *A Consolatorie Epistle to the Afflicted Catholics* (1579). *Missale parvum pro sacerdotibus in Anglia . . . itinerantibus* (Saint-Omer, 1626), p. 271.

[6]Maximilian von Habsburg, *Catholic and Protestant Translations of the Imitatio Christi, 1425–1650* (Farnham, 2011), p. 1.

Jesuits as paradigmatic of the Ignatian vocation. Protestants were attracted by its stress on interior religion, its diffidence about veneration of the saints and its sympathy for the vernacular. Protestant editions were purged of monastic terminology and excluded Book Four, on the Catholic Mass. Meanwhile, St Ignatius himself swore by it and bequeathed it through the 'Spiritual Exercises' to the Society of Jesus which became its principal promoter and oversaw editions published as far afield as Japan. Ignatius is said to have 'institutionalized the original vision of the Sisters and Brethren of the Common Life' through requiring Jesuits to live outside the cloister and to serve the world.[7]

What did *The Imitation* have to say about the essential Christian vocation which explained its popularity? Most obviously, the book was strongly scriptural and Christocentric. Its teaching chimed with the contemporary Catholic renewal and Protestant reformation, for it demonstrated the central ambidexterity[8] of the Christian vocation: prayer and action or 'contemplation in action', as the Jesuits defined their own vocation. If it appealed to the Ignatians, *The Imitation* was also to be found in every monastic library and had a place in every Benedictine *ratio studiorum*. The abbey of San Guistina in Padua, where the English Benedictine mystical writer, Augustine Baker (died 1641), had served his novitiate, had multiple copies, and it was he who was to encourage his later Benedictine disciples to become 'perfect ambidexters'. Baker quarried *The Imitation*, and spoke of God calling every soul interiorly and exteriorly. 'Consider your call that's all in all', is his famous rhyme. Baker taught that 'all the exercises of a Christian are to be founded on Our Saviour's Passion',[9] that, of course, was close to the message of *The Imitation*. Announcing the Year of Faith which began in October 2012, Pope Benedict XVI underlined, in agreement with the nature of the Christian vocation as outlined in *The Imitation*, the importance of faith as a personal encounter with Christ, being touched by Christ, being in touch with Christ.

---

[7] Ibid., p. 213.

[8] Ibid., p. 35.

[9] Augustine Baker, 'Doubts and Calls', ed. John Clark, *Analecta Cartusiana*, 119:10 (Salzburg: Institüt fur Anglistik und Amerikanistik, Universität Salzburg, Austria, 1999), p. 32.

7

'The Irreducible Particularity of Christ' – Hans Urs von Balthasar's theology of vocation

Sr Gill Goulding

Introduction

'[God's] love transforms all of life. It is a love that is limitless and that precedes us, sustains us and calls us along the path of life, a love rooted in an absolutely free gift of God. . . . Every specific vocation is in fact born of the initiative of God; *it is a gift of the Love of God!* He is the One who takes the "first step", and not because he has found something good in us, but because of the presence of his own love "poured out into our hearts through the Holy Spirit"' (Rom. 5:5).[1]

Pope Benedict's assertion that it is the love of God that is both the origin and the transformative principle of all life and the root of all vocations finds

---

[1] Pope Benedict XVI, Message for the 49th World Day of Prayer for Vocations 29 April 2012 Fourth Sunday of Easter. See 'Every ministerial action – while it leads to loving and serving the Church – provides an incentive to grow in ever greater love and service of Jesus Christ the head, shepherd and spouse of the Church, a love which is always a response to the free and unsolicited love of God in Christ'. Blessed John Paul II, *Pastores Dabo Vobis*, p. 25.

an echo in the work of the Swiss theologian Hans Urs von Balthasar. Both men understand every vocation to be a gift of the love of God. It is one of Balthasar's central assertions that love alone is credible. Indeed he asserts that the common destiny of every human person is a vocation of love in Christ. *Caritas Christi urget nos*. It is the love of Christ that impels us. Nowhere more so is this apparent than in Balthasar's theology of vocation. Indeed he endeavours to present the mystery at the heart of vocation from its rooting in divine love. It is this divine initiative that calls forth the human response, one which finds true authenticity in permanent commitment.[2]

In 2010 the journal *Communio* published a translated article that Balthasar had written in 1966. It was simply entitled 'Vocation'.[3] Here he raises three key factors that illumine the understanding of vocation. The background context is the divine initiative of love 'the freedom of God, on whose good pleasure all worldly being depends'.[4] He then stresses the importance of the Incarnation – the Word made flesh in Jesus Christ who calls and invites followers into His redemptive work. Thirdly he emphasized the relationship between the individual called, the Church and the world.

This paper explores his theological vision of vocation more expansively drawing from across his theological corpus and paying particular attention to two areas where contemporary passions swirl – truth and freedom. First I explore the dynamic divine initiative of Trinitarian love as the ground of the truth of a vocation. There follows a brief excursus on our contemporary cultural contexts in which this call is heard. In deference to the fact that the Lord always calls – even when we do not hear him – the third section considers the call of Christ. Here, we see clear links that Balthasar makes with the Ignatian *Spiritual Exercises*. It is the Eternal King, Jesus Christ, who died and rose and calls believers to enter into his joy, who issues a clarion call to contemporary

---

[2]John O'Donnell observes 'every genuine love has the form of a vow. Lovers wish to pledge themselves, to bestow themselves upon the beloved, and they wish to make this gift of themselves in a way which says "forever"'. John O'Donnell SJ, *Hans Urs von Balthasar* (New York, NY: Continuum, 2000), p. 127.
[3]It was from *Zur Pastoral der geistlichen Berufe. Zum Welttag der geistlichen Berufe*, 24 April 1966 (Freiburg: Informationszentrum Berufe der Kirche, 1966), pp. 3–15. Translated and published by kind permission of the Hans Urs von Balthasar Archive in Basel, Switzerland, *Communio* 37 Spring 2010, pp. 113–28.
[4]Ibid.

young people to enter into that personal relationship with God which lies at the heart of any vocation to the priesthood or religious life. This section concludes with an outline of the three-fold stages of a vocation according to Balthasar. An exploration of the interaction of human and divine freedom forms the fourth part leading into a consideration of identity person and mission. This concluding section emphasizes the centrality of a loving obedience and self-surrender for the prayerful discernment and the fruitful living out of a vocation.

The divine initiative

The profound truth of our existence is that all creation and in particular every human person is a result of the fecundity of God's loving activity, a love that we know from scripture, tradition and our own personal experience is without limit, faithful and everlasting. It is this love Balthasar maintains that is the transformative dynamic at the heart of any vocation.[5] God is not only Love, the eternal act of perichoretic indwelling between the Father and the Son hypostasized as the Spirit who is Love, but God also loves the human person on whom he freely chooses to disclose divine love in the fullness of the act of creating. The Trinity is love ad-intra and ad-extra. Accordingly, God's love is a mutual revelation of the divine Persons in whom they are Lover, Beloved and Love and an external revelation of love as God's nature to each human person. Such a revelation is grounded in mystery.

For Balthasar 'mystery' is intrinsic to truth, it is not an optional additional extra.[6] At the heart of this mystery is the truth of the Trinity. For Balthasar the

---

[5]See Pope Benedict XVI, 'God is indeed visible in a number of ways. In the love-story recounted by the Bible, he comes towards us, he seeks to sin our hearts, all the way to the Last Supper, to the piercing of his heart on the Cross, to his appearances after the Resurrection and to the great deeds by which, through the activity of the Apostles, he guided the nascent Church along its path. Nor has the Lord been absent from subsequent Church history: he encounters us ever anew, in the men and women who reflect his presence, in his word, in the sacraments and especially in the Eucharist'. *Deus Caritas Est* [17] The resonance in Pope Benedict's comments with the work of Balthasar is the fruit of the longevity of their relationship of esteem both as theologians and as friends.

[6] For Balthasar, everything that may be known must have some characteristic of mystery as all objects of knowledge have a *creaturely* character. This leads to the conclusion that the final truth of all things is 'hidden in the mind of the Creator who alone may utter [their] eternal names'. Hans Urs von Balthasar, *Theo-Logic I: Truth of the World* (trans. Adrian J. Walker; San Francisco, CA: Ignatius Press, 2000), p. 17.

reality of the Trinity is the source from which is derived a fullness of interpretation of human existence. From our understanding of the distinctions within the Trinity – Father, Son and Spirit – and the fullness of relationship inherent in one God we may postulate that distinction and otherness as well as communion may all be an integral part of such mystery bursting the bounds of any subjective identification. Such an assertion is important for our contemporary understanding where attention has been focused on the question of whether the transcendence that takes place in the knowing process and the search for truth is achieved only through the act of the subject or it is something that the object being known co-enables.[7]

The process of knowing – and specifically knowing the reality of a vocation, then, for Balthasar is primarily God's act of disclosing or unveiling objective content to the thought of the receptive human person who then awakens to knowing in wonder and amazement. It is the divine initiative that inspires the process of unveiling and true reception of such disclosure involves that spirit of wonder and gratitude that is as it were the 'natural' Christian response to God's gift of self. Through this process, the receptive human subject transcends personal limitations through grace by being opened to an 'other' who is beyond the knowing subject. The focus here is on engaged contemplation as the human subject contemplates in wonder the divine disclosure.

Receptiveness, an opening of one's self by grace, toward the revelation of God allows for entrance into the intrinsic mystery of truth itself. 'This revealed and revealing light, however, is being – the wonder that there is anything at all rather than nothing'.[8] Since this knowing subject is only gradually opened to the truth of the object, elements of mystery and obscurity always remain so that the subject never has total control or dominance over the object. 'Truth is being's property of unveiledness, uncoveredness, revealedness, non-hiddenness'.[9] This truth in being, for Balthasar, ever remains a

---

[7]See David C. Schindler, *Hans Urs von Balthasar and the Dramatic Structure of Truth: A Philosophical Investigation* (New York, NY: Fordham University Press, 2004), p. 4.

[8]Peter Henrici, 'The Philosophy of Hans Urs von Balthasar', in *Hans Urs von Balthasar: His Life and Work* (ed. David L. Schindler; San Francisco, CA: Ignatius Press, 1991), p. 165.

[9]Aidan Nichols, *Say it is Pentecost: A Guide Through Balthasar's Theo-Logic* (Washington, DC: Catholic University of America Press, 2001), p. 12.

gift.[10] Truth is not just a property of knowledge; 'it is above all a transcen-dental[11] determination of being as such'.[12]

Balthasar's premise for this whole process of knowing is that all meaning and all unity lie in God. We can only know God by being 'in' God. This is the goal of a vocation. It is God alone who brings about being, which unveils itself within the world. So the process of knowing is primarily God's action of disclosing or unveiling objective content to the receptive human person. In this revealing, there is ultimately what Balthasar calls, a 'poverty of Being and of its sensibility [which] reveals that the sole treasure Being contains, is noth-ing other than – love'.[13] This love is the divine dynamic operative deep within human reality calling to relationship and for the believing Christian this rela-tionship is an interaction with the divine life of the Trinity.[14]

> To say that love is the communion of Christians is not simply to enunciate an abstract principle; rather in the Christian communion of love we share in a personal act of God himself, the tip of which may be seen shining in

---

[10]As a gift its transcendental nature and its integral connection with goodness and beauty is most appreciated. Balthasar approaches the mystery of Being from the perspective of the transcendental properties of Being: the One, the True, the Good and the Beautiful. Balthasar deals with the transcendentals in his trilogy: *The Glory of the Lord* – Aesthetic (beauty); *Theo-Drama* – Dramatic (goodness) and *Theo-Logic* – Logic (truth). 'We start with a reflection on the situation of man. He exists as a limited being in a limited world, but his reason is open to the unlimited, to all of Being. The proof consists in the recognition of his finitude, of his contingence: I am, but I could also, however, not be. Many things that do not exist could exist. Essences are limited but Being is not. That division, the "real distinction" of St Thomas, is the source of all the religious and philosophical thought of humanity'. Hans Urs von Balthasar, *My Work: In Retrospect* (San Francisco, CA: Ignatius Press, 1993), p. 112.

[11]The sense here is of using the term in reference to a scholastic notion of the properties to be found in the *praedicamenta* of intelligible being rather than the post-Kantian condition for the possibility of 'x'.

[12]Balthasar, *Theo-Logic I*, p. 11.

[13]Hans Urs von Balthasar, *The Glory of the Lord I: Seeing the Form* (ed. Joseph Fessio and John Riches; trans. Erasmo Leiva-Merikakis; San Francisco, CA: Ignatius Press, 1982), p. 407. Also Hans Urs von Balthasar, *Love Alone is Credible* (trans. David C. Schindler; San Francisco, CA: Ignatius Press, 2004) which clearly explores throughout this short book how love is the leitmotif of Balthasar's work.

[14]Such an interaction though is not just focused upon relationship with the Trinity but in and through that relationship a renewed engagement with other human persons. 'The significant factor in being a Christian is that [one] does all with reference to and in dependence on the ultimate source of [one's] action, through loving first and above all things, the God who loves us in Christ in order that [one] may then, by means of and together with love, turn [one's] attention to the needs of those who are the object of the love of God'. Hans Urs von Balthasar, *Engagement with God* (trans. R. John Halliburton; San Francisco, CA: Ignatius Press, 2008), p. 40.

the person of Christ, but which in its depths contains the interpersonal life of the Blessed Trinity and in its breadth embraces the love of God for the whole world.[15]

Here we need to listen to the other and above all the 'Other' who is God. It is in this way that we come to know the truth about ourselves and to truly become ourselves. This is the progress of a vocation.

As Aidan Nicholls brings to our attention, Balthasar emphasizes within the Theo-Logic that 'A starting point generous enough to be congruent with its subject can only be the way God's triune being is reflected in the being of the world: *imago Trinitatis in ente creato*'.[16] It is love which is the final truth of being[17] – in the divine essence, in the reciprocal self-gift of the Persons, and so, since God the Trinity is the Creator, in the created world itself which bears God's mark. Supremely in human persons made in the image of God love is the final truth of human existence, for it is the creativity of divine love which pours itself out in a 'glorious self-sharing love of its own divine Source'.[18] In this graced sharing of divine love the human person is brought to a deeper expression of the creaturely reality of what it means to be both a creature and a beloved child of God. This lies at the centre of the covenant relationship to which human persons are invited and is a key recognition vital for the discernment of a vocation.

Balthasar's extraordinary theological vision attempts to speak words of beauty and honour to reflect the grandeur of the mystery of God's love for human beings made known in Christ. The foundation of his project is the very human experience of being struck by glory, of being penetrated by divine presence, to be elevated to God's own dignity. The *Herrlichkeit* is thus a 'theological aesthetics' that is, a theological reflection on how the enfleshed spirit is moved, is enraptured in seeing the form of God.[19]

---

[15]Ibid., p. 41.

[16]Nichols, *Say it is Pentecost*, p. 91.

[17]Truth is first and foremost a transcendental property of being – rooted in love.

[18]Nichols, *Say it is Pentecost*, p. 93.

[19]For Pope Benedict 'the appealing beauty of this divine love, which precedes and accompanies us, needs to be proclaimed ever anew, especially to younger generations. This divine love is the hidden impulse which never fails even in the most difficult circumstances'. Pope Benedict XVI, Message for the 49th World Day of Prayer for Vocations 29 April 2012 Fourth Sunday of Easter.

For Balthasar, the foundation of the God-human covenant is the paradox of God's glory as love – the divine desire to exchange love with human beings and for them to bear fruit.[20] In consequence it is not surprising that Balthasar's own theological project is inherently paradoxical. Indeed he excels at accentuating contrary – though not contradictory claims about God and the world, while holding them tenaciously in tension. To draw a musical analogy, if one begins an encounter with a piece by Mozart by analysing in the score the use of rhythms, time and key signature, entry points of the theme and counterpoint, one can hardly be said to have *heard* the piece. His method is one of 'integration not evolution'.[21] Nevertheless his project comes across as more piercing, incisive and decisive rather than smooth and melodious. Balthasar wants to shock, not invite to complacency, his message is profoundly penetrating and fiesty in order to awaken us – twenty-first-century Christians, entrapped in our end-of-modernity darkness and emptiness – to wake up to be attentive, to follow the master in embracing the reality of vocation.

The contemporary cultural context – seed ground for vocations?

It is in our contemporary context an overworked truism to say that contemporary society is dominated by technological advances and principally in the area of communications media. This does, however, raise certain fundamental questions with regard to the theology of vocation. Balthasar was very concerned about the way in which the mass media of his time – mainly focused through television – exerted a seductive influence on young people who 'assaulted by a multitude of chaotic images flitting across the screen, are no longer capable of asking questions about the meaning of life'.[22] The rapid increase of such 'chaotic

---

[20]See Jn 15.

[21]Hans Urs von Balthasar, *The Glory of the Lord IV: The Realm of Metaphysics in Antiquity* (trans. Brian McNeil et al.; ed. John Riches; San Francisco, CA: Ignatius Press, 1989), p. 18.

[22]He continues, 'I remember one of the last lectures of Gabriel Marcel, at which, leaving his notes aside and glancing up at the ceiling, he said that watching television reminded him of seeing a tiny patch of the ocean floor through the hatch of a submarine, imagining it to be the whole world'. Hans Urs von Balthasar, *Test Everything: Hold Fast to What is Good* (San Francisco, CA: Ignatius Press, 1989), p. 26.

images' and the increased hours spent in artificial computerized environments continue to raise serious questions about the possibility of any receptiveness and indeed recognition of a vocational call from God. In response to such questions it is interesting that amidst current research there is emerging the awareness that a right relationship to technology is attainable in part through the recovery of the priority of silence, understood as both an experience and an inner attitude characterized by active receptivity.[23]

Alongside these developments in technology which has brought about a radical immanentism, the popularity of the so-called New Atheists[24] and the concurrent atheistic movements manifest a deep cultural sense that 'truth' and 'freedom' are threatened by the existence of God (or – perhaps more accurately – the Abrahamic religions' teachings about God). Modern philosophy's characteristic 'turn to the subject' valorized human reason and conceived of truth as the correspondence between 'the world' and the human person's determined, innate structures for knowing the world. To know the truth of a thing, in this 'modern' paradigm, is therefore to have a clear and distinct concept of the thing, and therefore to overcome, as far as possible, any lack of clarity, difference or 'otherness' in knowing.[25] When this notion of truth informs

---

[23]'This attitude is not focused towards the digital field but to the Trinitarian God and to incarnate reality, and results from a recovery of the priority of "being" over "doing" or "making", an existential stance that acknowledges one's ontological contingency and creature-hood'. John D. O'Brien SJ, 'The Priority of Silence: Recovering an anterior sense of "active receptivity" to acquire right relationship with the new digital media environments of our technological society'. Unpublished M.A. Thesis Regis College, Toronto, 2012. See also Pope Benedict's message for World Communication Sunday 2012.

[24]Prominent among whom are: Richard Dawkins, Daniel Dennett, Sam Harris and the late Christopher Hitchens.

[25]The reductive notion of truth also leads to significant anxiety. Amidst the media pressure to focus attention on material wealth, success and sexual pleasure as the means of self-realization, economic well-being and immediate emotional satisfaction, still there is a pervading anxiety that these foci do not provide the lasting happiness that is sought. In his 1952 essay entitled in English, *The Christian and Anxiety*, Balthasar attempted to 're-value' Kierkegaardian anxiety so that it could be of use to the Christian, illustrating how anxiety, rightly understood, is a part of the Christian experience and making it 'possible for anxiety to participate in the fruitful anguish of the Cross'. Hans Urs von Balthasar, *The Christian and Anxiety* (trans. Dennis D. Martin and Michael J. Miller; San Francisco, CA: Ignatius Press, 2000), p. 79. Balthasar opens the horizon of anxiety beyond the merely human, to show its theological dimension, and in so doing integrates anxiety into the human-Divine relationship. In redeeming human anxiety, by integrating it into the Paschal Mystery and the Son's anxiety experienced in Gethsemane and at Calvary, Balthasar reclaimed anxiety from the monopolistic hold that existential philosophy had attempted to place on it and returned it to the loving view of the Creator.

discussions of human freedom (whether freedom as an inherent property of a person, or within the political realm), the notion of an absolute truth (held by God or an earthly authority) must somehow be opposed or resisted, since such a totalizing truth would necessarily homogenize the difference and otherness necessary for freedom.

But while knowledge and mystery are opposed in this 'modern' notion of truth, it is possible to conceive of truth in such a way that mystery and 'difference' are an intrinsic part of it. Grounded in Jesus' revelation of a Triune God, Balthasar has formulated a non-reductive 'dramatic' structure of truth capable of uniting independent terms into an intelligible whole, while simultaneously maintaining an abiding difference (mystery) between them. This is of considerable importance when trying to plumb the mystery of identity, person and mission that lie at the heart of a vocation.

The particular effect of the growth of digital media and the popularization of the new atheists concern that the notion of God undermines the reality of truth and freedom, on an understanding of vocation, is to undermine the understanding of permanent commitment. Indeed a life lived in this way is seen as unrealistic. By contrast David L. Schindler indicates that the only credible response to charges of a lack of realism is the witness of 'each one's entire way of life, as carried in the whole of one's countless concrete acts, thoughts and gestures'.[26] It is a reminder that fundamental to any vocation is the call to be a witness in person, word and deed in a permanent commitment. The contemporary volatility with regard to commitment results in qualified assents which undermine the very nature of vocation. As Balthasar states: 'today qualified contingent assents cripple vocations everywhere like mildew'.[27] For him: 'Only one thing can be of use for God, with a view to his Kingdom: total surrender,

---

[26]David L. Schindler, *Ordering Love: Liberal Societies and the Memory of God* (Grand Rapids, MI: Eerdmans, 2011), p. 287.

[27]He continues: 'People either want to commit themselves only for a time (and thereby take away from God the possibility of being able to dispose over the whole man), or only for a certain kind of work they have in mind, that attracts them or seems timely (and thereby bind the hands of their ecclesial superiors, preventing them from disposing over those under them)'. *Zur Pastoral der geistlichen Berufe. Zum Welttag der geistlichen Berufe*, 24 April 1966 (Freiburg: Informationszentrum Berufe der Kirche, 1966), pp. 3–15. Translated and published by kind permission of the Hans Urs von Balthasar Archive in Basel, Switzerland. *Communio* 37 Spring 2010, pp. 113–128 [117].

which posits no conditions'.[28] He asserts that in the Old and New Testaments the figures (he cites Abraham, Samuel, Isaiah and Saul) who received a call from God responded with 'unconditional unrestricted readiness' for wherever they might be sent. Likewise in our contemporary milieu a vocation requisitions the entire life of a human being, and demands a correspondingly whole answer, and the totality of the commitment belongs to the fundamental form of the life of everyone who is called.[29]

The call of Christ

'If Jesus is risen. . . . Then he is someone in whom we can put absolute trust; we can put our trust not only in his message but *in Jesus himself*, for the Risen One does not belong to the *past* but is *present* today, alive'.[30] On Easter Sunday 2012 Pope Benedict XVI asserted the logic of the resurrection. If Christ is risen then his followers across all time and space are able to entrust themselves to this living Lord and to wager their entire lives on his living presence and his gospel.[31] Such a way of life calls for great generosity and an openness to an encounter with Christ that leads to a growing faith.[32]

---

[28]Ibid. See also 'if this total surrender of the person into the function determined by God is the indispensable common foundation of all vocations, then with respect to it, all – even considerable – differences in the manner and goal of the vocation are secondary'.

[29]See Ibid. [119]. The clear gender inclusiveness of this statement pre-empts any suggestion of an unhelpful gender focus on female submission.

[30]Pope Benedict XVI *Urbi et Orbi* Greeting, 8 April 2012.

[31]This is the joy and freedom of the children of God. 'Jesus asks us to follow him and to stake our whole life on him. Dear young people, do not be afraid to risk your lives by making space for Jesus Christ and his Gospel. This is the way to find inner peace and true happiness. It is the way to live fully as children of God, created in his image and likeness'. Benedict XVI, Message of His Holiness Pope Benedict XVI for the Twenty-Seventh World Youth Day 2012, 15 March 2012.

[32]The fruit of that faith is a deep joy arising from the profundity of the relationship with Christ 'The fruit of that faith is a deep joy arising from the profundity of the relationship with Christ. This deep joy is the fruit of the Holy Spirit who makes us God's sons and daughters, capable of experiencing and savouring his goodness, and calling him 'Abba', Father (see Rom. 8:15). Joy is the sign of God's presence and action within us. . . . The discovery and preservation of spiritual joy is the fruit of an encounter with the Lord. . . . Contemplation of [his] great love brings a hope and joy to our hearts that nothing can destroy. . . . Christian joy is born of this awareness of being loved by God who became man, gave his life for us and overcame evil and death. It means living a life of love for him'. Ibid.

The present dynamic presence of Christ – that irreducible particularity across all generations is a key focus of Balthasar's theology of vocation. This presence Balthasar asserts is both exemplary of the fullness of commitment involved in the response of a vocation, Christ's own willingness to allow himself to be sent and led by the Father; and also the very imperative for the vocational call Christ addresses to men and women in each generation. The call of Christ and the appropriate human response are the focus of his work, *The Christian State of Life*. Balthasar maintains that being a Christian means to be 'in Christ', it is a participation in Christ's very being. 'The "where" of the Christian is in Christ himself, just as Christ's "where" is in the Father',[33] which means to be in the will of the Father. This will is revealed gradually through the Son by subsequent calls. The will of the Father has an eternal dimension which is the election of human beings in Christ before creation.[34] This eternal election is made known to the human person in a particular moment of time through a call. The call is followed – immediately or later – by a sense of being given a mission. Such a mission is a unique participation in the mission of Christ. The mission is inchoately present in the call 'but there are intermediary stages'.[35] Election, call and a sending forth are in God one unique act which is manifested to us in different historical moments. For Balthasar the reality of vocation embraces the eternal election of God, and the manifestations of divine will in history through subsequent calls. The reality of call has a fundamental importance in Balthasar's understanding of being a Christian. He asserts that the dynamic call 'is the very essence of the Christian state of life or even the Christian life as such'.[36]

Here we see Balthasar's indebtedness to St Ignatius Loyola. The clarion call of Christ resounds through the *Spiritual Exercises* of St Ignatius. That same call reverberates with crystal clarity throughout Balthasar's work. It is a call to

---

[33]Hans Urs von Balthasar, *The Christian State of Life* (trans. Sr. Mary Frances McCarthy; San Francisco, CA: Ignatius Press, 1983), p. 212.

[34]See Ibid., pp. 139–40 and Hans Urs von Balthasar, *Theo-Drama: Theological Dramatic Theory III: Dramatis Personae: Persons in Christ* (San Francisco, CA: Ignatius Press, 1992), p. 263.

[35]Ibid., p. 267. See Balthasar, *The Christian State of Life*, p. 405.

[36]Ibid., p. 391.

enter into the mission of Christ.[37] It was this same call of Christ experienced in a personal manner that marked the life of Balthasar, himself, causing him to enter the Society of Jesus after completing doctoral studies.[38]

In *The Christian State of Life,* Balthasar indicates that if there is any original-ity in his presentation of the theology of vocation it is to be found in his explo-ration of the mystery of a vocation from the standpoint of love. He makes clear that the primary call to human beings is the call to love – love of God and love of neighbour. This is an absolute call admitting of no exception.[39] This love is active 'shown more in deeds than in words'. 'A love that is not active, that is not ready to prove itself in ever new and different ways, is not love'.[40]

At the heart of this love is the mystery of self-giving, and consequently of choice. For Balthasar, true love is radically and fundamentally disposed to

---

[37]Thus Ignatius invites one making the Exercises in the meditation on the Kingdom of Christ to ask for the grace to be attentive to this call of Chrsit. 'I will ask of our Lord the grace not to be deaf to His call but prompt and diligent to accomplish His most holy will'. [*Spiritual Exercises* 91]

[38]The call of God struck von Balthasar 'like lightening'. After completing his doctoral work, he made the 30 days Spiritual Exercises with a group of fellow students. Of this time he said years later:Top of F Bottom of Form 'Even now. . . . I could still go to that remote path in the Black Forest, not far from Basel, and find again the tree beneath which I was struck as by lightening. . . . And yet it was neither theology nor the priesthood that came into my mind in a flash. It was simply this: you have nothing to choose, you have been called. You will not serve you will be taken into service. You have no plans to make, you are just a little stone in a mosaic which has long been ready'. Pourquoi je me suis fait prêtre. Témoignages recueillis par Jorge et Ramón Sans Vila, e. Centre Diocésain de Documentation (Tournai, 1961), p. 21. He saw his vocation as being to spend himself for the Church. Twenty years later he felt called to leave the Society in obedience to what considered to be a new mission, namely the founding and leadership of the Community of St John along with Adrienne von Speyr. Within this context there was a sense of a 'dual' mission 'a double mission which complement each like the "two halves of the moon" . . . In our case, the plan was that we should collaborate intensively on a common work'. Hans Urs von Balthasar, *Our Task: A Report and A Plan* (trans. Dr John Saward; San Francisco, CA: Ignatius Press, 1994), pp. 16–17. This complementarity was a living out of two distinct vocations through the medium of a significant collaboration in mission. Although he left the Jesuits in 1950, Balthasar still continued to live out of the spirituality of the Exercises and we can continue to trace Ignatian insight in Balthasar's theology. He continued to speak of the Society as his 'most dear and self-evident home'.

[39]'We are here to love – to love God and to love our neighbour." Balthasar, *The Christian State of Life,* p. 27.

[40]'The inner life of love is inconceivable without the rhythm of growth, of ever new openness and spontaneity. Love can never give itself sufficiently, can never exhaust its ingenuity in preparing new joys for the beloved, is never so satisfied with itself and its deeds that it does not look for new proofs of love, is never so familiar with the person of the beloved that it does not crave the wonderment of new knowledge'. Ibid., p. 28.

renounce everything so that everything may be held in readiness for the first sign of the will of the beloved.[41] Balthasar emphasizes that so true is this of God's love for human beings that the whole existence of the world is a demonstration and proof of God's unsurpassed love for the human creatures God has made. 'God's deepest love in the splendor of his dying is so that all might live beyond themselves for him'.[42]

The divine call of love is focused in the call of Christ.[43] So Balthasar explains 'the call that is heard individually and personally in attentive meditation on the word of God becomes the basis not only of the right direction of the Christian's progress, but also and explicitly of his [or her] "state" which Ignatius identifies with "way of life"',[44] and Balthasar equates it with the differentiated states of life – the priestly state, the state of the counsels, the married state and even more narrowly with the concrete situation in which each one finds himself [herself] in the here-and-now of the state chosen.[45] As, he or she makes their choice, the one chosen by God enters into the unity between Father, Son and Spirit. Every mission, every qualitative calling within the Church proceeds from the Father and, through the Spirit, leads the one called to the Son, who has been called from all eternity by the Father. Here it may be helpful to consider the different stages of a vocation as Balthasar outlines them.

---

[41]As Ignatius stresses in the Spiritual Exercises, 'Love consists in a mutual sharing of goods; for example, the lover gives and shares with the beloved what he possesses, or something of what he has or is able to give; and vice versa, the beloved shares with the lover', *Spiritual Exercises*, p. 231.

[42]'To display the Christian message in its unsurpassable greatness (*id quo maius cogitari nequit*), because it is God's human word for the world, . . .' Hans Urs von Balthasar, *My Work: In Retrospect* (San Francisco, CA: Ignatius Press, 1993), p. 50.

[43]In the contemplations on the life of Christ in the second and third weeks of the Exercises, it is primarily the contemplation of Christ's call, and the living out of that call in terms of his mission, which leads to his passion, death and resurrection. It is against this background that during the second week Ignatius prompts those making the Exercises to 'begin to investigate and ask in what kind of life or in what state his Divine Majesty wishes to make use' of them, and how they ought to 'prepare (themselves) to arrive at perfection in whatever state or way of life God our Lord may grant (them) to choose'. *Spiritual Exercises*, p. 135.

[44]Balthasar, *The Christian State of Life*, p. 170.

[45]See ibid., p. 392.

The three-fold stages of a vocation

Balthasar distinguishes three different stages of a vocational call. There is a baptismal call to the family of the Church, then to a particular state within the Church, and finally to a concrete situation within that particular state.[46] In his interpretation of the first stage the call into the Church, it is as we have seen a call to love, since this is the fundamental Christian vocation and the primary response to the divine initiative,[47] It is also, however, a call to holiness.[48]

The second stage of vocation leads to a definite state of life in the Church as it gives a concrete form to the mission in which the individual fulfils that primary call to love. Balthasar distinguishes two fundamental states of life: the secular state[49] and the so-called 'state of election'. The secular state is 'the primary and, at the same time, the fundamental state in the Church'.[50] The usual consequence of the call to this state finds expression in the decision to marry, to raise a family and to witness to Christ in the world.

The second state, 'the state of election', includes the priesthood and religious life.[51] Balthasar considers the priesthood as fundamentally a function to represent Christ through the ministry of teaching, guiding and sacramental service. Religious Life is considered more in terms of a subjective following of Christ in being poor, celibate and obedient. The task of this state is to be 'the leaven

---

[46]Ibid.

[47]'all [human persons] are called to perfect love'. Ibid., p. 57. In this work Balthasar gives an extensive excursus on the fundamental vocation of love see ibid., pp. 25–66.

[48]See Lumen Gentium, pp. 40–41 'Thus it is evident to everyone, that all the faithful of Christ of whatever rank or status, are called to the fullness of the Christian life and to the perfection of charity; by this holiness as such a more human manner of living is promoted in this earthly society. In order that the faithful may reach this perfection, they conform themselves to His image seeking the will of the Father in all things.'

[49]'the state of the Church itself, which, removed from the world by the fact of redemption and chosen by the call of Christ, has been empowered and called by the Holy Spirit to take its place with the Son in the presence of the Father'. Ibid., p. 386.

[50]Ibid., p. 333. For a fuller exposition of Balthasar's understanding of the different states of life see ibid., pp. 133–364.

[51]Balthasar's original terminology for this is the 'state of the counsels'. To avoid a confusion of terminology I shall use the term 'religious life' but in a more general sense to include also the secular institutes.

of the people',[52] and also to assimilate the 'yes' of the whole Church to the *fiat* of Mary who is the model of the fullness of obedient response. Balthasar maintains that priesthood or religious life require a distinctive qualitative call in contradistinction to the lay state.[53] For the lay Christian, the fundamental call to love which is the call into the Church is the operative principle of their whole life. The fact that someone is not called to one of the more specific vocations does not mean a life of less dedication since the primary call to perfect love is mandatory for all.[54]

For Balthasar the lay state means marriage. Like Ignatius[55] he does not consider the single life in the world as a positive option for an election of a state of life.[56] His analysis of the nature of love leads him to the conclusion that love requires a definitive commitment, a self-giving in a concrete way. Accordingly he maintains that to introduce a third state of life as a possible option would seriously endanger the radicalism of the other two states of life, due to the absence of such a commitment. Balthasar is aware, however, that there are persons who for different legitimate reasons do not marry. He considers them as exceptions and as persons belonging potentially to the marital status. They also have a specific place in the work of salvation and they are also called to a life of service and self-giving in the Church. Meanwhile the persons who have not yet chosen a state of life are in a state of preparation, which is not considered to be a definitive state in itself. The confirmed commitment to a particular state of life does not mean the

---

[52]Balthasar, *The Christian State of Life*, p. 278.

[53]Ibid., p. 148. 'The impulse lying behind Balthasar's reflections on the states of life is his desire to bring into relief the life of the evangelical counsels. Hence the weight of his reflection falls on the state of election. . . . For him election implies a twofold possibility, that of the religious life and hat of the priesthood. Although a person may be called to one or the other or both, it is important to see priesthood and religious life as two sides of a single election. These two sides of election have an inner dynamism toward each other'. O'Donnell SJ, *Hans Urs von Balthasar*, p. 129.

[54]Balthasar, *The Christian State of Life*, pp. 165, 420.

[55]See *Spiritual Exercises*, pp. 170–74.

[56]Balthasar, *The Christian State of Life*, pp. 236–38. By contrast Vocationcast, April 2012, stated that the Church teaches there are four vocations: Priesthood, Consecrated Life, Married Life and the single Life. Vocationcast is an online audio webcast and podcast inspired by the Holy Father's encouragement to bring the witness of faith to the digital world. It arose out of the question Pope Benedict XVI posed to young people on his visit to the United Kingdom in 2010 'what kind of a person do you really want to be?' Each 30-minute episode is produced by a team of trained seminarians from the dioceses of England and Wales. 'We aim to inspire, empower and equip young people in their search for life in Christ'. The monthly episodes include interviews, faith stories, prayer and reflection. www.vocationcast.org

end of the dynamic of call. There is a third stage which involves the refinement of a person's mission through a 'constant being led by the Holy Spirit'.[57]

At this juncture it is important to address the other major contemporary concern the question of the reality of human freedom within Balthasar's theology of vocation.

Freedom

To adequately address the subject of freedom in the theology of Balthasar would overwhelm the limitations of this paper.[58] Add to this Edward Oakes comment that 'Christian theology invariably shipwrecks itself when it confronts the issue of divine and human freedom'[59] and we might see the temptation to remain silent on the subject. This is not an option, however, as we must address the issue of freedom because of its significance to an understanding of vocation in our contemporary milieu. In the relationship between infinite freedom and finite freedom, which is how Balthasar frames the discussion, he says there is found 'the starting point of all Theo-drama'.[60] This starting point can be expressed in Aidan Nichols' question 'who else can act if God is on the stage?'[61] It is also not difficult to see how the question is related to concepts such as identity, vocation, mission and action. It is at the heart of the relationship between humanity and God. 'Having given freedom to the creature', Balthasar wrote early in the *Theo-Drama*, 'God, as Creator, is always "involved" in the world, and this means that there is always

---

[57]Balthasar, *The Christian State of Life*, p. 406.

[58]This is a crucial subject for scholars of Balthasar. Thomas G. Dalzell, *The Dramatic Encounter of Divne and Human Freedom in the Theology of Hans Urs von Balthasar* (New York, NY: Peter Lang, 2000) is a valuable book length study. Other scholars including Edward Oakes, Aidan Nichols and John O'Donnell each undertake chapter length examinations in their books.

[59]Edward Oakes, *Pattern of Redemption: The Theology of Hans Urs von Balthasar* (New York, NY: Continuum, 1994), p. 211.

[60]Hans Urs von Balthasar, *Theo-Drama, II Dramatis Personae: Man in God* (trans. Graham Harrison; San Francisco, CA: Ignatius Press, 1988), p. 271.

[61]Nichols, *No Bloodless Myth*, p. 63.

a divine-human dramatic tension'.[62] Indeed Balthasar's starting point is the dramatic tension that occurs when humanity recognizes that, although the God of infinite freedom exists, we are still free to act, albeit in a limited way. The question then becomes how are we to act both in the presence of God and in a way that neither seeks more freedom than we deserve (or want, if only we knew it) while living out all the freedom that is properly ours.

Balthasar's understanding of the relationship between human and divine freedom is grounded in a Trinitarian theology of persons in unity. In the Triune mystery, the three persons of God are each themselves and wholly distinct and yet fully interconnected and one.[63] Furthermore, for Balthasar the dramatic union of the persons of the Trinity is characterized by *kenosis*: the mutual self-giving, self-emptying, to and for each other. This giving of each person is undertaken in absolute freedom as gift, and the giving of each is 'understood differently and according to their proper roles within the divine life'.[64] It is through this infinite, kenotic, self-giving of the persons of the Trinity between and within each other, giving and sharing one another in infinite freedom and love, that they share themselves again and further in Creation.[65]

Just as the persons of the Trinity remain mysteriously one and distinct, so too we are free because we are made free by God, who guarantees our freedom. Our freedom is certain because we are created to be free by an infinite freedom.

---

[62]Hans Urs von Balthasar, *Theo-Drama I: Prologema* (trans. Graham Harrison; San Francisco, CA: Ignatius Press, 1998), pp. 128–29.

[63]As John O'Donnell states, 'the Trinity brings us face to face with the mystery that there is real otherness in God which is not incompatible with [God's] unity. . . . Oneness is not incompatible with otherness'. O'Donnell, *Hans Urs von Balthasar*, p. 66.

[64]Dalzell, *Dramatic Encounter*, p. 47.

[65]And therefore as O'Donnell states, 'this conception of divine life as the infinite self-giving of the persons thus makes possible the reality of a free creation as well as the interchange of freedom in the divine drama between God and the world. The goal of God's free dramatic action is, in Balthasar's judgement, the setting free of the creature. In the action of creation God first of all enables an autonomous creature to be. [God] lets it be and hence be free in its very being'. O'Donnell, *Hans Urs von Balthasar*, pp. 66–67. And according to Dalzell, 'the ultimate end of human freedom is understood as a taking part in God's Trinitarian life process'. Dalzell, *Dramatic Encounter*, p. 213.

Our createdness itself therefore does not endanger our freedom; something else did and does.[66] This is the reality of sin in our lives.

Humanity is caught within a web of paradoxes.[67] In the effort to be free without limitation humanity has become bound to sin and death on the one hand, and according to Balthasar, left with the feeling of 'emptiness and indifferent freedom' on the other when we recognize our freedom is in fact the 'space that God had originally created for himself'.[68] Our desire to have more freedom than was ours to have, to make human freedom absolute, has left us unable to enact the story we are created to live. We can only sense the presence of the lead role – of Christ – on the stage but are unsure of how to interact with Him. We recognize our freedom but do not know how to direct it toward our end, leaving all action, story and characters searching.

For Balthasar what is necessary to move humanity beyond its inertness is a recognition that human freedom is not absolute but rather related to another freedom. He asserts that both finite and infinite freedom find their full integration in the person of Jesus Christ, and this is nowhere more evident than in Christ's 'yes' to both the incarnation and his passion and death on the cross: 'as God's "yes" to the world and the world's "yes" to God, Jesus Christ seals and implements the truth of the relationship between God and the world in terms of

---

[66]'Although set by God in a state of rectitude, humanity, became enticed by the evil one, and abused its freedom at the very start of history. It lifted itself up against God, and sought to attain its goal apart from God. Although they had known God, they did not glorify God, but their senseless hearts were darkened, and they served the creature rather than the creator. What Revelation makes known to us is confirmed by our own experience. For when humanity looks into its own heart it finds that it is drawn towards what is wrong and sunk in many evils which cannot come from the good creator. Often refusing to acknowledge God as its source, humanity has also upset the relationship which should link it to its last end; at the same time humanity has broken the right order that should reign within himself as well as between himself and other men and all creatures. Man therefore is divided against himself. As a result, the whole life of man, both individual and social, shows itself to be a struggle, and a dramatic one, between good and evil, between light and darkness. Man finds that he is unable of himself to overcome the assaults of evil successfully, so that everyone feels as though bound by chains'. *Gaudium et Spes*, p. 13.

[67]Michael Buckley puts paradox at the centre of our questions about freedom then he says, 'the human person is fundamentally conditioned by a paradox: freedom is a question about yourself. It is not a question which the person has; it is a question which I am and with which I constitute what I am to become'. Michael Buckley, 'Freedom, Election and Self-Transcendence: Some reflections upon the Ignatian Development of a Life Ministry', in *Ignatian Spirituality in a Secular Age* (ed. George P. Schner; Canada: Canadian Corporation for Studies in Religion, 1984), p. 71.

[68]Balthasar, *The Christian*, p. 135.

a Covenant between infinite and finite freedom.'[69] Here Balthasar says, 'in concrete terms, infinite freedom appears on stage in the form of Jesus Christ's "low-
liness" and "obedience unto death", which shows humanity the way in which it
is to live out and fulfill its freedom'.[70] Or in Ignatian terms, freedom can now be
understood as the 'freedom for' that helps to make us 'indifferent to all created
things' and makes us ready to accept the invitation of Christ the King, the God
who labours, to give 'all liberty, my memory, my understanding my entire will'
in service to God and humanity.[71] Freedom is about potentiality and purpose,
possibility and identity.[72]

Identity person and mission – at the heart of vocation

Attention has been given to the subject of freedom to establish the basis of a
single assertion apparent within Balthasar's work 'absolute freedom has prepared a personal path for each of us to follow freely, in the liberated freedom
which alone permits true self-realization'.[73] This is the basic assumption at the
heart of an understanding of vocation. As Balthasar portrays this in the *Theo-
Drama* in life there is a story to be enacted by individual characters fulfilling
their roles.[74] For each one, there stands the questions 'who am I?' and 'what
am I to do?' These questions reveal the integrated themes that are the focus of
the *Theo-Drama* namely identity and mission.[75] They are the component parts
and the pathway to personhood in Balthasar's theological anthropology, for

---

[69]Nicholls, *No Bloodless Myth*, p. 72.

[70]Balthasar, *Theo-Drama, II*, p. 250. For humanity, freedom is nowhere more fully experienced than in participating in the life of Christ. Dalzell, *Dramatic Encounter*, p. 57.

[71]Ignatius, *Spiritual Exercises*, pp. 23, 91–100, 236, 234.

[72]See Buckley, 'Freedom, Election and Self-Transcendence', *Ignatian Spirituality*, pp. 70–71.

[73]Nichols, *No Bloodless Myth*, p. 105.

[74]Hans Urs von Balthasar, *Theo-Drama I: Theological Dramatic Theory: Prologomena* (trans. Graham Harrison; San Francisco, CA: Ignatius Press, 1988), p. 105.

[75]According to Nichols 'we must remember that in *Theodramatik* Balthasar is concerned above all with the missions that agents assume or are given in view of the working out of the divine drama whose dénouement is the Cross of Christ and that for his theology, mission and identity are co-related terms.' Nichols, *No Bloodless Myth*, p. 119.

as he said only 'when God addresses a conscious subject tells [him/her] who [he/she] is and what [he/she] means to the eternal God of truth and shows [him/her] the purpose of [his/her] existence – that is, imparts a distinctive and divinely authorized mission – that we can say of a conscious subject that [he/she] is a "person"'.[76]

But for many people in today's world, this pathway to personhood is far from clear. For many people there exists more than just questions and uncertainty regarding ideas such a role, identity, purpose and action in the world. Indeed there appears to be a crisis of identity and purpose. Identity and action have become completely detached from a sense of purpose and the contemporary world offers little to help define or integrate them. This can be a real source of anxiety.[77]

For Balthasar, mission, which guides and motivates activity in the world is grounded in and flows from the person whom God made. As Balthasar himself wrote, 'if the mission is the real core of the personality, it opens up the latter – because it comes from eternity and is destined for eternity – far beyond the dimensions of which it is conscious in the world or which others allot to it'.[78] There is, however, as Balthasar emphasizes a communal aspect to the search for personal identity and mission and neither can really be found in isolation from other people. It is only in true inter-subjectivity, in relationship with another, that we will come to know ourselves. Systems and social structures cannot tell us who we are. As Balthasar wrote, 'if the mission is the real core of the personality, it opens up the latter – because it comes from eternity and is destined for

---

[76]Hans Urs von Balthasar, *Theo-Drama III: Dramatis Personae: Persons in Christ* (trans. Graham Harrison; San Francisco, CA: Ignatius Press, 1992), p. 207.

[77]In *the Christian and Anxiety* Balthsar states that 'there is Christian anxiety before the mission – at the point where the soul is being cleaned out' and prepared for mission.' He goes on to say that there might also be a certain Christian anxiety 'while the mission is being carried out (if having anxiety belongs to the mission), but not in the act itself of being sent: here clarity, certainty, and agreement necessarily and unconditionally rule'. Balthasar, *The Christian*, p. 149. Balthasar suggests that this is a part of the contemporary experience of the theo-drama. If indeed personhood is beyond the reach of humanity before mission, then character and derivatively plot must be beyond their reach as well at this time. What that experience is like for the individual who is yet to become a character, who is an actor without yet knowing what they are to enact, is a moment fraught with anxiety and danger.

[78]Hans Urs von Balthasar, *Theo-Drama V: The Last Act* (trans. Graham Harrison; San Francisco, CA: Ignatius Press, 1998), pp. 393–94.

eternity – far beyond the dimensions of which it is conscious in the world or which others allot to it.[79] This idea of inter-subjectivity in the search for identity and mission is present also in the theology of Balthasar, not in the sense of human inter-subjectivity, but rather in the interrelationship of divine-human freedom.

The individual human mission, of which the individual's identity is a part, is only fully revealed as it is understood to be related to the divine mission of the Son. It is the interrelationship of the individual's sense of mission to the divine mission of the Son that permits the individual to act in true freedom and to fulfil the identity which they were given by God. For Balthasar then, the human individual must seek unity of personhood achieved when identity and mission come together (but are not equated) 'at some mysterious point' and become 'a kind of reflection on the mission of Christ'.[80] It is a dramatic mysterious point. Like the union of divine and human freedom, in the interrelationship between the individual human mission and the mission of Christ, there is a dramatic tension. And here, Balthasar's ecclesiology impels us to consider the nature of what it means to be *persons*-in-communion. Not just as biological beings, nor merely as a social group held together by commonly accepted customs, and courtesy, persons in communion means first and foremost persons grounded in love – a love originating from the depths of the Trinity.

The question then becomes how might the Christian make good choices in this drama of existence? How do we come to know who we are and what it is we should do? Here one method close to the heart of Balthasar is to use the *Spiritual Exercises* of Ignatius.[81] The connection between giving oneself to God

---

[79]Hans Urs von Balthasar, *Theo-Drama Theological Dramatic Theory V: The Last Act* (trans. Graham Harrison; San Francisco, CA: Ignatius Press, 1998), pp. 393–94.

[80]Hans Urs von Balthasar, *Theo-Drama Theological Dramatic Theory I: Prolegomena* (trans. Graham Harrison; San Francisco, CA: Ignatius Press, 1988), pp. 46, 69.

[81]The Exercises have as their stated purpose 'the overcoming of self and the ordering of one's life on the basis of a decision made in freedom from any ill-ordered attachment'. [21]. According to Michael Ivens in his guide to the Exercises, this summary statement by Ignatius 'associates the Exercises with making a decision', and that 'Ignatius preferred, other things being equal, to give the Exercises to persons having to choose a state of life', [Michael Ivens SJ, *Understanding the Spiritual Exercises: Text and Commentary, a Handbook for Retreat Directors* (Leominster, Herefordshire: Gracewing, 1998), p. 22] or in other words, an understood way of acting in the world or one who was discerning their vocation. What we can also note through the Exercises is Ignatius moving the individual toward union with Christ who is himself on mission for the Father. Throughout the Exercises Christ remains on mission and the exercitant is invited to join. The primordial act of love is the choice to give oneself to God.

in love and freedom and service in the world, grounds the Exercises. To follow Christ then means to give one's whole self, 'all that I have and possess', to God so that God may 'dispose of it entirely according to His will'.[82] This is to imitate Christ in his obedience even unto death.

Obedience

In Balthasar's theology of vocation obedience holds a central place. It is seen both as an activity which makes the individual more active and energized for mission and also as the disposition which makes the individual freer to accept being missioned. This should not be seen as promoting passivity. 'It is just the reverse', says Mark McIntosh, for Balthasar 'an attitude of obedience brings about a sense of worth and dignity, or having been entrusted with something unfathomably . . . significant to God, and the personal freedom and strength to see the commission through'. He continues 'from this standpoint obedience to mission is an essential contributing factor in the integrity of the human person'.[83] In becoming obedient to the will that God has for each of us we grow in both freedom and integrity. In this individual sense of mission that exists as part of the Son's mission for the Father is grounded our sense of participation in the building of the Kingdom of God.

Accordingly, Balthasar emphasizes that both self-surrender and obedience are crucial to the mission. Without the latter, the former runs the risk of being a deceptively self-transcending asceticism. So self-surrender is a prelude and a prerequisite for the active co-operation of human beings in the divine enterprise. In that self-surrender, individuals respond to an invitation to enter into God's creative and redemptive activity. Here obedience is a response of love to that invitation and always includes the divine gift of a greater interior freedom and energy, which in turn assists that response. Thus there develops a deeper intimacy with God through such obedience, and a deeper integrity of the human person. Indeed, Balthasar is insistent that obedience is only true when undertaken out of love in a joyful response to the divine initiative of love, not out of fear. It is love alone that prevents obedience from becoming oppressive;

---

[82]*Spiritual Exercises*, p. 234.
[83]Mark McIntosh, *Christology from Within: Spirituality and the Incarnation in Hans Urs von Balthasar* (Notre Dame Indiana: University of Notre Dame Press, 2000), p. 77.

love engenders life-giving energy and permanence of commitment. And the test of obedience to a vocation Balthasar asserts is 'fundamentally to be ready to stake everything on the one card of the call, and on the one who calls'.[84]

The movement toward cooperation with God that comes from the loving relationship of self-surrender and obedience helps the individual person to find and fulfil their own being. McIntosh notes that for Balthasar, 'obedience is so crucial because apart from it, and from the pilgrimage it entails, Christians might never claim for themselves what is truly theirs: the particular form of cooperation with God which they were created to enjoy'. In mission therefore we come to know who we are and to fulfil that by giving ourselves in loving service to the Beloved and to those the Beloved loves.[85] The gift of a vocation is never just for the individual nor for the individual as part of the Church but it is an invitation to enter into the redemptive work of Christ for the salvation of the world. In the enactment of a vocation both the Church and the individual come to awareness of the free gift of vocation that has been given by the one who calls. It is here that the vows of religious life become the means to more fully enter into that redemptive work.[86]

---

[84]*Zur Pastoral der geistlichen Berufe. Zum Welttag der geistlichen Berufe,* 24 April 1966 (Freiburg: Informationszentrum Berufe der Kirche, 1966), pp. 3–15. Translated and published by kind permission of the Hans Urs von Balthasar Archive in Basel, Switzerland, *Communio* 37, Spring 2010, pp. 111–28.

[85]'In this way too, human history remains open and vital and "cannot close in on [itself], since it is from the definitive mission of Jesus Christ that they take on their ultimate meaning'. Jacques Servais, 'Freedom as Christ's Gift to Man in the Thought of Hans Urs von Balthasar', *Communio,* vol. 29(3) (Fall 2002), p. 560.

[86]'If obedience is to be theologically relevant, it is always obedience to the "wholly-other", the one who disposes with a total freedom, never the God who has come to be at our disposition (e.g. through a law or a rule). The authoritative standard for Christians is the human obedience of Jesus' disciples to the Master. . . . This relation cannot be surpassed, it can only be made present (quasi-sacramantally) through the ecclesially sanctioned relationship of obedience of one of the faithful to his superior, who concretely represents Christ to him. [120] Virginity is indivisible, not only in its bodily, but also in its spiritual aspect. . . . the ethic of the one called, with regard to the sexual sphere, is entirely determined by the virginal bodily relation between Christ and the his Church: its exclusivity has nothing to do with prudery or exaggerated asceticism. It is the exclusivity of the Body of Christ eucharistically surrendered to the end and – as the response of the one called to this – the exclusivity of the body of the Christian handed over to Christ. From the grace-filled fruitfulness of the latter, the Lord can draw what he wills for the redemption of the world. . . . The poverty of the one called must, above all, makes visible the poverty of the people of God in the world that is to it a "desert" and a "foreign land". It is a poverty that, in the Old Covenant, is one with faith and in the New Covenant is one with love. The canonical regulations are important to the extent that they help to support this Spirit and not, to the contrary, darken or diminish its power as a witness of faith.' [121] *Zur Pastoral der geistlichen Berufe. Zum Welttag der geistlichen Berufe,* 24 April 1966 (Freiburg: Informationszentrum Berufe der Kirche, 1966), pp. 3–15. Translated and published by kind permission of the Hans Urs von Balthasar Archive in Basel, Switzerland, *Communio* 37 Spring 2010, pp. 113–28.

Conclusion

According to Balthasar, vocations are rooted in the divine Trinitarian initiative depending essentially on the one who calls. It is Christ who continues to call men and women in every generation to pay attention to the divine drama of existence and to offer themselves to engage with him in his redemptive work. Such action flies in the face of our contemporary cultural context and gives a renewed appreciation of the nature of truth and the reality of human freedom enfolded and guaranteed by the action of divine freedom. It is also perhaps to underline that the end of the Christian life is to love God for God's own sake and to participate intimately in the mission and life of Christ the one who continually calls. It is to 'praise reverence and serve God our Lord' and in and through such living to grow in the holiness that underlies St Thomas' ascent to perfection. Such a lived life is the way of blessedness – of more depth than our contemporary understanding of happiness – and a source of blessing for others. Those discerning vocation need to perceive that irreducible particularity of Christ at work in and through such lives and thereby be attracted to that self-surrender of unconditional commitment. For this sound guidance is required.

'The young Christians who grapple with the question of vocation urgently need guidance from experienced, praying and spiritually reflective persons, now more than ever in the history of the Church, since the whole atmosphere of the Church is contaminated by theologically unreflective short-winded and often downright "watered-down" catchwords and ideologies. It would be desirable if those in positions of responsibility from all states – priests religious lay – would come together in order further to clarify theologically the problems of vocation today and together seek paths towards workable solutions.'[87]

---

[87]Ibid.

Part Three

Discerning Vocation Today

8

What is distinctive about vocations to religious life?

Sr Cathy Jones

Until the twentieth century, the question 'what is a religious?' could be answered with some certainty: religious were people who made vows, lived communally and wore some form of identifiable clothing. Answering that question today requires a more complex response. Religious life, in its many and varied forms, is now one among several forms of ecclesial consecration and it is debatable to what extent religious life today is a distinct ecclesial form. The growth of new forms of consecrated life (as distinct from religious life in the strictly defined sense) now makes the discernment of a vocation to a religious community a more demanding process than in previous eras.

When considering religious life as a whole, attempting to identify what, if anything, distinguishes vocations to religious life is highly problematic. Not only is there immense diversity between different expressions of religious life but also other forms of ecclesial consecration are often understood to be 'religious' while not falling into the canonical category, while the self-understanding of many contemporary religious is at odds with the canonical definition.

Given this complex situation, it could be argued that a quest to express the distinctiveness of religious life will necessarily fail, and that only the lived expression of religious life is able to witness to the 'why' of this form of vocation. However, dispensing religious from reasoned reflection upon how and why they are living their consecration would lose the potential for deepening their sense of identity and purpose. For those discerning if they are called to this way of life, this uncertainty adds to the difficulty of responding to a religious vocation. This is particularly significant since those currently discerning a vocation to consecrated life are highly influenced by questions concerning identity and purpose.

Vocational trends and the variety of forms of consecrated life

Research shows that the most clearly defined ecclesial vocations are more attractive to discerners than those whose identity is less explicit. This is true both in the United Kingdom and in the United States.[1] In the United Kingdom this is most evident in non-clerical male apostolic religious life, which has only had eight new entrants in the past decade,[2] compared to almost ten times as many entrants to male priestly congregations and hundreds of seminarians for diocesan priesthood.[3] Similarly, the significantly higher proportion of men entering seminary (and male clerical institutes) to women entering religious life is almost certainly linked to the clear function or role of a priest. The 'why' of priestly existence has an obvious sacramental answer; the 'why' of non-clerical religious life is much harder to answer. In the past dedication to a particular work played a role in motivating people to join religious institutes, but today, with all non-ordained ministry being open to lay people, there are no specific activities only open to religious.

---

[1]While the vocational trends in the United Kingdom and United States have enough in common to enable them to be considered together, religious institutes in the United States are far more likely to have had members joining recently. The 2009 survey of the National Religious Vocations Conference in the United States found that 78 per cent of institutes of men and 66 per cent of institutes of women have at least one person currently in initial formation. The survey conducted by the National Office for Vocation for England and Wales for 2011 found that only 20 per cent of female institutes and 29 per cent of male have at least one member in initial formation.Sources: http://nrvc.net/english_version/?return_url=english_version and unpublished survey of the National Office for Vocation of England and Wales 2011.
[2]Furthermore, the vast majority of these entrants have not remained in religious life.
[3]See The statistics published by the National Office for Vocation: www.ukvocation.org/national-vocations-framework There have been approximately 150 entrants to male clerical congregations in the United Kingdom in the past decade.

Although on average in the United Kingdom about a third more women join apostolic congregations than enclosed convents, there are currently about 20 times more convents of apostolic sisters than of enclosed sisters.[4] Thus, an enclosed convent is 13 times more likely to attract a new member than a convent of apostolic sisters. However, perhaps more significantly, those entering apostolic congregations (both male and female) are practically all doing so in congregations where the majority (and often all) the members live in community and have a rhythm of communal prayer.[5] Therefore, considering vocational 'choice' from a purely human perspective, clarity of function or specificity of role, as well as communal life and common prayer are clearly significant influences.

Consecrated life today is expressed in countless different ways. While the lives of purely enclosed contemplatives are markedly different from members of secular institutes who express their consecration in a 'hidden' manner in the midst of the world, practically every conceivable variation exists on a spectrum between these two life-forms. A brief indication of some of the points on the spectrum illustrates this clearly: male contemplatives with significant apostolic engagement; religious whose life is ordered around common prayer and community life as well as active ministry; congregations with some common prayer and a flexibility as to whether they live in community or not and congregations where individual ministries and living alone are the norm. Alongside this great sweep of possibilities are members of secular institutes, some of whom are 'hidden' and some not, with some living in community, although the majority live alone. Adding even more variety to this mixture are Societies of Common Life which Canon Law describes as 'resembling' institutes of consecrated life, only some of whom profess the evangelical counsels.[6]

---

[4]Figures for 2010 show 1,066 convents in the United Kingdom, of which about 50 are of enclosed sisters (see the website of the Association of British Contemplatives www.abc.mydom.co.uk and the statistics complied by the Bishops Conference of England and Wales for the Papal visit in 2010 www.thepapalvisit.org.uk/The-Catholic-Faith/Some-key-statistics).

[5]For example, the recent comprehensive survey conducted on behalf of the National Religious Vocations Centre in the United States found that when asked about their decision to enter their particular religious institute, new members cite the community life in the institute as the most influential factor in their decision (followed closely by the prayer life or prayer styles in the community). Most new members indicate that they want to live, work and pray with other members of their religious institute, with the last being especially important to them. http://nrvc.net/english_version/?return_url=english_version.

[6]Canon 731.1 & Canon 731.2.

Within religious life, monastic communities, whether purely contemplative or not, have a more clearly defined identity than the vast majority of apostolic congregations. A life-long commitment to common liturgical prayer and fraternal communion in a given monastery or abbey provides a locus for expressing an identity; this is particularly so when the communities are purely contemplative or (for women) observe papal enclosure. Contemplative religious institutes as well as active ones were called to renewal of their life by *Perfectae Caritatis* but it is above all apostolic congregations who, 50 years after Vatican II, face the difficult challenge of identifying (and living out) a distinctive identity. These congregations rather than monastic or contemplative religious will be the focus of this essay.

The question of the particularity of religious consecration today will be addressed by comparing active religious life to three forms of ecclesial commitment which mark the Church of the twenty-first century: (1) consecration outside of an institute; (2) consecration within a secular institute; (3) commitment within new ecclesial movements. Precisely because these three have strong similarities to many forms of active religious life, an attempt to tease out how they can be distinguished will help to answer the question of how religious life can be said to be a distinctive vocation.

(1) Consecration outside of an institute

The New Testament and early patristic writings witness to the ecclesial categories of virgins and widows. Paul describes women who remained unmarried and devoted themselves to prayer (1 Cor. 7) and records the attributes required to be eligible to be 'enrolled' as a widow (1 Tim. 5). However, as religious institutes emerged, they gradually became the central form of consecrated life in the Church, supplanting consecrated virgins and widows.

Vita Consecrata describes the 'new flowering of the ancient Order of Virgins'[7] since Vatican II, where the women (no such state is available for

---

[7] *Vita Consecrata* 7.

men) are consecrated to virginity, to a life of prayer and penance, and to the service of the Church under the jurisdiction of the bishop, according to the proper liturgical rite. While it is not possible to know exact numbers (since the Vatican's *Annuario Pontifico* does not record figures) research suggests that there are approximately 3,000 consecrated virgins in about 42 countries.[8] This is an extremely small figure compared to the 730,000 religious women world-wide.[9] Although numbers of consecrated virgins are growing slowly world-wide, it remains a vocation which relatively few younger women discerning their vocation consider. Consecrated virgins have no rule or community and own their own property and care for their personal needs; in the eyes of many young discerners such characteristics do not express the radical distinctive-ness that they are looking for in consecrated life.

Although the Latin Church has no particular rite for consecrating widows and widowers or hermits who are not attached to a religious community, these ancient forms of consecration have also re-emerged after Vatican II and, like consecrated virgins, are slowly taking their place in the rich tapestry of con-secrated life in the twenty-first century. Hermits who are not attached to a religious institute are still a rare phenomenon, and while the numbers of those seeking consecration as widows and widowers appears to be growing, the lack of rite of consecration in the Western Church hinders the growth of this form of consecration.

While all these ancient expressions of consecrated life obviously have much in common with religious life, as all share the vow of celibacy which is often seen as the heart of religious consecration, the fact that they are not professed within an institute clearly distinguishes them from religious life. It is with another form of consecrated life, membership of a secular institute, that the closest similarities to religious life are to be found.

---

[8] http://consecratedvirgins.org/whoarewe. The figures are based upon information compiled in preparation for the Rome 2008 International Congress of Consecrated Virgins.

[9] The 2011 *Annuario Pontifico* records 729,371 members of women's religious orders at the end of 2009.

(2) Consecration within a secular institute

The Church only made provision for the formal establishment of secular institutes in 1947, when *Provida Mater Ecclesia* acknowledged the validity and particular contribution of the secular institutes which had emerged and 'quietly and without publicity' proliferated through the first half of the nineteenth century.[10] A sociological analysis of the emergence of secular institutes would note their creation at this time when religious (particularly religious women) were often hindered from engaging in 'worldly' ministries. While such external factors explain something of their origins, to reduce their existence to this historical situation would be to downplay their intrinsic worth and particular contribution to the Church's mission, as Pius XII's Motu Proprio *Primo Feliciter* (1948) makes abundantly clear.[11] As Beyer states:

> This document declared that secular Institutes were not camouflaged religious, which had got rid of all outward signs of their vocation and continued in private a work which would come out into the open when times 'got better'. No: these were Institutes providentially inspired, having their own place in all times, good and bad alike, founded by a special call of God, different in kind from that of religious Institutes and Societies of the Common Life, with a way of life all their own. 'This apostolate must be faithfully exercised not only in the world, but, as it were, by using the instruments of the world: that is, through the tasks, professions, and forms of life, the places and circumstances which correspond to this secular condition'. It was no longer a question of a supplementary apostolate which happened to be exercised 'in the world', but one fully adapted to all the circumstances of the essentially secular condition.[12]

Even among religious themselves, the distinction between religious and secular consecration is often misunderstood. This is not surprising given that the documents of Vatican II themselves send out conflicting messages. Although

---

[10]*Provida Mater Ecclesia* 22.

[11]See *Primo Feliciter* 2.

[12]Beyer, J. *Religious Life or Secular Institute*, Way Supplement 7; 1969 www.theway.org.uk/Back/s007Beyer.pdf [Hereafter, Beyer 1969].

chapter 6 of *Lumen Gentium* is entitled 'religious', it simply equates the profession of the evangelical counsels with religious life.[13] Beyer describes the 'vigorous protests' against this 'erroneous title' which 'unfortunately . . . led to the belief that secular institutes were religious',[14] and relates how Paul VI made a correction to *Perfectae Caritatis* the day before it was published to safe-guard the identity of secular institutes by explicitly declaring that secular institutes are not religious.[15] Subsequent documents have shown a clearer appreciation of the distinctive nature of religious and secular consecration, and the 1983 Code of Canon Law addresses each separately.

Thus, in theory the two types of consecration can be distinguished. Not only is religious consecration described as being marked by giving public witness to Christ,[16] but 'the apostolate of all religious consists primarily in the witness of their consecrated life'.[17] This witness involves public vows and the living of fraternal life;[18] wearing the habit of their institute[19] and a 'separation from the world which is proper to the character and purpose of each institute'.[20]

However these statements are to be interpreted, and whether or not religious are able to identify their lived experience in these descriptions, it is clear that Canon Law intends to distinguish religious life from secular consecration, and public witness and fraternal life in common are key to this. In contrast to religious, members of secular institutes 'express and exercise their special consecration in apostolic activity',[21] living 'in the ordinary conditions of the world, either alone, in their families or in fraternal groups'[22] and 'strive for the sanctification of the world, especially from within'.[23] Von Balthasar's theological

---

[13]*Lumen Gentium* 44; 'this state of life . . . which is constituted by the profession of the evangelical counsels'.

[14]Beyer, J, 'Life Consecrated by the evangelical counsels: Conciliar teaching and later developments', in *Vatican II: Assessment and perspectives: Twenty-five years after (1962–1987)* (ed. Latourelle, R.; vol. III; New York/Mahwah: Paulist Press, 1989), pp. 69, 79.

[15]See Ibid., p. 80; *Perfecta Caritatis* 11.

[16]Canon 607.3.

[17]Canon 673.

[18]Canon 607.2.

[19]Canon 669.

[20]Canon 607.2.

[21]Canon 713.1.

[22]Canon 713.2.

[23]Canon 710.

interpretation of the distinction between the two categories grounds the difference in an eschatological (religious) and incarnational (secular) emphasis.[24] While this comparison may aid a general understanding of the two groupings, it remains the case that for many active religious their spirituality and raison d'être are much more closely aligned to an incarnational model than an eschatological one. Similarly, with what Schneiders terms the 'evolution of community life' within religious life, such that community living is no longer perceived as a necessary part of religious life in many congregations,[25] the practical lived expression of some forms of active religious life, both male and female, appears to fit more neatly into the ecclesiastical category of lay (secular) consecration rather than religious.

In the initial decade or two after Vatican II, one current of thought suggested that the way forward for religious institutes whose founding charism fell into the relatively new category of secular consecration would be to change the nature of the institute.[26] This would be one way of responding to the call of *Perfectae Caritatis* for religious institutes to acknowledge 'the spirit and aims of each founder.'[27] However, few religious congregations have done this; most have simply refused to be constrained by the canonical categories. Ultimately, only time will tell which will out-live the other, the canonical categories or the 'secular' religious congregations.[28] In the meantime, secular institutes, which have only relatively recently achieved canonical recognition, and active religious institutes, many members of which disagree with the canonical account of their nature, co-exist in the Church, the distinction between them remaining something of a mystery to many.

(3) Consecration within new ecclesial movements

A significant number of new ecclesial movements, such as Communion and Liberation, the Neo-Catechumenal Way, Focolare and the Beatitudes, have

---

[24]See Von Balthasar, H., *Explorations in Theology: Volume II – Spouse of the Word* (San Francisco, CA: Ignatius Press, 1991), pp. 435–37. [Hereafter, Balthasar 1991].

[25]See Schneiders, S., *New Wineskins: Re-imagining Religious Life Today* (NJ: Paulist Press, 1986), p. 238.

[26]See Beyer 1969.

[27]*Perfecta Caritatis* 2(b).

[28]It is worth noting that the latter are receiving very few entrants, both in the United Kingdom and the United States, see footnote 17 above.

emerged unexpectedly in the Church since Vatican II. They have simultaneously invigorated and challenged the Church, bringing both renewal and controversy. As Ratzinger notes, 'there are always the new interventions of the Holy Spirit . . . yet this "making new" hardly ever happens without pain or without conflict', in the case of the new movements 'various infancy sicknesses' are present, such as 'tendencies towards being exclusive'.[29]

Whether one is inclined to support these movements or not, it is clear that they are a force to be reckoned with in the Church today. This is due to both the numerical size of the larger movements and the evangelical zeal which marks their members. For example, Communion and Liberation have 500,000 people attending their annual summer meeting and 2,400 business enterprises, with combined total revenues in excess of $1 billion,[30] and the Neocatechumenal Way has 78 *Redemptoris Mater* seminaries and a presence in more than 120 countries.[31] Alongside these large organizations many countries have locally based new ecclesial communities such as the Sion[32] and *Cor et Lumen Christi*[33] communities in the United Kingdom.

Unlike the comparison between secular institutes and religious institutes which are broadly of the same 'type', any attempt to assess the extent of the over-lap in function between religious and members of new movements is problematic since it is impossible to make generalizations about the latter. They range from the Neocatechumenal Way which resists being called a movement, although Bl. Pope John Paul II, one of its great supporters, repeatedly referred to it as such,[34] and the community of the Beatitudes where single, married, consecrated and ordained members live a strongly ordered community life.

Many of these new ecclesial movements were originally a lay movement with consecrated and priestly expressions of the charism of the movement

---

[29]Ratzinger, J., *New Outpourings of the Spirit: Movements in the Church* (San Francisco, CA: Ignatius Press, 2006), pp. 21–22. [Hereafter, Ratzinger].

[30]Hanna, T., *New Ecclesial Movements* (Staten Island, NY: Alba House/St Pauls Publications, 2006), p. 38. Although these figures are now several years out of date they nonetheless give an idea of the scope for influence the movement has. [Hereafter, Hanna].

[31]See www.camminoneocatecumenale.it/new/evento.asp?lang=en&id=110.

[32]www.sioncommunity.org.uk.

[33]www.coretlumenchristi.org.

[34]See Hanna, p. 55.

emerging over time, such as Communion and Liberation's *Memores Domini*, women members who are committed to celibacy and the clerical Fraternity of St Charles.[35] However, others like the Focolare movement began with a group desiring to live a consecrated life, the focolarini, consecrated men and women living in single-sex communities, putting their goods in common, and remaining clearly as lay people, immersed in the world.[36]

While the lives of many members of active religious congregations today are marked by the canonical signs of secular not religious consecration (living alone, without visible sign of witness), committed lay members of new ecclesial movements are often more externally 'religious' than consecrated religious. A community like the Beatitudes indicates the extremes of communal living that can be found in these new movements. An interview with members of a community of the Beatitudes in Denver from 2002 is worth quoting at length, as it clearly demonstrates how this community of lay and consecrated people is marked by many features of religious life – obedience, poverty, habit, witness, communal prayer, common mission:

> With their radical living arrangements, their monk-like daily routine, their simple habits and beautifully ethereal liturgies, community members are attracting a small but loyal following. . . . 'We are a family living like monks', says Christine Meert, a small woman in her mid-40s with a big smile and short, tousled hair. She and her husband, Christian – the tall, lanky man in the cowl at Morning Prayer – are the co-leaders of the Denver community. Married in 1977, they have five children. They began living this way – as married monastics, parents vowed to a life of prayer – in 1990 in France.
>
> . . . After a long period of prayer and reflection, Christian quit his job and they sold all their worldly belongings to join the community. . . . 'The obedience, the accountability – this is the intimacy that we were striving for', Karen explains. 'This is a place where you do share your whole being – your weaknesses, your strengths, everything.'

---

[35]Founded in 1985 by Monsignor Massimo Camisasca, the Fraternity of St Charles is born of the charism of Communion and Liberation's founder, Monsignor Luigi Giussani, who was Camisasca's former high school teacher.

[36]See www.focolare.org/en/movimento-dei-focolari/scelte-e-impegno/focolarini.

All members of the Denver community live simply. 'We need about $3,500 every month', says Christian. The community earns about half of that through various ministries: leading holy hours, school retreats and parish missions. . . . The other half comes from donations and the kindness of strangers. For instance, one man shows up every Friday, takes the household's weekly grocery list and buys every item for them.

. . . members of the Beatitudes Community are aware that their lives are a kind of sermon. They are a daily witness to the possibility of other priorities and values, to another purpose for living, another way of life.[37]

However this new form of life has not been without serious difficulties. On investigating the community in 2007, the Pontifical Council for the Laity found several unacceptable practices, such as referring to children living in the community as 'community children' and the lack of clarity over the canonical status of members. They were instructed that members had to choose whether they were monastic or lay and that families were to have independent housing. More recently, the Holy See took over leadership of the community to deal with various abuses, including sexual abuses by one of the married founders. Perhaps the lack of understanding of the difference between religious life and secular life by the Beatitudes' leadership contributed to the disordered state that led to these interventions by the Holy See.

Other communities where the daily life of lay members could be taken for religious life have not been so controversial. For instance, the *Cor et Lumen Christi* community in England has full Church backing; single, married and family members live together in a community house, mainly working full-time for the community mission, with shared common prayer, common purse and table. They expressly seek 'to be a sign of contradiction through their life style'.[38]

Apart from the absence of life-long vows and the mixture of states of life, the outward form of life is very classically 'religious'. It is as if, as active religious communities turned from witnessing to the world to solidarity with the world,

---

[37]www.americancatholic.org/messenger/mar2002/feature1.asp.
[38]www.coretlumenchristi.org/Site_stream/our_life_together.htm.

the vacuum was filled by these alternative forms of evangelical life. Similarly, as active religious tended to become less freely available to be sent on mission as the emphasis moved from obedience to dialogue and personal discernment of mission, many of the new ecclesial movements have a remarkable tradition of availability for mission. For example, there are currently nearly one thousand Neo-Catechumenal Way 'families in mission', who make up 'mission ad gentes' teams (three or four families together with a priest) who are sent to areas where a bishop has requested them.[39] Single people also make themselves freely available for mission, for example, at the end of a recent Neo-Catechumenal Way meeting, 200 young men and about 120 young women volunteered for the New Evangelization in China.[40]

Conclusion

The comparison of active religious life to other forms of consecrated life has demonstrated that the lived expression of many apostolic religious is hard to distinguish from secular consecration. In addition, some new ecclesial movements are marked by more 'religious' features than many active religious institutes. So young people seeking some form of consecrated life are confronted with a confusing landscape.

Given this lack of clarity about its own particularity, perhaps it should not be surprising that apostolic religious life is not attracting many new vocations. Research shows that those institutes of active religious life which are attracting new members have a clear identity and purpose precisely as religious and not secular. Contemplative religious life and priesthood, with their distinctive features, are more attractive options for the vocational discerner than many congregations of active religious life. While it is impossible to know how the new ecclesial movements and non-religious forms of consecration will develop in the future, it is clear that the strong expression of the distinctive nature of religious life will be integral to its future flourishing.

---

[39]See www.zenit.org/article-34154?l=english.
[40]See www.zenit.org/rssenglish-34833.

In seeking to identify the distinguishing features of a vocation to a particular religious congregation there are several possible starting points, including the community's history, spirituality and ministry as described in the note by Susan O'Brien that follows this chapter. While these may well be unclear, complex or disputed, they each provide something of a pathway into appreciating what it is to have a vocation to live according to the charism of a particular religious community. So discerning a vocation to religious life will be more than ever a personal encounter with a community living out a distinctive spirituality and a clear ministry both of which have evolved from a particular history. For discerners, this spirituality and mission will be an encounter with the Lord calling them out into the deep. There may not be so much excitement as in some new forms of consecrated life but the discerner may well find more depth.

A note on apostolic religious life

Dr Susan O'Brien

*We must indeed insist that the only adequate reflection on
the concrete church is that of theology. But if ecclesiology is
to contribute to the health of the church . . . it must examine our
human activity as it concretely is: thoroughly human.*[1]

The history of religious life captures the interest of many students of religion
but it nonetheless seems a good candidate for a 'least compelling approach'
among those concerned with the future of religious life and to those younger
Catholics discerning their vocation. There are good reasons why this might be
so. Conscious of the paradigm shifts that have taken place in culture during
the past 20 years and only too conscious of the imperative of discerning the
signs of today, the past can seem like a diversion, even a dangerous diversion.
For some religious the past has already occupied much time and energy since
the Second Vatican Council as they responded to the call to return *ad fontes*:
effort that has not always created the expected clarity of identity and renewal
of life. Hence it is theology, not history, that has been identified by seasoned
religious as the approach most likely to 'awaken religious to the beauty, dignity
and glory of their vocation' and to 'equip contemporary religious for living and
working where they ought to be – on the frontiers of the church's mission to
the world.'[2] Similarly, for those discerning a vocation there are many issues and

---

[1]Nicholas M. Healy, *Church, World and the Christian Life: Practical-Prophetic Ecclesiology* (Cambridge:
Cambridge University Press, 2000), p. 5.
[2]Gregory Collins, 'Giving Religious Life a Theology Transfusion' in *A Future Full of Hope* (ed. Gemma
Simmonds; Dublin: Columba Press, 2012), p. 23.

questions to be explored, but the history of religious life *per se* does not seem to be one of them.

Nevertheless, in the present context, history can be of assistance in thinking through current issues in religious life, paying particular attention to those identified as the concerns of younger generations of vocational searchers: distinctiveness and purpose. Jesuit historian John W. O'Malley has argued that history is the key to thinking through at least one issue of this kind – the distinctiveness of ministry associated with particular states of life. Writing in 1988, in 1990, and again on the same topic in 1997, O'Malley has been worrying away at this trouble spot which, he believes, should concern anyone attending to consecrated life in the church, whether they are doing so theologically and ecclesiologically[3] or whether, one might add, if they are engaged in aiding others to discern vocation. His conclusion is that, despite significant new work and understanding in the realm of religious and social history, the church's magisterium (and others in the church) operate with 'some inadequate but popular and widely appropriated historical grids' of the religious life. His starting point (and his conclusion) is quite stark:

> The categories with which we customarily think about religious life
> are inadequate to the historical reality and that inadequacy is to a large
> extent responsible for some of the confusion in the Church today about
> religious life.[4]

The confusions that O'Malley is particularly concerned to approach from the standpoint of a sound (revised) historical framework and well-researched historical particularities are those of priesthood, ministry and the religious life. He describes the question 'How do religious priests fit in the ministry of the Church?' as a critical one for the present era, made urgent by the 'sense of

---

[3] John W. O'Malley, 'Priesthood, Ministry, and Religious Life: Some Historical and Historiographical Considerations', *Theological Studies*, 49(2) (June, 1988), p. 233. See also John W. O'Malley, 'Diocesan and Religious Models of Priestly Formation: Historical Perspectives', in *Priests: Identity and Mission* (ed. Robert Wister; Wilmington: Michael Glazier, 1990), pp. 59–70 and 'One Priesthood: Two Traditions', in *A Concert of Traditions* (ed. Paul K. Hennesey; Conference of Major Superiors of Men's Institutes of the United States, 1997).

[4] O'Malley, 'Priesthood, Ministry and Religious Life', p. 225.

dislocation in some religious at the present time', a confusion that 'has roots deep in our past, [that] remained latent or at least virtually unnamed until quite recently'.[5] Recent events which have brought the confusion to the surface have included the promulgation and implementation of key post-conciliar Church documents on priesthood and priestly formation.[6] It is worth taking a little time to study his argument before applying it to the main focus of this essay which is the situation of apostolic women religious and their distinctiveness.

In O'Malley's view conciliar and post-conciliar documents about priesthood (*Presbyterorum ordinis* and *Optatum totius*) underrepresent the ways that ministries and charisms have been constitutive for the friars and apostolic male religious. Instead they emphasize the evangelical counsels, or three traditional vows, as the 'real' or defining element of religious lives and religious institutes. Even though the vows are 'absolutely constitutive' to apostolic religious life, O'Malley wants to show that they 'do not express the full reality [because] . . . ministry is not something one adds to one's vocation as a Franciscan or Jesuit upon ordination to the priesthood, but something which was central and intrinsic from one's very first moment in the order, no matter how imperfectly this might be expressed by the ceremony of the vows'.[7] Over-emphasis on the vows runs the risk of abstracting or 'essentialising' the nature of apostolic religious life away from ministry to a new idealized model that continues to link it to the history of asceticism rather than the history of ministry. Such a 'category error' can occur because the history of ministry as it is referenced in the church's documents, more or less ends in the sixth century, and does not reflect what happened in the next 1500 years. Any later history of ministry that *is* so referenced concerns *ideas about priesthood*, such as those of Aquinas or the Council of Trent, rather than *practice* on the ground and in the historical realities of different eras.

A second consequence is the way in which the documents define the parish and diocese as normative for priestly ministry whereas the history of O'Malley's two exemplars, the friars in the thirteenth century and the Jesuits

---

[5]Ibid, p. 233.
[6]*Presbyterorum ordinis* and *Optatum totius* as well as *Perfectae Caritatis*
[7]O'Malley, 'Priesthood, Ministry and Religious Life', p. 256.

in the sixteenth century, shows their radical and prophetic *innovations* in ministry and the astonishing changes in church order that were agreed by Popes for the sake of evangelization and the Church's mission. Moving from these 'historical realities' back to the framework of the Council and post-conciliar documents on religious life, he asks whether the 'traditional way of *interpreting* religious life fully correspond to the tradition of religious life'.[8] In more recent documents, happily, the emphasis has moved in the general direction of recognizing charism and ministry.[9]

While none of O'Malley's essays have a focus on apostolic women's congregations (a topic he describes as 'ravishingly important') he has indicated confidence in the application of his arguments to them[10]: indeed, in one essay he went so far as to say that they were even more distinctive of Catholicism (when compared with Protestantism) than were men's institutes and that ministry is an ecclesiological issue for them as much as for ordained men and nonclerical congregations of men. By implication, then, the traditional historical framework given to women's apostolic life should be examined to see how far its interpretation and understanding corresponds to historical realities. In turn, this examination is closely connected to clarity of purpose – a clarity which is vital not only for the apostolic congregations themselves but also for people seeking to enter these congregations.

If 'we cannot examine "what happened"' until we examine 'the categories in which we frame what happened' there are at least two significant aspects of historical understanding about women's apostolic life that might repay some re-framing: (1) the traditional historical periodization of religious life, with the schemas and emphases accompanying it (2) the issue of boundaries and definitions.

(1) *Periodization, schematization and emphases in religious life history*. A particular 'historical pattern' of religious life, for both men and women, has become familiar through repetition in many of the books and essays reflecting

---

[8]Ibid., p. 249. See also, Thomas P. Rausch, 'What is Dominican Priesthood?' www.spiritualitytoday.org.
[9]*Vita Consecrata* 9, 19, 30.
[10]O'Malley, 'One Priesthood: Two Traditions', p. 3.

on religious life in the post-Vatican II era and the pattern underpins what is said in church documents since that Council. It has led to the division of the past into a number of eras, each given a name characterizing its dominant trend. So, we have the eremitic cycle from 200 to 500, followed by the shift to the monastic era from ca. 500 to 1200 (often divided into two parts); the mendicant era of the thirteenth and fourteenth centuries succeeded by the apostolic orders of the sixteenth to late eighteenth centuries and the post-French Revolutionary era from 1800 to 1960 which has been named by some as the missionary era and by others as the era of the teaching congregations.[11] With the *possible* exception of the last era where the sheer number of female congregations was a remarkable reality, each of the others is defined by a movement that began with male religious charisms gifted and acted upon as responses to needs of the day: each is predominantly characterized in the literature by reference to those male orders and their ministries. Acknowledgement is made of their female counterparts, sometimes springing up in parallel and sometimes at a later date.

But is this chronological and typological framing adequate for the history of women religious? So settled is this historiographical framework that key church documents on consecrated life, *Vita Consecrata* (1996) and *Starting Afresh from Christ* (2000), draw on it without question. One consequence is a refreshing insistence in the historiography and in church teaching on holding together male and female religious within the one historical narrative and schema. It would seem that when it comes to religious life, general Catholic teaching about the essential differences between male and female, manhood and womanhood, appear to be of less importance than in other domains of human experience.[12]

Refreshing though this common narrative may be, in the diffused light of O'Malley's critique of traditional historiography and under the spotlights of

---

[11]Raymond Hostie, *Vie et Mort des Ordres Religieux* (Paris: Desclee de Brouwer, 1972); Lawrence Cada et al., *Shaping the Coming Age of Religious Life* (New York, NY: Seabury Press, 1979); Patricia Wittberg, *The Rise and Decline of Catholic Religious Orders: A Social Movement Perspective* (New York, NY: State University of New York Press, 1994); Diarmid O'Murchú, *The Prophetic Horizon of Religious Life* (London: Excalibur Press, 1989), Chapter 5.

[12]See Ivy Helman, *Women and the Vatican: an exploration of official documents* (Maryknoll, New York, NY: Orbis, 2012).

detailed historical research undertaken in the past 25 years, it seems likely that this familiar periodization and its emphases will repay fresh examination. Writing in 1995, Craig Harline noted that 'study of religious women in early modern Catholicism is now an indisputable growth industry'[13] and so it has continued to be. From being a sadly neglected topic that did not interest the social, structural or women's historians of the 1960s to 1980s, religion, gender, identity and culture are hot topics for newer generations of historians. Perhaps it is not surprising that the impact and implications of their findings has not yet been assimilated by those thinking and teaching about religious life. As O'Malley notes 'the historiography of any phenomenon falls into patterns that form at certain moments and then tend to persist for decades, generations, or even longer'[14] until our assumptions become, according to Harline, 'like favourite old clothes in middle age . . . of questionable fit'.[15]

What would a new framing, derived from a focus on apostolic women's life look like? As a starting point we might consider two refinements to the traditional periodization of female religious life indicated by recent research.

Contrary to the general assumption that 'with the rise of the *male* mendicants and of the male and female apostolic orders, external ministerial foci became – *for the first time* – essential components of the dominant frame for religious virtuosity',[16] historians now make the case for an earlier chronology for women's apostolic life. How early is a matter for debate. Sandra Schneiders takes it back to the early church.

> Down through the ages various groups have felt called to live that pattern, not just interiorly or in spirit but in concrete historical fact. Beginning with the original band of Jesus' itinerant disciples, through the consecrated virgins in the earliest Christian communities, the mendicants in the middle ages, the apostolic congregations of men and of women in the early modern

---

[13]Craig Harline, 'Actives and Contemplatives: The Female Religious of the Low Countries before and after Trent', *Catholic Historical Review* 81(4) (October 1995), pp. 541–67.
[14]O'Malley, 'Priesthood, Ministry, and Religious Life', p. 225.
[15]Harline, 'Contemplatives and Actives', p. 555.
[16]Wittberg, *Rise and Fall of Religious Orders*, p. 134. The emphases are mine.

period, down to the ministerial Religious of today the Church has always had members who embraced this lifeform.[17]

What Schneiders is doing here parallels O'Malley's revised framework by placing the interpretation on the connection between consecration and ministry (or mission or evangelization), although it is of the essence of her argument to focus on what she terms consecrated ministerial life rather than consecrated life in community as the lifeform. But medieval historians *have* taken the existence of women's apostolic life in community back to at least the thirteenth century, which is a good deal further than is traditionally ascribed. Moreover, they have shown that its presence from this earlier date was the start of a continual lineage rather than being a brief appearance followed by total suppression or abandonment. It was sufficiently vibrant to have made a significant impact and for historians to be able to trace continuity in certain locations, such as the southern Netherlands. The fact that monasticism was the only officially legitimate religious life for women did not prevent a flowering of communities where women were dedicated to following Christ's model of love of neighbour through the practice of a range of ministries that were constitutive (not an add-on) of the identity of the life they were leading. Finding that women, in significant numbers and to concrete effect, persisted in a ministry-based community form of self-giving, adapting and innovating within it, might be one good reason to nuance the schema and paradigms in a more thorough going and positive way.

Conversely, recent research has made clear how the contemplative life for women was as vibrant and characteristic of the post-Trent so-called Apostolic Era as were apostolic congregations: where it was not disbanded by rulers and governments this life flourished and it did so not simply because it was mandated by the Church.[18] This too is highly significant and, taken together, both narratives disturb the traditional historiographical framework.

In particularizing themes and emphases as gifts from the religious life to the whole church in the course of history, there is much to be learned from

---

[17]Sandra Schneiders, 'The past and future of ministerial religious life', *National Catholic Reporter*, 2 October 2009. See also Sandra Schneiders, *Finding the Treasure: Locating Catholic Religious Life in a New Ecclesial and Cultural Context* (New York, NY: Paulist Press, 2000).

[18]Harline, 'Actives and Contemplatives', pp. 563–66.

the rich research undertaken recently on the history of devotions in the lived experience of lay Catholics and in mission and evangelization.[19] With this new emphasis we can see more clearly that many powerful devotions came into the life of the church through religious, particularly female religious, several of these being women from humble origins living in communities that participated in the apostolic religious life of their era: in the thirteenth century Augustinian nun Juliana of Liège with whose petitions the Feast of Corpus Christi originated; in the seventeenth century Marguerite Marie Alocoque of the Visitation order who promoted the modern devotion to the Sacred Heart of Jesus that was taken up by the Jesuits; in the mid-nineteenth century we note the apparition of the Blessed Virgin to Catherine Labouré in the chapel of motherhouse of the Company of the Daughters of Charity led the Company to promote and sustain devotion to the Miraculous Medal globally, while the devotion that is today so meaningful in the prayer lives of many contemporary Catholics, the Divine Mercy, came to them through Sister Faustina Kowalska of Our Lady of Mercy Congregation in Poland in the 1930s. The point being made here is about how, if we bring into the foreground a vital dimension in the historical and lived experience of the whole church (whether this is mystical theology, devotions, support of vulnerable individuals and families or care of the sick) rather than place firmly in the foreground either the vows themselves or emphases more traditionally derived from men's apostolic life (such as preaching or apologetics), the result might be to discover a fresh and illuminating historiography of religious life. In turn, this might lead to a deeper understanding of the place and purpose of consecration and the charismatic dimension in the life of the church.[20]

---

[19]See, for example, Alana Harris, 'Undying devotions' *The Tablet* 15 December 2012, p. 11. See her *Faith in the Family: a lived religious history of English Catholicism before and after Vatican II* (Manchester: Manchester University Press, 2013). Also Nathan D. Mitchell, *The Mystery of the Rosary: Devotion and the Re-invention of Catholicism* (New York, NY: New York University Press, 2009); René Laurentin, *The Life of Catherine Labouré* (London: Collins, 1980) and Robert Orsi, *Between Heaven and Earth: The Religious Works People Make and the Scholars Who Study Them* (Princeton and Oxford: Princeton University Press, 2007).

[20]See for example the way that the emphasis in Pope Benedict XVI's Encyclical Letter, *Deus Caritas Est* (2005) in the section 'Charity as a responsibility of the Church' is placed on the diaconia during the first centuries of Christian history (20–24) and also discusses episcopal responsibilities, particularly as they have been defined in the most recent decades. There are some exemplars from early monasticism but no detailed reference to apostolic religious in the medieval, early modern and modern era who would generally be perceived as the church's main and most innovative agents of charity though history.

(2) A second lens through which we might review the traditional historiography so as to sharpen our understanding of women's apostolic life is the vexed and very confusing business of definitions and boundaries: that is to say, what was recognized as religious and consecrated life by whom in the church, and what was not, in which periods of history. If there is a crisis of identity for religious today, there is also a history concerned with precisely the question of identity. It is at least possible that the former, as O'Malley says of the crisis of identity of ordained religious, 'has roots deep in our past, [that] remained latent or at least virtually unnamed until quite recently'.[21]

As is generally known, but has recently been laid out in fascinating detail, from the thirteenth century onwards (and perhaps before) there was as much 'religious life' for and by women taking place outside the formal category recognized by the Church as within it. Debates and controversies over the definition of the category 'religious' and 'nun' are crucial to understanding and analysing the history of women's call to Christian discipleship in the vowed life. Similarly, the controversy over female leadership and authority in women's congregations and institutes is an important part of their history.[22] Such debates have been sufficiently significant in the history of apostolic women to constitute an essential element in it and, perhaps, in the ecclesiology of the church, particularly if we follow Nicholas Healy's approach that 'ecclesiology is not a doctrinal theory to be worked out without close attention to the concrete life of the church'.[23] While there are some similarities in the history of men's apostolic religious life, this aspect of female apostolic life cannot be subsumed within the normative meta-narrative.

Historians and women religious have charted aspects of the ups and downs and the slow expansion of the ecclesial status for women dedicated to apostolic life as it has occurred in the period they were studying, or as it pertained

---

[21]Ibid., p. 233.

[22]Council of Major Superiors of Women Religious, *The Foundations of Religious Life: Revisiting the Vision* (Notre Dame, IN: Ave Maria Press, 2009), pp. 2–9; Lynn Jarrell, 'The Development of Legal Structures for Women Religious between 1500 and 1900: A Study of Selected Institutes of Religious Life for Women' (doctoral thesis, Catholic University of America, 1984); Elizabeth Makowski, *Canon Law and Cloistered Women: Periculoso and its Commentators 1298–1545* (Washington, DC: The Catholic University of America Press, 1997).

[23]Nicholas M. Healy, *Church, World and the Christian Life*, p. 50.

to their institute. Perhaps the profound shift from seven centuries (ca. 1200 to 1900) of official exclusion but much actual practice to a century of progressively widening inclusion (1900–2000) and a decrease in practice would merit more reflection as a theme, particularly in relation to the latter period. The modern era, starting with *Conditae a Christo* in 1900, the 1917 Code of Canon Law 'which took into account a great number of Congregations with simple Vows . . . and places them among the states of perfection canonically recognised',[24] but did also exert a baleful influence through its homogenizing of charisms, and followed by the expansion of categories of consecrated life since the 1940s, together form an interesting and important era for interpretation in the history of women religious. It is striking, for example, that it was not until 1954 that the largest religious institute of all, the Company of the Daughters of Charity (founded 1633), finally had a category of consecrated life created for it that corresponded to its historical and concrete reality.[25] This history of consecrated life running ahead of the canonical categories is of great relevance for people discerning a consecrated vocation today. As is made clear in the next essay, new but not yet settled forms of consecration are a marked feature of the Church's life in recent decades.

A greater emphasis than is traditional on the relationship between the magisterium and its responsibility for church order on the one hand and the persistent charismatic and often suppressed outcroppings of apostolic or ministerial women's religious activity on the other hand, seems warranted. While the story of some individuals, such as Mary Ward, have now come to be told as fully as possible from the sources available,[26] there are many other stories that, as Gemma Simmonds noted, 'proved problematic' when women's congregations responded to the call to return *ad fontes* and 'found that they had been subsumed into an identity, construct and lifestyle at odds with the spiritual impulse of their origins'. The structures they had developed over time had been 'imposed

---

[24]*Genesis of the Company 1633–1968* (Daughters of Charity of St Vincent de Paul, 1968), p. 144.

[25]This category was 'A Society of Pontifical Right', subject to the authority of the Superior General of the Congregation of the Mission and, by special apostolic privileges, exempt from the jurisdiction of the local Ordinaries. Since the 1983 Code of Canon Law their status has become that of Society of Apostolic Life.

[26]M. Wright, *Mary Ward's Institute: The Struggle for Identity* (Sydney: Crossing Press, 1997).

on them from without by a church anxious to control the impulses of its more charismatic groups and members'.[27] What matters here is to find a process for renewing the historiography that is dialogic between apostolic women religious and the magisterium, for such a dialogue in itself would carry the burden of this aspect of history. Such a process was developed by the Holy See for the history of the Inquisition[28] and such a dialogue is currently being engaged between Catholics and Protestants in anticipation of the quincentenary of the Reformation in 2017. Where it can be developed in such highly contentious historical fields with all the meaning they carry into the present day, there are real grounds for hope that such a process could be developed within the church between those whose longing is the same, and that, like the other processes, it would be grounded in what Blessed John Paul II called 'historical science'.

The call for an integration of a revised historiographical framework into a theology of apostolic religious life, particularly apostolic women's religious life, should be part of the process for clarifying the confusions about identity and purpose expressed by a younger generation of Catholics. The question of sustaining and then sharing memory is not only the work of history but also the work of the future. Interviewed in October 2012 for his reflections as a participant in the Synod of Bishops on 'The New Evangelisation for the transmission of Christian Faith', Father Adolfo Nicolás, General of The Society of Jesus made a number of remarks about the 'positives' and the 'insufficiences' of the Synod. Among the latter he commented that the whole Synod showed 'Very little awareness and/or knowledge of the history of evangelization and the role of religious men and women in it. At times Religious Life was ignored and at times it was mentioned only in passing. Not that we, Religious, need further affirmation, but I express a concern that the Church risks losing its own memory'.[29] The denial and the loss of memory are both serious matters for the future. 'Without remembrance', said Nicholas Lash, 'we are incapable of living consciously in time. And those who cannot live consciously in time can have no future'.[30]

---

[27]Gemma Simmonds, 'Religious Life: A Question of Visibility' in *A Future Full of Hope* (ed. Gemma Simmonds; Dublin: Columba Press, 2012), p. 117.

[28]Address of the Holy Father Pope John Paul II to an International Symposium on the Inquisition, 1998.

[29]www.catholicnews.com/data/stories/cns/1204382.htm.

[30]Nicholas Lash, 'Remembering Our Future', *The Month*, 'The End of History' January 2001, p. 4.

9

Vocation to the diocesan priesthood

Fr Stephen Wang

Introduction

There is an ambiguity at the heart of the vocation to the diocesan priesthood –
one that can create a particular confusion for those discerning this path. The
ambiguity presents itself in different ways.

Theologically, there is an ongoing debate about the relationship between
the diocesan priest's interior consecration and his apostolic mission, between
his ontological status as one who stands in the person of Christ the Head and
his pastoral activity as leader and servant. Where should we put the emphasis?
Which comes first?

Ecclesiologically and canonically, the diocesan priest is never quite sure
about his place in the Church and in the world. He is, clearly, not a lay person.
He is in many ways 'set apart', not least by his commitment to celibacy.[1] He is
concerned with the *negotia ecclesiastica*, the affairs of the Church, rather than
with the *negotia saecularia*, the things of the world. Yet his vocation, unlike
that of priests who belong to religious congregations, is not defined by a profession of the evangelical counsels and a withdrawal from the world, and he is
explicitly called to live in the midst of his people and to share their concerns.

---

[1]Referring to the situation in the Latin Church.

At the level of spiritual theology and vocational discernment, the diocesan priest often feels that his identity is defined in negative terms. He is someone who has chosen *not* to enter a religious order; he is *just* a priest; he is called to get on with the nuts and bolts of priestly ministry *without* having a particular focus or charism. There is obviously a positive attraction to the priesthood in itself, and to the activities that constitute his ministry. But there is also, strangely, an attraction to what the priest is not.

The intention of this article is to show how there is a single ambiguity at issue here, and that it is constitutive of the identity of the diocesan priest. It doesn't arise through some failure to create an adequate theological synthesis, or through some fault in the genetic makeup of the diocesan priest. The tension between consecration and mission, between living in the world yet not belonging to it, between having no particular charism and having to discover whatever charism the pastoral situation demands – this tension is what actually defines the diocesan vocation. It is not something to be resolved; it is something to be understood theologically and treasured in everyday experience. It is meant to animate rather than frustrate the life of the diocesan priest. And for those discerning a call to diocesan priesthood, the *eureka* moment comes when they realize that they are called not to one aspect of the vocation or to the other but to both at the same time: to consecrate their lives, yet to do this *in the world*; to stand both *with* their brothers and sisters in the body of Christ and *before them* in the person of Christ the Head.

This article looks at the ambiguity more closely, through the question of 'secularity', and then explores how it has been addressed at the Second Vatican Council and in Pope John Paul II's *Pastores Dabo Vobis*, with special reference to 'pastoral charity'. Finally, some conclusions are drawn about whether or not the ambiguity needs to be resolved in order to present an adequate theology of diocesan priesthood for those discerning a vocation. Some extremely important topics are hardly touched on (incardination, obedience, celibacy, praying the Divine Office; the three *munera* of the priestly office: teaching, sanctifying, leading), since the focus of the article is this defining ambiguity about diocesan priesthood.

The secularity of the diocesan priest

In one of the wisest books on the subject, George Aschenbrenner writes about the elusive search for the identity of the diocesan priest:

> Benedictines, Franciscans, Jesuits, and other religious congregations do indeed have their own unique spiritualities that somehow flow from the original vision of their founders. Such is not the case for the diocesan priesthood. Nothing special distinguishes that priesthood – or so goes the common misconception. I have often heard this claim from diocesan priests as well as from many other people. It is one of the most serious problems facing diocesan priesthood at this time.[2]

Aschenbrenner describes an encounter between Fr Paul Keyes and a woman who worked in St Paul's Passionist Monastery in Pittsburgh. When she realized he was a secular priest, she blurted out, 'Oh, I'm sorry . . . you are just one of those "ordinary" priests', and then realized what she had said and in her embarrassment offered an apology. But Fr Keyes reflected that she had actually paid him a great compliment, which helped him to appreciate 'the great dignity there is in being a priest who lives intimately in the life and concerns of common, everyday people'.[3]

Stephen Rossetti expresses it this way:

> More than any other priest or religious, the diocesan priest is called to be 'in the world'. Indeed, he is a 'secular' priest. But since he is in the world, the danger is that he will be converted to a completely secular perspective.

---

[2]George A. Aschenbrenner, SJ, *Quickening the Fire in Our Midst: The Challenge of Diocesan Priestly Spirituality* (Chicago, IL: Jesuit Way/Loyola Press, 2002), p. 4.
[3]Ibid., pp. 29–30; quoting Paul Keyes, *Pastoral Presence and the Diocesan Priest* (Whitinsville, MA: Affirmation Books, 1978), p. 17.

He is constantly tempted to lose his Gospel vision and to become a slave of materialistic and worldly values.[4]

Is it accurate to say that the diocesan priest is a *secular* priest? It depends what you mean, and what kind of secularity you are talking about. This is where the telling ambiguity lies.

The term 'secular' is used to distinguish those priests who do not belong to the 'regular' clergy who have professed the evangelical vows in religious congregations. It was developed at a time when, broadly speaking, most regular priests lived in monastic enclosures, and it made sense to speak about secular clergy having a particular vocation to live and minister in the world. But since the arrival of the mendicant orders in the thirteenth century, and the profusion of forms of religious life that have emerged since then (many of them fully engaged in the life of society), it hardly makes sense to say that diocesan priests can be defined by their place in the world.[5]

More and more, 'secular' seemed to denote not their positive place in the world but their lack of a defining religious charism. Cardinal Manning, Archbishop of Westminster in the late nineteenth century, despaired of hearing his parochial clergy say, 'I am only a secular', echoing the sentiments of many lay people: 'He is only a secular priest'.[6] The diocesan clergy were 'cowed, discouraged, depressed, weakened' by the belief that there was nothing higher to aim at; it was only the religious who were expected to seek perfection.[7] Bishop Ullathorne, Manning's interlocutor, believed that the very name 'secular' was part of the problem, since (writes Peter Doyle):

> [...] it misled people into thinking that the parochial clergy were worldly, less spiritual, whereas it just meant that they worked in the world but were

---

[4]Stephen J. Rossetti, *The Joy of Priesthood* (Notre Dame, IN: Ave Maria Press, 2005), pp. 137–38.

[5]Antoine-Marie Charue, *The Diocesan Clergy: History and Spirituality* (New York, NY: Desclee Company, 1963), p. 186.

[6]Peter Doyle, 'Pastoral Perfection: Cardinal Manning and the Secular Clergy', in *The Ministry: Clerical and Lay (Studies in Church History, Vol. 26)* (eds W. J. Sheils and Diana Wood; Oxford: Blackwell, 1989), pp. 385–96, at 385; referring to E. D. Purcell, *Life of Cardinal Manning, Archbishop of Westminster* (vol. 2; London, 1896, repr. New York, 1973), pp. 784–85.

[7]Ibid., p. 385; quoting Letter to Bishop Ullathorne, in C. Butler, *The Life and Times of Bishop Ullathorne* (vol. 2; London, 1926), p. 153.

not of it. They should be known as the Pastoral Order, of which Christ himself was the founder, and they should have their vocation spelled out in spiritual laws and customs as the Religious Orders had.[8]

The ambivalence about the word 'secular' remains in the theology of the Second Vatican Council and in the Code of Canon Law. On the one hand, according to *Lumen Gentium*, the call to live out their vocation in the world belongs properly to the laity alone:

> What specifically characterizes the laity is their secular nature. It is true that those in holy orders can at times be engaged in secular activities, and even have a secular profession. But they are by reason of their particular vocation especially and professedly ordained to the sacred ministry.[9]

In the 1983 Code of Canon Law, all clerics, including diocesan priests, are in some sense set apart. They have 'a special obligation to seek holiness in their lives, because they are consecrated to God by a new title through the reception of orders'.[10] They are not bound by the poverty of religious clerics, but nevertheless called 'to follow a simple way of life and avoid anything which smacks of worldliness',[11] and to give to the Church or to charity any superfluous goods they receive through their ministry.[12] They wear distinctive ecclesiastical dress and are forbidden to assume public office, to trade, or to have an active role in party politics.[13] So in many ways they are denied the possibility of entering fully into the ordinary life of the world. It is the vocation of lay people, as noted above, to be occupied with the *negotia saecularia* (the affairs of the world); clerics, and therefore diocesan priests, are responsible for the *negotia*

---

[8]Ibid., p. 387.

[9]*Lumen Gentium*, Dogmatic Constitution on the Church of the Second Vatican Ecumenical Council, Art. 31.

[10]*Code of Canon Law: Annotated* (eds Ernest Caparros, Michel Thériault and Jean Thorn; 2nd edn; Montréal: Wilson & Lafleur Limitée, 2004), Can. 276:1. Henceforth referred to as CIC.

[11]CIC, Can. 282:1.

[12]CIC, Can. 282:2.

[13]CIC, Can. 285–7.

ecclesiastica (the affairs of the Church).[14] The diocesan priest, in the theology and ecclesiastical law of the Conciliar Church, does not seem to be defined by his secularity.

On the other hand, in the same Code of Canon Law, it is the nature of the religious vocation and not the diocesan clergy to give a public witness to Christ and the Church that involves a 'separation from the world'.[15] This *fuga mundi* (withdrawal from the world), although it is expressed more intensely in contemplative orders, is common to all forms of religious life.[16] Members of religious institutes, according to the Second Vatican Council, have responded to a call so that 'not merely being dead to sin but renouncing the world as well [*sed etiam mundo renuntiantes*], they might live for God alone'.[17] In this sense, theologically and canonically, it is quite right to consider the diocesan priest as a secular priest. He does not take religious vows. Despite his consecration, and the many 'limitations' imposed on his full participation in secular life, he nevertheless lives and minsters in the world.

The Second Vatican Council

This ambiguity and tension is expressed nowhere better than in *Presbyterorum Ordinis*, the Decree on the Ministry and Life of Priests of the Second Vatican Council.[18] Article 1 of the Decree states that it is addressed 'to all priests and especially to those who are engaged in the care of souls'. Given, however, that the following line reads, 'It is to be applied to religious priests insofar as its provisions suit their circumstances', it seems reasonable to assume that the primary subject in mind is the non-religious (i.e. secular) priest. James A. O'Donohoe notes:

> Many bishops (139) who had submitted suggested changes (*modi*) on an
> earlier draft felt that the document should be entitled 'On the Ministry and

---

[14]CIC, editorial note at 168, commenting on Can. 207.

[15]CIC, Can. 607:3.

[16]CIC, editorial note at 493, commenting on Can. 607–709.

[17]*Perfectae Caritatis*, Decree on the Up-To-Date Renewal of Religious Life of the Second Vatican Ecumenical Council, Art. 5.

[18]*Presbyterorum Ordinis*, Decree on the Ministry and Life of Priests of the Second Vatican Ecumenical Council; henceforth referred to as PO.

Life of Priests, Especially Diocesan Priests'. They were of the opinion that the text did not treat of the priesthood as such but of diocesan priests and only analogously of religious priests who serve in the diocesan ministry.[19]

Far from being a compromise text, or an unsatisfactory jumble of conflicting theologies, *Presbyterorum Ordinis* perfectly expresses the paradoxical identity of the ministerial priesthood as it is lived in the world. Notice, in this passage from Article 3, the constant back and forth between the language of being 'set apart from the world' and of being 'called into the world'.

> Priests of the New Testament, by their vocation and ordination, are in a certain sense set apart in the bosom of the People of God. However, they are not to be separated from the People of God or from any person; but they are to be totally dedicated to the work for which the Lord has chosen them. They cannot be ministers of Christ unless they be witnesses and dispensers of a life other than earthly life. But they cannot be of service to men if they remain strangers to the life and conditions of men. Their ministry itself, by a special title, forbids that they be conformed to this world; yet at the same time it requires that they live in this world among men.[20]

If Article 3 of *Presbyterorum Ordinis* is more like a pastoral exhortation, the theological heart of the Decree lies in Article 2. There is a carefully placed double emphasis on *consecration* and *mission*, on being called away from the world in order to fulfil the sacred duty of offering sacrifice and forgiving sins, and on being sent out as Christ himself was sent by the Father. Priestly ministry is orientated to the secular space of the world (it 'begins with the announcement of the Gospel'), yet it is fulfilled in the sacred ecclesial space of the Eucharist (it 'draws its force and power from the sacrifice of Christ and tends to this').[21]

The dual emphasis on consecration and mission is explicit in the text of *Presbyterorum Ordinis*: the bishops are 'sharers in [Christ's] consecration and mission'; and the very first line of Article 2 quotes John 10:36, referring to Jesus

---

[19]'Vatican II and the Secular Priest' in *Secular Priest in the New Church* (ed. Gerard S. Sloyan; New York, NY: Herder and Herder, 1967), pp. 77–91, at 83.

[20]PO, Art. 3.

[21]PO, Art. 2.

as the one 'whom the Father consecrated and sent into the world'. These two aspects of priesthood were very consciously in the minds of the participants as they drafted the texts.

Archbishop François Marty, as the first draft was being discussed, summarized the divergence of views on the ministry and life of priests:

> On this matter, there have been expressed two conceptions which seem to differ at first glance. For one of them insists more on the consecration of the presbyter worked by the sacrament of Orders, and on the personal union of the presbyter with Christ, who is the font of holiness and spiritual efficaciousness. The other conception, however, insists on the mission of the presbyter, which mission he receives from Christ through the sacrament [. . .]. Our commission will take care to show how these two conceptions combine with one another harmoniously and indeed complete each other, so that they go together in the unity of the presbyteral ministry.[22]

So the question before those producing the document was: Should it emphasize the ministry of sanctification, especially of celebrating the Holy Eucharist, or the ministry of the word and evangelization? Is the ministry of the priest primarily sacred or secular? The answer is both. Guy Mansini and Lawrence J. Welch comment: 'At this distance, one may wonder what the great difficulty was. Marty himself says carefully [. . .] of these positions only that they "seem to differ" and that only "at first glance".[23] They believe that doctrinally 'the synthesis is not difficult', and note how Yves Congar, who helped produce the text, already identifies a theological synthesis between sacred consecration and secular mission in the thought of Saint Vincent de Paul of the French School and in St Thomas Aquinas.[24]

Mansini and Welch are critical of those who would characterize the text of *Presbyterorum Ordinis* as merely a juxtaposition of two theses or viewpoints,

---

[22]Concluding *relatio* of François Marty, 16 October 1965, presenting the 'textus recognitus', in *Acta synodalia*, vol. 4, pt. 5, pp. 70–71; quoted in Guy Mansini and Lawrence J. Welch, 'The Decree on the Ministry and Life of Priests, *Presybterorum Ordinis*', in *Vatican II: Renewal Within Tradition* (eds Matthew L. Lamb and Matthew Levering; Oxford: Oxford University Press, 2008), pp. 205–27, at 206.
[23]Mansini and Welch, 'The Decree on the Ministry', pp. 205–27, at 207–08.
[24]Ibid., p. 208.

or who would see the background debates as a battle between conservatives ('consecration') and progressives ('mission'). The genius of the final Decree is that it explains theologically how the consecration and mission of the priest flow one from the other:

> Consecration is for the purpose of extending the mission of Christ, whose own end is the glory of the Father in a redeemed humanity. The priest-presbyter is sent forth as one consecrated *in persona Christi capitis* authoritatively to proclaim the Gospel to the world, to extend the offer of salvation in the sacraments, and to build up the Church.[25]

Mission is fulfilled in the Eucharistic sacrifice, where the Christian life passes sacramentally into the eternal sacrifice of the Lamb, and the world is understood in its true eschatological light. And despite the mission, the presence in the world, and a profound solidarity with lay people, still the priest remains a 'man apart', by reason of his consecration, so that he may have something to bring to the people in whose midst he lives and works.[26]

James O'Donohoe explains the success of the synthesis more in terms of a spiritual or pastoral theology. He writes that while recognizing the tensions in the priest's life:

> [. . .] the decree tells him quite forcefully that he is not to be torn by the dichotomy of work and holiness; [. . .] it is adamant in teaching that this union of action and spirituality is not achieved by 'merely gluing the external works of his ministry to his interior life' by the empty gesture of a few practices of piety. Even though the fathers of the Council were convinced that their priests are 'plunged into a diversity of problems and duties in today's world', they [. . .] will surmount the area of tension between action and spirituality by giving themselves in serene union with Christ to the service of the people.[27]

---

[25]Ibid., p. 220.
[26]Ibid., p. 221.
[27]'Vatican II and the Secular Priest' in *Secular Priest in the New Church* (ed. Gerard S. Sloyan; New York, NY: Herder and Herder, 1967), pp. 77–91, at 90–91.

The holiness of the priest, in other words, comes through his pastoral ministry, not before it or after it or despite it. This is put forward in Articles 12 to 14 of the Decree, and it is expressed beautifully in the Code of Canon Law. Canon 276 speaks about the special obligation that clerics have to seek holiness, because of their consecration and their stewardship of the mysteries.[28] Then in the second paragraph of Canon 276 there is a long list of spiritual exercises that should help them in their search for holiness, and most of these could apply to almost anyone, ordained or lay (Sacred Scripture, the Eucharist, retreats, mental prayer, sacrament of penance, devotion to Our Lady, etc.). What's significant, however, is that the first item mentioned in the second paragraph, before all the other exercises, is this: 'In order that they can pursue this perfection: They are in the first place faithfully and untiringly to fulfil the obligations of their pastoral ministry'.[29] So pastoral ministry is not just a canonical duty for the priest, it is the primary means of his sanctification. There is a unity in the life of the priest between the inner search for holiness and the outer faithfulness to ministry. Personal spirituality and public ministry are united in his priestly identity.

This is an important insight for those considering a vocation to the diocesan priesthood, who may at first be drawn to just one part of this identity. A single-minded attraction, for example, to the liturgy or to teaching the faith or to pastoral care of the needy, is meant to draw the diocesan candidate into a more comprehensive appreciation of the fullness of pastoral ministry.

Pastores Dabo Vobis

If *Presbyterorum Ordinis* succeeded in constructing a coherent synthesis of the apparently conflicting elements of priestly identity, why was there so much confusion and controversy about the nature of the priesthood in the years after the Council? That question, which touches on sociology and psychology as

---

[28] CIC, Canon 276:1.
[29] CIC, Canon 276:2:1.

much as theology, is beyond the scope of this present article.[30] One brief comment, however, is needed: It is not at all clear that the post-conciliar crisis was caused by any failure on behalf of the Council to present an adequate theology of priesthood, as if another formulation could have contained the centrifugal forces that were about to fracture the unity of priestly vision that had just about held until then.

What is not in doubt is that there was a post-conciliar crisis in priestly identity. It was in part to address this crisis that the Eighth Ordinary General Assembly of the Synod of Bishops was convened in 1990, 25 years after the closing of the Second Vatican Council, to discuss 'the formation of priests in the circumstances of the present day'. In Pope John Paul II's Post-Synodal Exhortation *Pastores Dabo Vobis*,[31] he explicitly refers to:

> [. . .] various forms of 'crisis' to which priests are subjected today in their ministry, in their spiritual life *and indeed in the very interpretation of the nature and significance of the ministerial priesthood* [emphasis added].[32]

This recognition takes up an earlier statement from his Final Address to the Synod:

> This crisis arose in the years immediately following the Council. It was based on an erroneous understanding of – and sometimes even a conscious bias against – the doctrine of the conciliar magisterium. Undoubtedly, herein lies one of the reasons for the great number of defections experienced then by the Church, losses which did serious harm to pastoral ministry and priestly vocations, especially missionary vocations. It is as though the 1990

---

[30]See, for example, the different US perspectives offered by David L. Toups, *Reclaiming our Priestly Character* (Omaha, NE: IPF Publications, 2008), ch. 2, 'Post-Conciliar Confusion', pp. 97–132; Paul Philibert, 'Issues for a Theology of Priesthood: A Status Report', in *The Theology of Priesthood* (eds Donald J. Goergen and Ann Garrido; Collegeville, MN: Michael Glazier/Liturgical Press, 2000), pp. 1–42; and Dean R. Hoge and Jacqueline E. Wenger, *Evolving Visions of the Priesthood: Changes from Vatican II to the Turn of the New Century* (Collegeville, MN: Liturgical Press, 2003).

[31]See the Editor's Introduction to *Pastores Dabo Vobis* in *The Post-Synodal Apostolic Exhortations of John Paul II* (ed. J. Michael Miller; Huntington, IN: Our Sunday Visitor, 1998), pp. 463–90; and the extensive pre-1998 bibliography at pp. 490–92.

[32]*Post-Synodal Apostolic Exhortation* Pastores Dabo Vobis, Pope John Paul II, 1992 in *The Post-Synodal Apostolic Exhortations of John Paul II* (ed. J. Michael Miller; Huntington, IN: Our Sunday Visitor, 1998), pp. 494–616, Art. 9:7. Henceforth referred to as PDV.

synod [. . .] has striven to instil hope in the wake of these sad losses. These statements showed an awareness of the specific ontological bond which unites the priesthood to Christ the high priest and good shepherd. This identity is built upon the type of formation which must be provided for priesthood and then endure throughout the priest's whole life.[33]

Pope John Paul himself is thus convinced that the roots of the crisis lie not in a failure on the part of conciliar theology, but in a failure to understand 'the doctrine of the conciliar magisterium', and even in a conscious bias against it. *Pastores Dabo Vobis* offers a deeper understanding of *Presbyterorum Ordinis* and the other conciliar texts, rather than correcting or repudiating them.

The Exhortation understands the constitutive ambiguity at the heart of priestly identity: the unresolvable tension between the sacred and the secular, between consecration and mission, between ontology and activity. It brings a new clarity to the theology developed by the Council.

Throughout the document the priest's identity is defined in terms of his configuration 'to Christ the Head and Shepherd, the Servant and Spouse of the Church'.[34] It is the inseparability of these images that is so significant. Jesus Christ is Head in a new and unique sense only because he is Servant: 'The Son of man came not to be served but to serve, and to give his life as a ransom for many'.[35] The authority of Jesus Christ as Head 'coincides then with his service, with his gift, with his total, humble and loving dedication on behalf of the Church'.[36] As Shepherd of the Church, Jesus searches for the lost sheep, gathers them together and protects them, offering his life for them through his own Death and Resurrection. As Bridegroom and Spouse, Jesus stands before the Church, loving her, nourishing her and giving his life for her.[37]

---

[33]Address at the Closing of the Synod of Bishops, Eighth Ordinary General Assembly (27 October 1990), 4: *AAS* 83 (1991), p. 496; quoted in PDV, Art. 11:3.
[34]PDV, Art. 3:7.
[35]PDV, Art. 21:3 quoting Mk 10:45.
[36]PDV, Art. 21:3.
[37]PDV, Art. 22.

Pastoral charity

The priest, therefore, is configured to Christ in all these different ways. The key to the whole vision of priesthood presented here, the inner principle that brings coherence to these apparently conflicting images, is *pastoral charity*. Pope John Paul is deeply troubled by the post-conciliar idea that there can be some sort of conflict between the sacramental and pastoral roles of the priest, as if one has to choose between the 'cultic' model of priesthood and the 'servant-leader' model, as if the building up of the Church and the sanctification of the world are somehow at odds with each other.[38] Stephen Rossetti expresses the same frustration:

> Could we not have a priest who loves the sacraments and has a high theology of the priesthood, dresses in clerical garb and is faithful to the breviary, and at the same time, is pastorally sensitive, one who empowers the laity and is among them as servant? Are these two models mutually exclusive?[39]

This would indeed offer a rounded identity to those approaching the vocation of the diocesan priest. But Pope John Paul, instead of simply asserting that both of these models are legitimate characterizations of priestly identity, or calling an uneasy truce, looks into the heart of the priest and explains that there is a single source that gives rise to every manifestation of priestly identity, which is the gift of oneself to others in humility and love in union with Jesus Christ.

> The internal principle, the force which animates and guides the spiritual life of the priest [. . .] is pastoral charity, as a participation in Jesus Christ's own pastoral charity, a gift freely bestowed by the Holy Spirit and likewise

---

[38]For an analysis of the post-conciliar swing from 'cultic' model to 'servant-leader' model and back again in the United States see Dean R. Hoge and Jacqueline E. Wenger, *Evolving Visions of the Priesthood: Changes from Vatican II to the Turn of the New Century* (Collegeville, MN: Liturgical Press 2003). Hoge and Wenger, at 10–11, point to James J. Bacik's characterization of the cultic model, 'The Practice of Priesthood: Working Through Today's Tensions', in *Priesthood in the Modern World* (ed. Karen Sue Smith; Franklin, WI: Sheed and Ward, 1999), pp. 51–65; and to Robert Schwarz's characterization of the servant-leader model in *Servant Leaders of the People of God* (New York, NY: Paulist Press, 1989).
[39]'The Priest as Man of Communion', in *Vocation Journal 2002* (Little River, SC: National Conference of Diocesan Vocation Directors, 2002), p. 60; quoted in David L. Toups, *Reclaiming our Priestly Character* (Omaha, NE: IPF Publications, 2008), p. 210.

a task and a call which demand a free and committed response on the part of the priest. [. . .] 'Pastoral charity is the virtue by which we imitate Christ in his self-giving and service. It is not just what we do, but our gift of self, which manifests Christ's love for his flock. Pastoral charity determines our way of thinking and acting, our way of relating to people. It makes special demands on us'.[40]

It is no longer possible (if it ever was) to believe that there is some kind of conflict between consecration and mission in the life of a priest. Jesus himself was consecrated by the anointing of the Holy Spirit so that he could be sent forth to announce the Gospel.[41] The key passage comes at the beginning of Article 24:

> The priest's mission is not extraneous to his consecration or juxtaposed to it, but represents its intrinsic and vital purpose: Consecration is for mission.

The vital unity between sacramental consecration and ministerial activity lies not in a new theological synthesis, but in the spiritual life of the priest himself, whose self-offering underlies every aspect of his ministry. There is a single self-gift, which is a participation in the self-gift of Jesus Christ the Head and Shepherd, and this is the unifying foundation of everything that the priest is and does.

> In this way the exercise of his ministry deeply involves the priest himself as a conscious, free and responsible person. The bond with Jesus Christ assured by consecration and configuration to him in the sacrament of orders gives rise to and requires in the priest the further bond which comes from his 'intention', that is, from a conscious and free choice to do in his ministerial activities what the Church intends to do. This bond tends by its very nature to become as extensive and profound as possible, affecting one's way of thinking, feeling and life itself: in other words, creating a series of moral and spiritual 'dispositions' which correspond to the ministerial actions performed by the priest.[42]

---

[40]PDV, Art. 23:1–2, quoting his own Homily at Eucharistic Adoration, Seoul (7 October 1989), p. 2: *Insegnamenti* XII/2 (1989), p. 785.
[41]PDV, Art. 24:1; see Lk. 4:18.
[42]PDV, Art. 25:3.

The unity between consecration and mission

Pope John Paul shifts the grounds of the debate. For him, the tensions and ambiguities about priestly identity will be resolved not through ecclesial politics or theological innovation, but in the spiritual lives of priests themselves. The tensions are on the surface. The priest doesn't have to choose between offering the Holy Sacrifice of the Mass in the parish church and being present in the homes and schools and shopping centres of his local area; between mission and maintenance; between prayer and work; between his own interior life and his pastoral commitments. Externally, in terms of his diary, it is certainly difficult to balance all these demands. But in terms of his priestly identity, there is a unity to his life and a serenity about his choices, because everything flows from his desire to love the Lord and be of service to others in pastoral charity.

To put this in terms of the three priestly *munera* of teaching, sanctifying and ruling, there is no need to prioritize one over the other two; pastoral charity – the love of Christ the Good Shepherd in the heart of the priest – is at the root of each of the *munera*.[43] The only reason for the priest to teach or celebrate the sacraments or be a pastoral leader to others is so that they may know the love of Christ and grow in that love.

This is reflected in the fourth and final promise made by the candidate in the 1968 Rite of Ordination of a Priest. The bishop asks the ordinand:

> Are you resolved to consecrate your life to God for the salvation of his people, and to unite yourself more closely every day to Christ the High Priest, who offered himself for us to the Father as a perfect sacrifice?[44]

---

[43]See Mansini and Welch, 'The Decree on the Ministry', pp. 205–27, at 208: 'After the Council, synthesis of the two views [priesthood as "consecration" or "mission"] took the form of picking one or another of the three numera of the priest and making it architectronic or deriving the other two from it, and there were many essays in this vein'. See the summary and references on 208.

[44]*Catholic Rites Today: Abridged Texts for Students* (ed. Allan Bouley; Collegeville, MN: The Liturgical Press, 1992). The revised 1990 Rite, as yet without an approved English translation, did not include any significant alterations to this promise. For differences between the 1968 and 1990 Rites see Susan K. Wood, *Sacramental Orders* (Collegeville, MN: The Liturgical Press, 2000), ch. 4, 86–116.

This is a commitment to an interior offering, a continual gift-of-self in union with the sacrificial love of Christ, for the sake of his people – a unity of consecration and mission.

This final promise refers to the interior consecration required by the priest, which animates the other promises.[45] The interior offering of oneself, in union with Christ the High Priest, is what allows the priest to teach, govern and sanctify in his 'external' ministry.

This is why whenever priestly celibacy is mentioned it is explained in terms of both following Christ with an undivided heart and dedicating oneself to the service of his people – the two are inseparable. So in the Code of Canon Law it states: 'Celibacy is a special gift from God by which sacred ministers can more easily remain close to Christ with an undivided heart, and can dedicate themselves more freely to the service of God and their neighbour'; and in *Pastores Dabo Vobis* celibacy is portrayed 'as a choice of a greater and undivided love for Christ and his Church, as a full and joyful availability in his heart for the pastoral ministry'.[46]

Conclusion

So in one sense there is a resolution, an end to the ambiguities about priestly identity, a unity to the life of the diocesan priest. It's not about spiritualizing away genuine theological problems, but appreciating how different and potentially contradictory aspects of a priest's ministry have a coherence, because they all flow from his love for the Lord and his desire to give his heart in love for others. Being set apart and being immersed in the world; praying, teaching, sanctifying, leading; standing with others as a brother and standing before them in the person of Christ the Head; having a very definite ministry or having what seems like nothing to do and nothing to give: it is all one thing, the pastoral charity of Christ; or in the language of St Paul, the preaching of the Gospel:

> For though I am free with respect to all, I have made myself a slave to all, so that I might win more of them. [. . .] I have become all things to all people,

---

[45]It is kept as the final promise (of five) in the 1990 Rite. See Wood, *Sacramental Orders*, p. 95.
[46]CIC, Can. 277; and PDV 50:2.

so that I might by any means save some. I do it all for the sake of the gospel, so that I may share in its blessings.[47]

But in another sense, the ambiguities remain – and that is a sign that the diocesan priest is being faithful to his vocation. The fact that he is constantly torn between different pastoral commitments, that he feels obliged to do everything at once without gaining the satisfaction of doing anything especially well, that he is a father to a parish community even though at any moment he can be moved away from that very community, that he longs to spend more time in prayer and to spend more time in the service of others, that he lives in the world and holds the world in his heart but must not be defined by the world, that he often feels adrift without the support of a community or a rule of life – this means he is fully living the constitutive tensions within the diocesan identity. His 'vow of stability' (See the Benedictines) is actually a promise to remain perpetually unstable, undefined, open. Of course there is a certain stability given by the interior dedication to Christ and by the pastoral charity that inspires his ministry; and there is a certain direction given to his activity by incardination in the local church and the promise of obedience to his ordinary. But none of this takes away from the essential ambiguity.

Cardinal P. M. Richaud described the work of the diocesan vocation in this way:

> The diocesan priest is unique in that he has no speciality. His holiness consists in his not being restricted to any special form of spirituality and in his not having to choose his field of endeavour. Instead, he is all things to all men and is completely at the disposal of souls wherever and whenever there is a need.[48]

What is the vocation of the diocesan priest? The short answer is: to be *just a priest*. His charism is to have no specific charism, which creates a unique and extraordinary kind of availability. It is a vocation that finds its coherence when the inner call to pastoral charity matches the external demands of priestly

---

[47]1 Cor. 9:19–23.
[48]*Y a-t-il une spiritualité du clergé diocésain?* (Paris: 1944), 15; quoted in Charue, *The Diocesan Clergy*, p. 187.

ministry; when the gift-of-self in one's heart and prayer flows into a dedication to others in the world. In vocational discernment, for both enquirers and those supporting them, there is no need to obscure the inherent ambiguities about the diocesan priesthood, or to pretend that there is a single way into this vocation. The fact that someone is torn between wanting to pray more and wanting to serve more, between a desire to be a priest among priests and to be a priest for others, between a call to a new kind of consecration and to a deeper identification with the needs of the world: these apparent contradictions can be a sign that someone may have a vocation to the diocesan priesthood.

10

How is marriage to be understood as a vocation? How is it connected to the clerical state?

Fr Yuriy Kolasa

The principal aim of this essay is to present marriage as a vocation. To this end, I will first explore some ancient prayers from the betrothal service of the Byzantine Rite. With this I would like to establish that, even though prior to Vatican II the idea of marriage as a vocation was not explicitly formulated in the pronouncements of the Magisterium of the Catholic Church, the Byzantine liturgical tradition contained an implicitly vocational understanding of marriage. We will then look at the relevant magisterial statements and seek to demonstrate that the Church's teaching on marriage has gradually shifted its emphasis from marriage as a natural institution elevated to a sacramental state to matrimony as a personal, covenantal relationship of the spouses based on conjugal love, and in this process the term 'vocation' became more and more prominent. Finally, we will look at the teaching of John Paul II, in order to elaborate on the 'personalistic norm'[1] for the idea of marriage as a vocation.

---

[1]Karol Wojtyla develops the concept of 'personalistic norm' as he reflects on the human person. 'Personalistic norm' has its origin in the relationship between God and man. See Karol Wojtyla, *Love and Responsibility* (trans. H. T. Willets; San Francisco, CA: Ignatius Press, 1993), pp. 245–46. (hereafter abbreviated as *Love and Responsibility*).

This paper will then conclude by offering some very brief remarks on the way in which marriage understood as a vocation is connected to the clerical state.

How is marriage understood as vocation?

One preliminary remark before proceeding: today, in the beginning of the twenty-first century, as we try to define marriage as a vocation, we are confronted with the fact that some are still critical of this idea. There is no simple formula for marriage as vocation in the official teaching of the Church. As a matter of fact, the phrase 'marriage as a vocation' appears only in recent texts and it involves a juxtaposition of several different ideas and an appropriation of analogous terms. There are certain theologians who have been eager to underline that since marriage is a natural institution, created by God, it cannot be placed in the category of vocations. Prior to the Council the term vocation was principally applied to a calling to the practice of the evangelical counsels in the religious state. Most preconciliar manuals of theology, when speaking about marriage, do not even consider the question of vocation in the context of matrimony.[2] According to Donald P. Asci, the Magisterium's recognition of marriage as a vocation is a consequence and an extension of *Lumen Gentium's* teaching on the so-called 'universal call to holiness'. Consequently, today when we say that marriage is a vocation, we have to explain what exactly we mean by the word 'vocation' and where we place marriage within the context of our understanding of vocation.

The service of betrothal in the Byzantine rite

Since there are diverse – and sometimes contrary – views among contemporary theologians from within the Church's Latin tradition on whether

---

[2] See A. Vermeersch, SJ, *De Religiosis, Institutis & Personis, Tractatus Canonico-Moralis, tomus prior,* pp. 79–81. Here Vocation is properly restricted to the call to a more excellent state. Marriage is written in the nature of man and therefore does not need a supernatural call. However, it is important to notice that some manuals prior to Vatican Council II clearly affirm marriage to be a vocation. See George Anthony Kelly, *The Catholic Marriage Manual* (New York, NY: Random House, 1958).

one can consider marriage as a vocation, I have decided to explore some ancient prayers from the betrothal service of the *Byzantine* rite in order to see whether Eastern Christianity, with its remarkable ability to interpret Scripture through its liturgical practice, would have at least an implicit understanding of marriage as a vocation. As a complete study of the texts of the liturgical rites for the sanctification of marriage in the Byzantine rite is beyond the scope of this paper, I will limit myself to the first few prayers in the service of betrothal.

The service of betrothal is composed of an initial great litany, which includes special petitions for the couple, two short prayers, an exchange of rings, and a somewhat longer concluding prayer. The two prayers are very ancient and, as indicated by Theodore Stylianopoulos,[3] already occur in the *Codex Barberinus*, dated to the late eighth or the early ninth century. The first prayer calls upon God to bless the couple and to lead them to every good work.[4] This blessing is invoked against the background of references to the eternal God, the one having brought together into unity things which have been separated and – specifically in the case of betrothal – having established an indissoluble bond of love:

Ὁ Θεὸς ὁ αἰώνιος, ὁ τὰ διῃρημένα συναγαγὼν εἰς ἑνότητα καὶ σύνδεσμον διαθέσεως τιθεὶς ἄρρηκτον· ὁ εὐλογήσας Ἰσαὰκ καὶ Ῥεβέκκαν, καὶ κληρονόμους αὐτοὺς τῆς σῆς ἐπαγγελίας ἀναδείξας· αὐτὸς εὐλόγησον καὶ τοὺς δούλους σου τούτους, ὁδηγῶν αὐτοὺς ἐν παντὶ ἔργῳ ἀγαθῷ[5]

Priest: (aloud): You, eternal God, the One having brought together into unity things which have been separated, and in so doing impose on them an indissoluble bond of love, Who did bless Isaac and Rebecca, declaring them

---

[3]See Theodore Stylianopoulos, 'Toward a Theology of Marriage in the Orthodox Church', *Greek Orthodox Theological Review* 22 (1977), p. 252.

[4]According to Theodore Stylianopoulos, the biblical background for this prayer can be found in the St Paul's letter to Col. 1:9–10 'And so, from the day we heard of it, we have not ceased to pray for you, asking that you may be filled with the knowledge of his will in all spiritual wisdom and understanding, to lead a life worthy of the Lord, fully pleasing to him, bearing fruit in every good work and increasing in the knowledge of God'.

[5]The Greek text is taken from the book of Anastasios Kallis, *Gottesdienst der Krönung*, Griechisch – Deutsch, Theophano Verlag Münster, 2000, p. 8.

to be the inheritors of Your promise: do You Yourself (+) bless these Your
servants, *(Name)* and *(Name)*, directing them into every good work.[6]

This first prayer of the betrothal service emphasizes the most important affirmation regarding the origin and nature of marriage. The prayer accentuates
that marriage is the result of God's divine creative action, and it affirms the
essential properties of marriage – its unity and indissolubility. This affirmation
is being repeated again in the last prayer of betrothal which follows the giving of the rings. It calls upon God to bless the couple and to make firm their
spoken vow. This last prayer refers to God's creation of man, male and female,
and to God as the one who unites the woman to the man for the purposes of
mutual support and procreation. It asks God to establish the couple in a holy
union and to seal their betrothal in faith, in oneness of mind, in truth and
in love. This theocentric orientation emphasizes that marriage is not a purely
human institution but originates from God. God is the Creator of man and
woman, the one who brings them together, and finally joins them in an indissoluble bond of love. The reminder that God is the author of marriage and that
it is God who brings the two together is not only a theological position, it is an
affirmation of the holiness of the married state, and thus implies two elements
which are essential for a vocation: a divine invitation and a human acceptance
or response. The phrase Ὁ Θεὸς ὁ αἰώνιος, ὁ τὰ διῃρημένα συναγαγὼν εἰς
ἑνότητα καὶ σύνδεσμον (You, eternal God, the One having brought together
into unity things which have been separated) deserves special attention. The
word συναγαγὼν (One having brought together) denotes a call by God for
and to man. God calls together those who have been separated. The word

---

[6]Taken from the official website of the Greek Orthodox Archdiocese of America, Ecumenical
Patriarchate, http://paul.goarch.org.

Paul Evdokimov, in his book *The Sacrament of Love,* p. 149, makes an interesting observation. He
compares this prayer to the oldest Eucharistic prayer of the Didache, *The Lord's Instruction to the
Gentiles through the Twelve Apostles*: 'As this broken bread was scattered upon the mountains, but was
brought together and became one, so let thy Church be gathered together from the ends of the earth',
demonstrating how the love of the betrothed is linked to and oriented toward the Mystery of the Holy
Eucharist, the source of our salvation. Theodore Stylianopoulos finds this comparison very interesting
but not satisfactory. For Theodore Stylianopoulos the prayer in Didache speaks more about God's
promise to gather His people from all nations rather than about the betrothed couple.

συναγαγὼν implies that God not only invites but also moves the subject to respond. Thus God wills for certain men and women to enter into marriage.

The Old Testament account of the betrothal of Isaac and Rebecca, a bride from the distant Mesopotamia, mentioned in the first prayer and again at the beginning of the last and somewhat longer prayer following the exchange of rings, further elaborates this theological concept of divine call:

> **Priest:** O Lord our God, Who accompanied the servant of the patriarch Abraham to Mesopotamia, when he was sent to espouse a wife for his lord Isaac, and did reveal to him a sign by the drawing of water to betroth Rebecca; do You Yourself bless the betrothal of these Your servants . . .[7]

The narrative of the betrothal of Isaac is the longest chapter in the Book of Genesis.[8] In the context of our paper one special feature of the narrative deserves special mention. When a question is put to Rebecca whether she wills to go at once, she firmly declares in response 'I will go'. Nahum M. Sarna

---

[7]Taken from the official website of the Greek Orthodox Archdiocese of America, Ecumenical Patriarchate, http://paul.goarch.org.

[8]Gen. 24:1–67. I will briefly present here the narrative using the hints provided by Claus Westermann and Nahum M. Sarna in their commentaries on the Book of Genesis. For more detailed commentary, see Claus Westermann, *A Comentary, Genesis 12–36*, pp. 377–92 and the JPS Torah Commentary, *Genesis*, the Traditional Hebrew Text with the New JPS Translation, commentary by Nahum M. Sarna. Philadelphia, New York, Jerusalem: The Jewish Publication Society, 5749 / 1989, pp. 161–70. The main action of the narrative unfolds in five scenes. First scene – Abraham commissions his servant (Gen. 24:1–9). To fulfill the divine promise of posterity, Abraham commissions his trusted servant to set out for far-off Aram-naharaim, a region on the middle Euphrates in central Mesopotamia, in order to find a wife for his son Isaac from among Abraham's own kinfolk. Abraham's commission takes the form of a demand for an oath. The second scene is the servant's encounter with Rebekah (Gen. 24:11–27). The meeting with Rebekah begins with the stop at the well in front of the city gate and the servant's prayer to God for a sign. As the girl comes to the well, she complies with the servant's request for a drink and, albeit quite unsolicited, waters the camels. In reply to the servant's question she informs him that she is related to Abraham, and the servant thanks God. The next scene moves from the inquiry about the girl's family to the welcome they give (Gen. 24:27–33). Forth scene – the betrothal (Gen. 24:33–55) is in the center of attention. This part is the actual execution of the commission that the servant received from Abraham. This he does in a long speech which begins with an exposition of the situation followed by a detailed account of the commission from Abraham right up to the meeting with Rebekah, and ends with a request for an answer to his quest. The brief and favourable reply is followed by rendering thanks to God, and the bestowal of presents. The fifth and the last part – Rebekah and Isaac, Gen. 24:55–67 begins with the servant asking leave to depart. He remains firm despite an invitation to stay longer. She receives her dismissal with a blessing from her brother. The arrival at Beer-lahai-roi, a well situated in the Negeb, is narrated as a meeting between Isaac and Rebekah. In the end the servant makes his report to Isaac, and Isaac takes Rebekah as his wife.

in the JPS Torah Commentary points to the remarkable parallel between Abraham's original exodus and Rebecca's departure for Canaan: 'The divine call to Abraham, "Go forth", and his unfaltering response (Gen. 12:1–4) are paralleled here by Rebecca's unquestioning willingness to go at once. "I will go", she firmly declares in response to the calling: "Will you go?"'[9]

Some early writers saw in the betrothal of Isaac and Rebecca a type of the call of the Gentiles to Christ. For example, Origen and Caesarius of Arles describe the encounter of the servant of Abraham with Rebecca as a mystery that prefigures the mystery of Christ's call to the Gentiles. They also saw a figure of Baptism in the fact that Rebecca was identified by the servant when she drew water out of the well.[10] For both Origen and Caesarius of Arles, the servant represents the prophetic word and in the same line of interpretation, the story foreshadows the Church finding Christ in the sacrament of Baptism:

'Now, dearly beloved, let us briefly see, as far as we can, what these facts mean. When blessed Abraham directed his servant to take a wife for his son, he portrayed an image of God the Father. Just as when he offered the boy as a burnt offering, he then presented an image of God the Father, so also his servant signified the words of prophesy. For this reason Abraham sent his servant into distant land to take a wife for his son, because God the Father intended to send his prophetic word throughout the world to search for the Catholic Church as a spouse for his only-begotten Son. Just as through Abraham's servant a bride is brought for blessed Isaac, so by his prophetic word the Church of the Gentiles is *called* to Christ the true bridegroom from distant lands. But where is found that spouse who was to be joined to Christ? Where, unless near the water? It is true, dearly beloved: If the church had not come to the waters of baptism, it would not have been

---

[9]See the JPS Torah Comment, *Genesis*, the Traditional Hebrew Text with the New JPS Translation, commentary by Nahum M. Sarna. Philadelphia, New York, Jerusalem: The Jewish Publication Society, 5749 / 1989, p. 161.

[10]See Ancient Christian Commentary on Scripture, Old Testament II, Gen. 12–50, edited by Mark Sheridan, general editor Thomas C. Oden, Downers Grove, Illinois: Inter Varsity Press, 2002, pp. 126–28.

joined to Christ. For this reason Rebecca found Abraham's servant at the well, and the Church finds Christ at the sacrament of baptism'[11]

This very brief examination of the ancient prayers from the betrothal service of the Byzantine rite demonstrates that even though the idea of marriage as a vocation was not specifically formulated in the doctrines of the Magisterium of the Catholic Church prior to Vatican II, the Byzantine liturgical tradition contained an implicit understanding of marriage as a vocation. The reader is left with the absolute conviction that the guiding hand of Divine Providence is present from first to last. The idea of marriage as a vocation stands out in the prayers of the betrothal service of the Byzantine rite, particularly as they employ the Old Testament account of the betrothal of Isaac and Rebecca, which manifests how God providentially steers the course of events.

Magisterial pronouncements on marriage in the Catholic Church

In this chapter, I would like to provide a brief summary of the magisterial teaching on matrimony, closely following the more comprehensive study of Donald P. Asci, associate professor of theology at the Franciscan University of Steubenville. In the course of an excellent analysis of the Magisterium's teaching on marriage Dr Asci has provided a detailed account of the development of the theology of marriage in the Catholic Church.[12] We will try to demonstrate that as the Church's teaching on marriage shifts its accent from marriage as a natural institution and places stronger emphasis on the importance of conjugal love, the term 'vocation' has more and more come to the foreground.

In his presentation Donald P. Asci begins by reviewing the teachings of the encyclical *Casti Connubii* of Pope Pius XI (31.12.1930) and the 1944 statement of the Sacra Romana Rota. Dr Asci states that these documents focus

---

[11]Caesarius of Arles, Sermon 85:3, *Sermons Volume 2:81–186* (trans. Sister Mary Magdeleine Mueller; FC 47; Washington, DC: The Catholic University of America Press, 1954).

[12]Donald P. Asci, *The Conjugal Act as a Personal Act, a Study of the Catholic Concept of the Conjugal Act in the Light of Christian Anthropology* (San Francisco, CA: Ignatius Press, 2002).

on marriage as an objective reality, a natural institution in which man freely participates according to God's plan.[13]

> 'Therefore the sacred partnership of true marriage is constituted both by the will of God and the will of man. From God comes the very institution of marriage, the ends for which it was instituted, the laws that govern it, the blessings that flow from it; while man, through generous surrender of his own person made to another for the whole span of life, becomes, with the help and co-operation of God, the author of each particular marriage, with the duties and blessings annexed thereto from divine institution.'[14]

Pius XI points out that although matrimony is, of its very nature, a divine institution, the human will, too, enters into it, and performs a most noble part. This freedom, however, regards only the question whether the contracting parties really wish to enter upon matrimony or to marry this particular person. According to Pope Pius XI the nature itself of matrimony is entirely independent of the free will of man, so that once a person has contracted matrimony he is thereby subject to its divinely made laws and its essential properties.[15]

Next, Dr Asci draws our attention to the teaching of Pope Pius XII on marriage and sexuality. Donald P. Asci observes that while Pope Pius XII still focuses on the objective, divinely instituted reality of marriage, he explicitly addresses the question of the 'personal values' of marriage, demonstrating a greater appreciation for these values than was explicitly present in previous magisterial pronouncements.[16] To the newlyweds Pius XII said: 'The sacrament makes of marriage itself a means of mutual sanctification for the

---

[13]See Donald P. Asci, *The Conjugal Act as a Personal Act,* p. 81.

[14]'Papal pronouncements on marriage and the family from Leo XIII to Pius XII', p. 6. All quotations of papal pronouncements are taken from the book: 'Papal pronouncements on marriage and the family from Leo XIII to Pius XII', by Alvin Werth and Clement S. Mihanovich, Milwaukee: The Bruce Publishing Company, 1982. In turn, the quotations in 'Papal pronouncements on marriage and the family from Leo XIII to Pius XII', are taken from documents that have been translated into the English language in their entirety or in major part. The pronouncements of Pius XI are taken from the volumes of Social Wellsprings by Joseph Husslein, S. J. (ed.), *Social Wellsprings* (Milwaukee: The Bruce Publishing Company, 1949). Quotations of pronouncements by Pius XII are taken from *The Holy Father Speaks to Newlyweds*, 3 January to 23 October 1940.

[15]See 'Papal pronouncements on marriage and the family from Leo XIII to Pius XII', p. 5.

[16]See Donald P. Asci, *The Conjugal Act as a Personal Act,* p. 81.

married and a source of inexhaustible supernatural helps; makes of their union a symbol of that between Christ and His Church; makes them collaborators with the Father in His creative works, with the Son in His redeeming work, with the Holy Spirit in His work of illumination and education . . .'[17] In the document *Woman's Duties in Social and Political Life, 1945*, Pope Pius XII teaches that:

> In their personal dignity as children of God a man and woman are absolutely equal, as they are in relation to the last end of human life, which is everlasting union with God in the happiness of heaven. But a man and woman cannot maintain and perfect this equal dignity of theirs, unless by respecting and activating characteristic qualities which nature has given each of them, physical and spiritual qualities, which cannot be eliminated, which cannot be reversed without nature itself stepping in to restore the balance . . . The two sexes, by the very qualities that distinguish them, are mutually complementary to such an extent that their co-ordination makes itself felt in every phase of man's social life.[18]

According to Donald P. Asci, Pope Pius XII confirms the intrinsic link between the objective requirements of the institution of marriage and the personal values available in marriage: 'They are intrinsically linked by "the very meaning of the conjugal life" and by the nature of the human person'.[19]

The thesis that the sacramental marriage is a means of sanctification, presented in the writings of Pope Pius XII and his predecessors,[20] found a new development in the dogmatic constitution on the Church, *Lumen Gentium*,

---

[17]"Papal pronouncements on marriage and the family from Leo XIII to Pius XII", p. 10.
[18]Ibid., p. 22.
[19]Donald P. Asci, *The Conjugal Act as a Personal Act*, p. 81.
[20]Leo XIII, as he spoke about the dignity of Christian marriage said: '. . . To the Apostles, indeed, as our masters, are to be referred the doctrines which 'our holy Fathers, the councils, and the Tradition of the Universal Church have always taught', namely – that Christ our Lord raised marriage to the dignity of a sacrament; that to husband and wife, guarded and strengthen by the heavenly grace which His merits gained for them, He gave power to attain holiness in the married state; and that, in a wondrous way, making marriage an example of the mystical union between Himself and His Church, He not only perfected that love which is according to nature, but also made the natural union of one man with one woman far more perfect through the bond of heavenly love (Leo XIII, 1880, Arcanum). 'Papal pronouncements on marriage and the family from Leo XIII to Pius XII', p. 7.

promulgated by Pope Paul VI on 21 November 1964. In their teaching on the universal call to holiness within the Church, the Fathers of the Council include Christian married life as a specific path to holiness, thus designating marriage as a vocation. Placing Christian marriage in the light of the true sacrificial love of Christ, which He revealed on the Cross, they underline that the basis of personal communion in marriage is the self-sacrificial love of the spouses for each other. In other words the Church teaches that the daily actions that comprise married life are actions that can lead to holiness through their performance in true sacrificial love and in accord with the requirements of marriage as divinely instituted.[21] According to *Lumen Gentium* 40, 'all the faithful of Christ of whatever rank or status, are called to the fullness of the Christian life and to the perfection of love'.[22] The constitution continues that: 'married couples should follow their own proper path to holiness by faithful love. . . . By such lives, they are a sign and a participation in that very love, with which Christ loved His Bride and for which He delivered Himself up for her'.[23] In this sense Christian marriage is a means to grow in virtue and in love of God and neighbour and as such, in the context of the universal call to holiness, qualifies the idea of vocation.

As the next step in the development of the Magisterial teaching on marriage, Asci points to the pastoral constitution on the Church in the modern world, *Gaudium et Spes*, promulgated by Pope Paul VI, on 7 December 1965. Here, Asci argues, while recognizing marriage as a natural institution, endowed with laws and ends by the author of nature, *Gaudium et Spes* also describes marriage as a personal, covenantal relationship grounded in love that embraces the good of the whole person.[24]

The biblical Word of God several times urges the betrothed and the married to nourish and develop their wedlock by pure conjugal love and undivided

---

[21]See, Donald P. Asci, *The Conjugal Act as a Personal Act,* p. 78.

[22]Dogmatic constitution on the Church, *Lumen Gentium,* promulgated by His Holiness Pope Paul VI on 21 November 1964, p. 40. Taken from: www.vatcan.va.

[23]Ibid., p. 41.

[24]See Donald P. Asci, *The Conjugal Act as a Personal Act,* p. 82. See, *Gaudium et Spes,* p. 48: 'The intimate partnership of married life and love has been established by the Creator and qualified by His laws, and is rooted in the conjugal covenant of irrevocable personal consent'.

affection . . . This love is an eminently human one since it is directed from one person to another through an affection of the will; it involves the good of the whole person, and therefore can enrich the expressions of body and mind with a unique dignity, ennobling these expressions as special ingredients and signs of the friendship distinctive of marriage. This love God has judged worthy of special gifts, healing, perfecting and exalting gifts of grace and of charity. Such love, merging the human with the divine, leads the spouses to a free and mutual gift of themselves, a gift providing itself by gentle affection and by deed, such love pervades the whole of their lives: indeed by its busy generosity it grows better and grows greater. Therefore it far excels mere erotic inclination, which, selfishly pursued, soon enough fades wretchedly away.[25]

In this way, according to Asci, the text of the constitution neutralizes any opposition between the two orders of this sacred reality: marriage as a natural institution and marriage as a personal, covenantal relationship grounded in love that embraces the good of the whole person. It is this theology of the conjugal life, according to which man freely cooperates with God but does not proceed in a wholly autonomous way, that provides a 'personalistic norm' for the idea of marriage as a vocation. Consequently, in addition to qualifying marriage as a path to holiness, the term vocation denotes a personal relation of God to man, a personal call and personal response. This second extension of the term vocation is explained by Joseph Bolin in his book *Paths of Love* as follows:

We can speak of marriage as vocation insofar as God, by means of grace, the infused virtues, and the gifts of the Holy Spirit, does not lead and guide us only to the act of love itself, but also to the means by which we act in accordance with love and grow in love. When the love of God moves someone to commit himself to a state of life, we can say that he is called to that state of life. Therefore, if one can be moved by the love of God and neighbour to marriage, and if marriage is a means to grow in love of God and neighbour, then men and women are called to marriage, and marriage is a vocation.[26]

---

[25]Pastoral constitution on the Church in the modern world, *Gaudium et Spes*, promulgated by Pope Paul VI, on 7 December 1965, p. 49. Taken from: www.vatcan.va
[26]Joseph Bolin, *Paths of Love*, The discernment of vocation according to the teaching of Aquinas, Ignatius, and Pope John Paul II, 2008, p. 42.

To elaborate this 'personalistic norm' for the idea of marriage as a vocation, I will now look at the teaching of John Paul II, who has made very significant contributions to the Church's understanding and appreciation of marriage and the family. Certainly, in the context of this paper I will limit myself to two texts, which present marriage as a vocation. First, I will look at the pre-conciliar arguments of Karol Wojtyla in his *Love and Responsibility*, second I will consider his magisterial teaching in the apostolic exortation *Familiaris Consortio*.

'Personalistic norm' for the idea of marriage as a vocation

Karol Wojtyla's complex and profound concept of vocation is confined to the world of persons and the order of love. Wojtyla begins to develop the concept of vocation, first looking at the fundamental principle of justice towards the Creator, 'vertical justice' as he defines it, that provides the rationale for personal relation between God and man. This fundamental principle revolves around the idea that God is a Personal Being, with whom man must have a personal relationship.[27] Karol Wojtyla explains justice towards the Creator in terms of the rights of God and the duties of man which derive from the fact that God is the Creator and man is His creature. Wojtyla then presents another dimension of man's dependence on God which is specified by love. He sees this dimension through the lenses of Divine Revelation:

> Revelation enables us to understand God's work of redemption and sanctification, from which it is most apparent that God relates to man as a person to a person, that his attitude to man is one of love.[28]

In Wojtyla's conception man's relations with God cannot be based on justice alone, because justice demands equality, and perfect equality is possible only where the two sides are fundamentally equal, thus man as a creature cannot do full justice to God as the Creator.[29] Therefore a relationship with God based on justice alone is, of necessity, incomplete and, as such, longs for love which aims

---

[27]See, *Love and Responsibility.*
[28]Ibid., p. 245.
[29]Ibid., p. 250.

at the unification of persons.[30] Wojtyla alludes to the fact that a full under-standing of a relationship with God, which is rooted in love, is possible only in the light of the Person of Jesus Christ, 'Who taught humanity a religion based on love'.[31] According to the mystery of Christ, the basis of the personal rela-tionship between God and man is self-sacrificial love. This, says Karol Wojtyla, 'is perfectly comprehensible, especially as the religious man knows that God gives Himself to man, in a divine and supernatural fashion (a mystery of faith revealed to mankind by Christ)'.[32] This self-sacrificial love, therefore, raises man's relation with God to a higher level than mere justice could.[33] It is this personal relationship between God and man, understood as a relation of self-sacrificial love that provides us with the foundation for the 'personalistic norm' in relation to the idea of marriage as a vocation. According to the teaching of Karol Wojtyla:

> It is not sexuality which creates in a man and a woman the need to give themselves to each other but, on the contrary, it is the need to give oneself, latent in every human person, which finds its outlet in matrimony. The need to give oneself to and unite with another person is deeper and connected with the spiritual existence of the person.[34]

Ultimately, each human person has an essence, which entails an objective call from God to love: 'This is the fundamental appeal of the New Testament, embodied in the commandment to love and in the saying "Be ye perfect", a call to self-perfection through love'.[35] According to the teaching of Wojtyla, the per-son fulfils itself most effectively when it gives itself most fully.[36] Thus a person who has a vocation, says Wojtyla, must not only love someone but be prepared to give himself or herself for love. Now, because the process of self giving is an essential aspect of wedded love, Karol Wojtyla concludes that: 'Hence both

---

[30]Ibid., p. 250.
[31]See ibid., p. 250.
[32]Ibid., p. 251.
[33]See ibid., p. 250.
[34]Ibid., p. 253
[35]Ibid., p. 257.
[36]See ibid., p. 257.

virginity and marriage understood in an uncompromisingly personalistic way are vocations.[37]

Karol Wojtyla explicitly addressed the idea of marriage as a vocation during his pontificate in his apostolic exhortation *Familiaris Consortio*.[38] According to Bd. John Paul II:

> God created man in His own image and likeness: calling him to existence through love, He called him at the same time for love. God is love and in Himself He lives a mystery of personal loving communion. Creating the human race in His own image and continually keeping it in being, God inscribed in the humanity of man and woman the vocation, and thus the capacity and responsibility, of love and communion. Love is therefore the fundamental and innate vocation of every human being.[39]

John Paul II teaches that Christian revelation recognizes marriage as one specific way of realizing the vocation of the human person, in its entirety, to love. In marriage man and woman are called by God to give themselves to one another in a total personal self-giving in which the whole person, including the temporal dimension, is present.[40] John Paul II identifies two dimensions of the realization of the fundamental vocation of the human person in marriage. Man and woman, says John Paul II are called by God to form a community of persons and to serve life.[41]

By virtue of the sacrament Christian spouses are assisted by the gift of the Spirit to fulfil the call to progress toward an ever richer union with each other, 'union on all levels – of the body, of the character, of the heart, of the intelligence and will, of the soul',[42] thus, according to John Paul II, revealing in this way to the Church and to the world the new communion of love, given by the

---

[37]Ibid., p. 257.

[38]Apostolic Exhortation of John Paul II, *Familiaris Consortio*. The role of the Christian family in the modern world, Boston: Pauline Books & Media (hereafter abbreviated as FC).

[39]FC, p. 11.

[40]See ibid., p. 11.

[41]Ibid., p. 17.

[42]Ibid., p. 19.

grace of Christ. Furthermore, John Paul II sees the gift of the sacrament of marriage as a vocation to remain faithful to each other forever, beyond every trial and difficulty, in generous obedience to the holy will of the Lord, thus to be a 'sign' of the unfailing fidelity with which God and Jesus Christ love each and every human being.[43] A call to the communion of persons, according to John Paul II, extends also to a brotherly communion, that of the family. It is a call to implement the lofty idea of the true sacrificial love in the daily life of the family: 'where there is care and love for the little ones, the sick, the aged; where there is mutual service every day in a spirit of sacrifice; where there is a sharing of goods, of joys and of sorrow's.'[44]

A call to serve life, according to Blessed John Paul II, is a call, by which man and woman are called by God to a special sharing in divine love and God's power as Creator and Father, through their free and responsible cooperation in transmitting the gift of human life.[45] However, a call to serve life is not restricted solely to the procreation of children, but as the Pope explains, it extends to the moral, spiritual and supernatural life which the father and mother 'are called to hand on to their children, and through the children to the Church and to the world'.[46]

---

[43]See ibid., p. 20.

[44]Ibid., p. 21. The thought of endlessly serving husband or wife, children, or elderly can bowl us over, or even strike terror in our hearts, but we must first clarify what this service entails. The service God has in mind is not slavery. The definition of 'to serve' centres on the concept: to work for or meet the needs or requirements of the other. Thus, authentic service would require that the one who serves knows what the one he serves truly needs – and further, to know what the other needs requires true sacrificial love for the good of the other, which is the essence of God Himself. Our service must have the good of the other in mind, which sometimes means acting, and sometimes means refraining from acting. It can be as simple as providing a smile, or it can demand years of labour, for example with an ill family member. Some service is as simple as listening; other service is complex, such as engaging a difficult personality on an important topic. Service must be backed up by prayer and its essential element is fidelity – we serve for as long as God would have the service rendered. God will provide the grace, provided that we are serving out of love. Just as Christ the Bridegroom served His beloved Bride, the Church, and laid down His life for her, so is the vocation of the family to realize the royal office of Christ, and Pope John Paul II reminds us: 'Family become what you are!' Do not be afraid to serve the needs of others. Be sensitive to the difficulties and problems and sufferings of others. Even if you feel that you do not need the help of others, others might need you. Thus, we as Catholics will serve to build the Kingdom as Christ intends us to do.

[45]See FC, p. 28.

[46]FC, p. 28.

Conclusion

I believe that today, like never before, when people seem to have lost the meaning of marriage or are very confused about what matrimony entails, it is necessary to fill the void and to give the human need for companionship, mutual support and love a spiritual dimension. Great changes have taken place in the last century. The revolution in birth control challenged, not in theory but in fact, the very core of conjugal life – its inseparability from procreation and the personal loving union between husband and wife. This separation, which fundamentally changed the idea of marriage, is now well established in society, so much so, that sexual intercourse is promoted as a form of recreation, and a call for the tolerance of homosexual partnerships was granted a legal recognition. The fundamental truth regarding marriage must be proclaimed today with greater zeal than ever.

Obviously, a single study cannot fulfil such a purpose, and so it should be immediately evident that it is only an attempt, in brief, to present how marriage may be understood as a vocation. We began this study by exploring some ancient prayers from the betrothal service of the Byzantine rite, which reveal to us that already in the late eighth or the early ninth century the Byzantine liturgical tradition contained an implicit understanding of the idea of marriage as a vocation. Then, by looking at the development of the magisterial teaching on marriage in the Catholic Church, we pointed out that the Magisterium gradually acknowledged that marriage possesses both a legal and a personal dimension. *Gaudium et Spes*, in particular, recognizes marriage as a natural institution, endowed with laws and ends by the Author of nature, and also describes marriage as a personal, covenantal relationship grounded in love that embraces the good of the whole person. At this point we established that the idea of marriage as vocation belongs to this personal dimension of marriage. Christian married life as a vocation is then placed in the context of the universal call to holiness within the Church, and the fundamental vocation of man for love. Consequently, the Church teaches that God calls husband and wife to perform their daily actions that comprise married life in true sacrificial love and in accord with the requirements of marriage as divinely instituted. If one lives the married life understanding that what he or she does is the will of God, doing those activities will sanctify him or her. If the spouses order their love for each other within a love of God and they give that priority to the love of God, it becomes charity; and every act of charity advances us on the path to holiness. Lastly, Bl. John Paul II teaches that Christian revelation recognizes marriage as one specific way of realizing the fundamental vocation of the human person, in its entirety, to love. In marriage man and woman are called by God to give themselves to one another in a total personal self-giving in which the whole person, including the temporal dimension, is present. Man and woman, says John Paul II, are called by God to form a community of persons and to serve life.

How is marriage, understood as a vocation, connected to the clerical state?

Thus far we have offered a brief examination of how marriage may be understood as vocation. There is no simple formula identifying marriage as a vocation in the official teaching of the Church. We must also concede that the Magisterium has precious little to say about how marriage, understood as vocation, is connected to the clerical state. As a priest of the Eastern Catholic Church, who is also married, I would simply revert to the Byzantine tradition and try to demonstrate the connection between marriage and the clerical state as it is stated in the Code of Canons of the Eastern Churches.

Before we begin, it is well that we review a few facts surrounding the tradition of married clergy in the Eastern Churches. The tradition of the Eastern Churches has encompassed the ordination of married man to the deaconate and the priesthood from the time of the early Church. Those who were not married before the ordination could not marry afterwards. Please note that not a single validly ordained and practicing priest in the Church has ever been allowed to marry; it has always been a question of married men who were admitted to sacerdotal ordination. The death of the wife or separation from the wife always obliged married clergymen to remain celibate.

Although the history of married clergy is rather complicated and it is currently a hotly debated topic in the West, Paul VI recognized the Eastern discipline of the ordination of married men to the deaconate and the priesthood not as an aberration of church discipline or a corruption of the *sensus fidelium* but as something that, given the particular circumstances, has been guided by the Holy Spirit.

> If the legislation of the Eastern Church is different in the matter of discipline with regard to clerical celibacy, as was finally established by the Council of Trullo held in the year 692, and which has been clearly recognized by the Second Vatican Council, this is due to the different circumstances of things and places pertaining to that most noble part of the Church, *which all, we believe, the Holy Spirit has presided over by his providential and supernatural help.* We Ourselves take this opportunity to express Our esteem and Our respect for all the clergy of the Eastern Churches, and to recognize with pleasure the examples in them of fidelity and pastoral diligence which make them worthy of sincere veneration.[47]

This is the strongest praise yet given for the Eastern discipline. The same Holy Spirit which Pope Paul invokes as guiding the Church into a deeper appreciation of the Apostolic Tradition in regard to clerical celibacy is also said to be behind the development of different traditions in the Eastern Church, a tradition which was both established at Trullo and recognized by the Second Vatican Council. As a result of this tradition, the Pope says that he is moved to praise the priests of the East, both married and celibate, who give examples of fidelity and pastoral diligence. For all the fittingness of celibacy for pastoral work and as an image of fidelity to the Church, married priests continue to offer a venerable witness of these things in their own ministry as well.

Now to demonstrate a connection between marriage and the clerical state we will employ the Code of Canons of the Eastern Churches. In fact there are only two canons which are located in the section on the rights and obligations of clerics, which specifically mention married clergy:

> Canon 374 – Clerics, celibate or married, are to excel in the virtue of chastity; it is for the particular law to establish suitable means for pursuing this end.

---

[47]Encyclical Letter *Sacerdotales Caelibatus.*

Canon 375 – In leading family life and in educating children married clergy are to show an outstanding example to other Christian faithful.[48]

Consequently, we can conclude that the connection between marriage and the clerical state is such that a cleric, be that a priest or a permanent deacon, is called to live out his Christian marriage and family life in an exceptionally exemplary way.

Bl. John Paul II, in his address to men ordained to the Permanent Diaconate, eloquently describes this exceptional opportunity to combine the witness of family life and the hierarchical witness in a single agent, namely, the married cleric. Although he specifically addresses married permanent deacons, his teaching can be extended to all forms of married clergy, be they Protestant converts serving as married presbyters in the Latin Rite or Eastern Catholic married clergy.

> Taking an active part in society belongs to the baptismal mission of every Christian in accordance with his or her state in life, but the permanent deacon has *a special witness to give*. The sacramental grace of his ordination is meant to strengthen him and to make his efforts fruitful . . . the fact that he is an ordained minister of the Church brings a special dimension to his efforts in the eyes of those with whom he lives and works . . . Important is the contribution that a married deacon makes to *the transformation of family life*. In particular, the deacon and his wife must be a living example of *fidelity and indissolubility in Christian marriage* before a world which is in dire need of such signs. By facing *in a spirit of faith* the challenges of married life and the demands of daily living, they strengthen the family life not only of the Church community but of the whole of society. They also show how the obligations of family, work and ministry can be harmonized in the *service of the Church's mission*. Deacons and their wives and children can be a great encouragement to all others who are working to promote family life.[49]

---

[48]Code of Canons of the Eastern Churches, Latin – English edition, Canon Law Society of America, Washington, DC, 20064, 1992.

[49]John Paul II, *Address to Men Ordained to the Permanent Diaconate.* Detroit: 19 September 1987. Taken from: www.vatican.va/holy_father/john_paul_ii/speeches/1987/september/documents/hf_jp-ii_spe_19870919_diaconi-permanenti-detroit_en.html.

Similarly, the Congregation for Clergy, in the Directory for the ministry and life of permanent deacons, stresses that the deacon and his wife are given a special grace to be a living example of interpersonal giving of self, mutual fidelity, a source of new life, a support in times of joy and sorrow.[50] Specifically, the Congregation for Clergy states:

> Married deacons should feel especially obliged to give clear witness to the sanctity of marriage and the family. The more they grow in mutual love, the greater their dedication to their children and the more significant their example for the Christian community. 'The nurturing and deepening of mutual, sacrificial love between husband and wife constitutes perhaps the most significant involvement of a deacon's wife in her husband's public ministry in the Church.'[51]

Much more time and effort could and should be devoted to a detailed study on how a married cleric, be that a priest or a permanent deacon, is called to give a witness to the sanctity of marriage and the family, yet the treatment here must be limited. There are two more aspects, which could be explored in the theological sense, as we try to connect marriage and the clerical state. These two aspects are: the idea of fatherhood and marriage as the image of the spousal love of Christ for his Church, both of which are found in St Paul's Letter to the Ephesians.

To consider the idea of fatherhood, we will look at the Pauline passage in Eph. 3:14–15: 'For this cause I bow my knees to the Father of our Lord Jesus Christ, of whom all paternity in heaven and earth is named'. Based on this passage it seems clear that paternity (or fatherhood) is primarily – *par excellence* – in God. (1) He is Father from all eternity, and His generation (of the Son) is perfect. (2) When He creates (generates life outside of Himself), he creates *ex nihilo*, whereas our generation presupposes God for the soul and pre-existent matter for the body. That is why human generation is not called creation but procreation. Men are only fathers insofar as they participate, in

---

[50]Congregation for the Clergy, *Directorium pro Ministerio et Vita Diaconorum Permannetium*. Rome: 22 February 1998. Taken from: www.vatican.va/roman_curia/congregations/ccatheduc/documents.
[51]Ibid., p. 61.

an imperfect and far removed sense of the term, in God's paternity. In fact, the priesthood is a kind of spiritual paternity which – precisely because it is spiritual and is in the realm of the supernatural – is closer to God's fatherhood, is an even richer participation of divine paternity. Nevertheless, a priest's human fatherhood seems to be a further participation in the likeness of our Heavenly Father, insofar as it adds an aspect of fatherhood to the one already possessed in virtue of sacerdotal consecration which was not there before, and by which what was in the supernatural order becomes a reality in the natural (corporeal) realm as well.

Now, to consider the idea of marriage as the image of the spousal love of Christ for his Church, we will look at Eph. 5:22–33. This Pauline passage says that matrimony is a sacramental image of the love between Christ, the divine Bridegroom and the Church, His mystical Bride. It is true that traditionally celibacy is considered to be a symbolic representation of Christ's faithful, undivided and sacrificial love for the one people of the New Covenant, the Church. Accordingly, the celibate priest has no wife or family except a spotless bride with whom he has been mystically wed through consecration. Yet, we have to admit that marriage, as elevated to a sacramental level by Christ, must also participate in this likeness or bridal imagery. In virtue of the priest being consecrated as 'another Christ', the Pauline comparison applies even more clearly to priestly families, where the husband is made Christ-like in an entirely unique and truly sacramental way. Thus the marital union of a priest and his wife– in a certain way – shines forth even more clearly as a sacrament, that is, a mystery that applies to the union between Christ and the Church.

These two are aspects of the relationship between the clerical state and the married state which could be developed further but to do so now would be beyond the scope of the present study. They seem to be indications, however, that the married priesthood, as it is traditionally practised by the Eastern Churches, shouldn't necessarily be considered as an obfuscation or degradation of the supernatural meaning of the priesthood as a sacramental sign. There is a way of looking at it which suggests that the marital union and human fatherhood of married priests does not lessen, on the contrary, supplements the innate sacramental connotations of the priesthood.

11

The psychology of vocation: nurturing the Grail quest

Dr Peter Tyler

Introduction: What does the psychologist do?

Before embarking upon the task of looking at the psychology of vocation it's worth describing the role of the psychologist and how he/she might help the discernment of spiritual vocation. This is no easy task, but, for simplicity's sake, the role of the psychologist can be described as that of providing an alternative view of the world. The therapist, counsellor or spiritual director is not a second-rate scientist or empiricist but is working from a different 'world view'. One, perhaps, where 'all possible world views' are held in balance. The therapist is allowed an insight into all world views and then presents them to the listener. In the same manner the spiritual director has to offer a 'transcendental position' that holds the possibility of the eternal perspective or what Wittgenstein terms the view *sub specie aeterni* (*Tractatus*).[1] In this respect

---

[1]"The sense of the world must lie outside the world. In the world everything is as it is, and everything happens as it does happen: *in* it no value exists – and if it did exist, it would have no value'. T 6.41, see also T.6.45 'To view the world *sub specie aeterni* is to view it as a whole – a limited whole. Feeling the world as a limited whole – it is this that is mystical'.

Wittgenstein saw the value of Freud's contribution to our understanding of the mind being not the observations of a pseudo-scientist but of someone who 'changes the perspective' of their interlocutor:

> When a dream is interpreted we might say that it is fitted into a context in which it ceases to be puzzling. In a sense the dreamer re-dreams his dream in surroundings such that *its aspect changes* . . .
>
> In considering what a dream is, it is important to consider what happens to it, the way its aspect changes when it is brought into relation with other things remembered, for instance. (LC: 45–46)[2]

Following this thought-way, we should view the practice of spiritual direction, counselling and therapy as unlike other modes of healing, in particular, scientific based modes. There is a tendency today to relate counselling to scientific and observable, quantifiable and empirical 'outcomes'. I would argue such a position is doomed to failure as therapy, counselling and spiritual direction themselves are modes of operation other than and in many ways alien to the operations of the dividing and cutting cognitive mind.

The nature of vocation

Having given some indicator of how I locate the role of psychology in our quest I turn now to the second part of our investigation: the nature of vocation. In this respect the key scriptural text for any consideration of vocation is St Paul's First Letter to the Corinthians:

> Christ is a single body which has many parts; it is still one body, even though it is made up of different parts . . . there are many parts but one body . . .
>
> There are different kinds of spiritual gifts, but the same Spirit gives them. There are different ways of serving, but the same Lord is served. . . . The

---

[2]*Lectures and Conversations on Aesthetics, Psychology and Religious Belief* (ed. C. Barrett; Oxford: Blackwell, 1989).

Spirit's presence is shown in some way in each person for the good of all. . . .
As he wishes he gives a different gift to each person. (1 Cor. 12: 4–20)

As St Paul makes clear we must *all* consider our vocation for the building up of the Body of Christ. All are involved and no-one is excluded.

Having said that the next question many people will ask is 'Well, what exactly *is* my vocation? – How do I discern it?' This, of course, is a different and trickier question and refers to the whole nature of discernment.

Over ten years ago I was asked to write an article for *The Way* journal about vocation and commitment for the contemporary generation (Tyler, 2000). As I thought about what to write in this article I felt myself drawn to the figure of Thomas Merton (1915–68) and how he too had struggled with a vocation to the celibate monastic life, especially in the light of (then) recently published journals which showed his intimate relationship with a woman known as M. What Merton's journals revealed to me at the time was what St Ignatius of Loyola would call 'indifference to all created things'. Merton, through his discernment of vocation began to understand that the most important thing for him as a human being and member of the Body of Christ was to find God in his own authentic self. This 'authentic self' was the key to vocation, as opposed to what he called at the time (contemporary with the Second Vatican Council) a 'false' or even (and shockingly) 'religious self'. What he meant by this was our strange desire as humans, as Christians, as Catholics, to do what we think we *ought to do* for some (usually imaginary) fictional entity. As a psychologist I would call this nowadays the 'superego' – that residue remaining from our parental upbringing which encourages guilt and 'drivenness' in our desires and actions.

How difficult it is for many of us to get some distance from this 'religious' or 'false' self. Indeed, it can become a demon driving us into false alleyways. I believe too that this can be one of the factors that blurs the spiritual perceptions of people when they consider their vocations in the building up of the Body of Christ. The drivenness of the false self may prompt initial moves into the seminary or religious life, but ultimately it will be a deceptive mirage that will lead to increased isolation, alienation or worse.

Vocation, then, I would define as the search for the true self – not some false, or even 'religious' self that is often a hangover from unresolved childhood parental complexes. Professor Price, in an earlier essay, suggested that the search for 'vocation' was not unlike the search for some 'small, furry beast'. I would go further and suggest that the word 'vocation' is not a denotative or informative word but a *performative* word. 'Vocation' in this sense thus becomes a way of describing a new 'point of view' which a person finds themselves adopting to the world and their lives. They will now 'see the world arite' in a way they did not before. This we can describe as the 'discernment of the true self', or, perhaps better, 'finding right relationship with the world'.

How then can we facilitate the discernment of this true self or help people to find their 'right relationship' with the world? This brings me back to my first remarks regarding the view *sub specie aeterni* – for, as believers we understand human anthropology as being essentially grounded in *transcendent* terms. True self identity can only be found when viewed *sub specie aeterni* in the light of faith and God's gentle presence.

I propose, then, to explore the nature of this encounter with the transcendent, especially by a young person, with the help of a foundational text of the Western psyche – the twelfth Century *Romance of the Grail* by Chrétien de Troyes.[3] Why this text? Beginning with Carl Jung and then following on through his students such as Marie-Louise von Franz, James Hillman and Robert Johnson, many twentieth-century psychologists saw the 'mythic' texts of Medieval Europe as offering a pre-modern insight into the Western psyche that underlies so many of our contemporary concerns. In this respect, I would see the contemporary 'search for the sacred' – of which the individual search for vocation is part – as a wider 'search for the Spirit' that haunts the Western mind from its inception in the High Middle Ages. If we study the text of the Grail-search carefully – and I propose here to concentrate on the call of the young Perceval, the 'pure-fool', to the transcendent Realm of the Grail – we have in microcosm a view of how the Western mind views the transcendent and clues as to how we can deal with the present 'crisis of vocation' within which we find ourselves. In this way we can develop another key theme of

---

[3]Chretien's song probably dates from the 1180s.

this book – the use of the imagination and its role in developing a theology of vocation. In this respect this chapter can be viewed as a 'thought experiment' to help us understand the dynamic of the encounter with the transcendent for the young person as well as drawing some (clinical) observations of how this process can inform the contemporary discernment of vocation.

The quest begins

Chrétien of Troyes begins his account of the Grail legend thus:

> It was in the season when trees flower, shrubs leaf, meadows grow green, and birds in their own tongue sing sweetly in the mornings, and everything is aflame with joy, that the son of the widow lady of the Waste Forest arose, effortlessly placed the saddle upon his hunter and, taking three javelins, left his mother's manor. (Chrétien: 62)

Now, as a psychotherapist, I know that beginnings are very important (as are endings). When the client comes in the room I look to see how they arrive: What are the features? What is their appearance? How do they enter? Likewise we can look at this medieval tale in the same way. How does it begin? Who is it about? Where does it happen?

Well, the first thing we notice is that it is the time of youth – the sap is rising, the birds are singing and all is full of promise and hope. This description of the Grail quest seems as good a description of the 'glad confident morn' of youth as we can hope to get. Everything, we are told, 'is aflame with joy'. This is the world of the young men and women who come to us seized with the vocation. Or at least it is the pool of life out of which the vocation director must fish.

What is the next thing we notice? Well, that our young hero has no name. He is simply described as 'the son of the widow lady of the Waste Forest'. The book of Chrétien is called the 'Song of the Grail', in its title the name of the hero is not included. Later we shall know him as Perceval or Parzifal (which means, literally 'pure fool') but at this stage in the story he has no name. This is significant as we shall see. Those who come to us seeking a vocation have at this stage of their lives no name . . .

Secondly, we need to note that this is the story of a boy not a girl. Our hero is a boy. Now, on one level we can just put this down to pre-modern prejudice. Yet, recent commentators such as Richard Rohr and Robert Johnson have seen in the story of the Grail a blueprint or, if you prefer, archetype, of the pattern of male spirituality (see Johnson, 1989 and Rohr, 1994). Whereas we must remain cognisant of the critiques of writers such as Nichola Slee, I think we must bear in mind that the legend has something to offer men in particular. However, having used the legend with groups and adapted it in my writings over the past few years, I think it has relevance for both men and women and make no apology for using it here to draw wider conclusions.

The third thing to note is that this is an ordinary boy. He is a simple boy. At this point the story of vocation is not that to a religious group or to the priesthood. The false sense of Merton's 'religious self' has not asserted itself yet. The boy has not been initiated into a particular religious elite. As mentioned above, in this context, I would like to suggest that the process of discovering vocation is the same for lay people, clergy and religious. In fact, I would go further to suggest that too often the word 'vocation' is used as shorthand for 'vocation to the priesthood'. What I will be discussing here are archetypal views of how the individual is encountered by the Transcendent and then works through that encounter. That, for me, is the theme of the *Song of the Grail*, and why it is of such help for our deliberations on vocation. From this I derive:

First lesson for the discernment of vocation

The fundamental question for the person discerning their vocation is that of St Benedict (and indeed the Psalmist):

> Is there anyone here who yearns for life and desires to see good days? (Rule of St Benedict, RB Prol.:15, see Ps. 33:13)

Essentially, seeking advice on vocation is seeking advice on how to live a fulfilled and happy life. The question of the Vocation Guide should not be 'what can you do for us?', but rather, 'what can we do for you?' Her/his role is to help someone to live a happy and fulfilled life, regardless of whether that life is lived out as a lay person, a member of the clergy or of a religious order. Abbot Christopher talks in this book of developing a 'culture of vocation' in the present day climate. This 'culture of vocation' should, I feel, embrace help to young Christians to explore how their authentic self is manifest in whatever role they adopt for the bringing about the Kingdom of God on earth. As well as priesthood, religious life and married life I contend that this should also include helping young people to discern vocations to be teachers, artists, healthcare workers or whatever role will bring 'life in its fullness' and fulfilment in the mystical Body of Christ.

The son of a widow lady

As we said above, the beginning of the adventure is significant. The next thing we discover about our hero is that he has no father. How interesting this is, and also how relevant to our situation in the United Kingdom in the early twenty-first century. Last August, I watched on a warm evening from the garden of a house in South London as buildings went up in flames caused by the notorious August 2011 riots. As I later watched these people being arrested on TV I kept finding myself saying, 'these children have no fathers', 'Where are the fathers?' On one level this should come as no surprise. In the 1950s and 1960s the British Object Relations theorist Donald Winnicott, made a fascinating link between delinquency and non-attachment to the parental figure (see Winnicott, 2000). I have often been struck by the prescience of Winnicott's thought (surely one of the greatest British psychologists of the twentieth century?). Richard Rohr has recently referred to this as the 'father wound' and cites the sad story of the prison chaplain who in her first week was overwhelmed by requests from the inmates for her to write Mothers' Day cards for them. As Fathers' day approached some months later she prepared herself with a big box of cards in readiness for their requests. To her surprise not one of the inmates approached her, for, as she realized later, they had no fathers. Daddy was absent. The father wound was deep, and in Rohr's words 'this was why they were in prison in the first place' (see Rohr, 2004).

We live now in the West in the era of the father wound. And this time I direct my comments directly to those looking at the vocation of men (I shall return to the vocation of women in more detail at the end) when I make my next observation:

Second lesson for the discernment of vocation

Discernment of vocation requires good role models.

The advances of feminism have been the most wonderful thing to behold as years of oppression of women begin to be lifted. However, as commentators such as Rohr and Bly point out, this has left a gap where the role of the man is involved. The young male does not have the immediate role models and sureties of a generation ago. What we are witnessing with our new generations are a flexibility towards gender and role.

We hear in the Grail legend that Perceval 'left his mother's manor'. This is shorthand for the most difficult journey all men must make – the journey from the 'mother's manor' to the 'father's manor'. This encompasses much of what the vocation journey is, for the man at least (and to a certain extent for the woman too). Traditionally this journey has been overseen by the tribe or society by initiation, work in the church, state or army. As Rohr points out (and I make no apology for referring frequently to his work – as any who have heard him talk will agree, he is one of the few contemporary Christian commentators who can talk directly to the hearts of the young and sees this aspect of the psycho-spiritual journey with peculiar clarity) we are the first human society to live without this process of male initiation – and look at the consequences! It is as though for human society to function successfully, the young male needs to be 'bested' or at least shown his place in the cosmic order before they can enter into full and satisfying adult life.[4] Let's see now how this happens to our young 'pure fool' . . .

---

[4] In a recent article (Rohr, 2012), Rohr points out how in the Gospels Christ usually calls men 'down' (Peter, Zacchaeus, James and John) and women 'up' (Mary Magdalen, The Woman with the Haemorrhage, The Woman Taken in Adultery).

The beautiful knights

Returning to our young hero, I'm afraid he still hasn't made much progress! What do we know so far? He is a motherless boy without a name. Where does he reside? Again, we have another key medieval trope for the life of the hero – he is from the 'Waste Forest'. Once more this should make our psychological antennae begin to twitch! The forest is the traditional manifestation of the unconscious, the unknown. Made more significant here by the use of the word 'waste'. We are reminded immediately of the 'desert places' that we have already heard about in this book, the realm of the earliest Christian contemplatives – the Desert Fathers and Mothers (see, for example Ward, 2012). Again, as any good scripture scholar will tell you, it is always from the least expected, most out-of-the-way places that salvation comes. The Grail legend is a little un-PC when it comes to its description of the boy by the knights he later encounters in the forest: he is dismissed as an uneducated Welshman – Wales, I'm afraid to say, being shorthand for the medieval writers for a backwards, uncultured place. As Robert Johnson puts it: 'Who would ever think of Wales as possibly providing an answer to our suffering?' (Johnson, 1989). But from the wasteplaces of Horeb, to the Empire fringe of Nazareth, and even from Pontypool or Aberystwyth, the unlikely places, in the outer world or the psychic world, are often or not the place where our healing comes from.

Returning to our story, our young hero heads off into the forest, as we have heard to attend to his mother's business, when all of a sudden he encounters something quite unexpected:

As soon as he entered the forest his heart leapt within his breast because the gentle weather and the songs he heard from the joyful birds; all these things brought pleasure. Because of the sweet calm weather he lifted the bridle from this hunter's head and let it wander along grazing through the fresh green grass. Being a skilled thrower he began to cast his javelins all around him: sometimes behind him, sometimes in front, sometimes low and sometimes high, until he heard five armed knights, in armour from head to toe coming through the woods . . . and when he beheld the green and vermilion glistening in the sunshine and the gold, the blue and the silver, he was captivated and astonished, and said: 'Lord God I give You thanks! These are angels I see before me.' (Chrétien 62)

The first thing to notice is that our young boy still has no name. In the coming encounter he will have his first discourse with representatives from an outer, more sophisticated world. This is the unformed unconscious slowly becoming aware of itself. Sometimes humorous, sometimes sad, the young boy will have to learn a new level of discourse. And this is the process of discerning vocation. For our young hero it will be a process of learning a name, which leads to my next lesson:

Third lesson for the discernment of vocation

The process of discerning a vocation is the process of learning our name. The role of the vocation director is to help a young person discover their name in God's eye.

This was beautifully illustrated in the BBC TV series 'The Monastery' when one of the young men was deeply moved by the request to pick up a stone with his name on. Just the act of naming was significant for him and echoed Isaiah's words 'that we are called by name' (Isa. 43). The young person approaches the Vocation Director, as it were, nameless before God. It will be the Director's job to help that person discern that name.

Back to our boy, we realize that he has set out now into the world, he has 'left his mother's mansion' and what does he find? Well, first that this is a world of pleasure: 'As soon as he entered the forest his heart leapt within his breast because the gentle weather and the songs he heard from the joyful birds; all these things brought pleasure'. And what pleasure we live in today! We live in a world fine-tuned to develop and assuage every minute aspect of pleasure from the moment we switch on our i-pods, i-phones or i-pads (always 'I' at the centre!). How do we react to this world in which we are trying to help young people discern the 'transcendent call'. I think a fatal mistake that has crept into Western theology over the past century or so is to make a false dichotomy between the life of the spirit and the life of pleasure. After Freud, psychology has realized that all thought and mental life is imbued with libido. When researching the twelfth century theological writings that are contemporary with the Grail legend for a recent book I was pleasantly surprised to see how balanced and sophisticated was the psycho-spiritual notions of pleasure deployed by these writers (see Tyler, 2011). A notion, I realized, that stretches throughout the medieval Latin west and finds wonderful expression in the sensual, libidinal writings of Ss Teresa of Avila and John of the Cross. From my study of those writings I draw out the:

Fourth lesson for the discernment of vocation

One of the key roles of vocation discernment today is to teach young people the 'education of desire'. Prayer, as writers such as Ronald Rolheiser have pointed out, has a key 'libidinal' aspect and only when we return to the sources of desire can we discern true vocation.[5]

Lets return, then, to our encounter in the woods . . .

The boy has met these unexpected knights. Who are they and what do they signify? Whenever a number appears in a medieval manuscript we know that it represents a code. The boy had taken out three lances from his mother – the three the symbol of the male telling us this will be a boy's journey to manhood. The boy's first encounter is with five knights – the symbol of perfection and the beyond. Four is the complete number, the number of the four elements, temperaments, Gospels etc. Five is the number beyond four – literally the quintessence. So, the boy is encountering the transcendent for the first time.

One of the main arguments of this chapter, and it is clear in the Perceval legend, is that at any early stage in our life we all have an encounter with 'the beyond' or 'the transcendent'. And this, I would suggest, is what brings young men and women to the Vocation Guide . . . if they are lucky.

As we can read from the Perceval legend, this encounter is literally crucial, and, if the person is not prepared or guided correctly through it, it can also be disastrous. Later, after a few chapters, Perceval will enter the Grail

---

[5]See, for example, Rolheiser, 2005.

Castle itself where, at a young tender age, he will be privileged to witness the mysteries of the Grail ceremony. However, the boy is ill-prepared. His own personal Vocation Director, the old knight Gurnemanz, has given him instruction but the boy fails to heed it. At the crucial moment, as we shall see, he fluffes it up. For many of our young people today, they have had no formation to prepare them for the encounter with the transcendent (this, we can take to usually happen in the late teens/early twenties). For anyone growing up in England in the 1960s and 1970s (and this would hold for many other parts of the world too), it would have been very difficult to avoid getting some sort of spiritual formation and education, even of the most rudimentary kind. As I have directed young people and worked with psychological disturbance over the past two decades I have noticed that a whole generation has now grown up in this country who have received little or no religious formation at all. My job as a spiritual director and retreat guide is often now as much catechetical as helping people discern the spirits: they need teaching about basic aspects of Christian doctrine and theology, nothing can be assumed in today's young people. Thus, when the inevitable encounter with the transcendent does occur – and occur it must – many young people today will have no conceptual framework with which to make sense of it. It may appear weird, an irrelevance, or indeed a mental pathology or psychosis. Like Perceval, they will stumble into the transcendent 'Grail Castle' totally unprepared. That is not to say psychosis etc. doesn't occur, just to say that much of what is in fact a spiritual emergence is too quickly pathologized as a 'spiritual emergency' (see Grof, 1989). Thus, a key argument of this chapter is that the role of Vocation Guides in today's Western world is to help educate young people to discern this encounter with the transcendent and to help steer them through it. Unless this recognition is made and articulated (which was done so well in the 'Monastery' film) there can be no progress in helping young people discern their vocations at this moment of time of widespread spiritual illiteracy.[6]

---

[6]I say, 'in the West', because on recent visits to India I have been struck by how seriously the religious quest is still taken by its young people. Attending the junior seminaries in Bangalore and Kerala I was amazed at the serried ranks of young people who were discerning the spiritual quest in their lives at a very deep level.

Returning to our young hero, we can learn a lot about how we manage this encounter with a spiritually untutored young person and what lessons we can take from it. When faced with the five knights, Perceval's first reaction is to think they are devils and to want to make the sign of the cross or throw lances at them to protect himself: 'these devils are more frightening than anything else in the world!' The knights are not the transcendent itself – Perceval will encounter that later in the Grail Castle – but rather they are its *representatives* – which leads us to our next lesson:

Fifth lesson for the discernment of vocation

For many young people the encounter with a Vocation Guide will be their first real acknowledgement of the realm of the Transcendent. How these guides act and deport themselves can make a crucial difference to how the young person perceives their vocation.

Rudolf Otto writing in the *Idea of the Holy* (1917) described one of the key attributes of the divine as the *fascinans* (the others are the *tremendum* and *numen*). Like Perceval seeing the glorious knights there remains in us all, as human beings, a fascination, an allure of the transcendent. It may be masked or perverted by gross consumerism into strange twisted ends, but at the end of the day the *fascinans* for the transcendent remains. Which gives rise to our sixth lesson:

Sixth lesson for the discernment of vocation

The spiritual seeker will project all their transcendental aspirations onto the Vocation Guide – for good or ill. This is what we can term the 'spiritual transference'. Likewise, the Guide will inevitably respond with what we can call the 'spiritual countertransference'. Aspects of the Guide's own journey and seeking will be evoked and they may come to embody aspects of the seeker's own journey that have been lost, for example, the wise old man, the hermit etc.

From a psychological point of view it is helpful for Vocation Guides to be aware that they are part of a wider 'archetypal' realm and their very presence will evoke this realm in the seeker. The feelings evoked in the guide will often be a clear window into how the Holy Spirit is operating in the seeker's life.

In this context we come to our:

Seventh lesson for the discernment of vocation

Discerning a vocation in a young person is a humbling business. To be the most help to young people we must often put aside our theological assumptions and sophistications. The self must be unlearnt as we allow the Holy Spirit to flow uninterrupted in a young person's life: in the words of Meister Eckhart, 'God's in, I'm out' (see Smith, 1987).

Space does not permit us to go through the whole Grail legend here. However, before we finish with some concluding reflections, it is necessary to describe that crucial encounter Perceval has with the transcendent to which I referred earlier – the entry into the Grail Castle. As I have said already, the young man is tutored by his mentor and enters the Castle, almost by chance stumbling upon it, but once there he 'fluffes it up'. This says much about the nature of the encounter with the transcendent for the young person in their teens/early twenties. Most of us, I'm afraid, fluff it up. It is too much. Even with a religious formation such as was available some years ago, most of us are not prepared for what we encounter when we enter the Realm of the Grail: its sheer beauty is astonishing and perplexing. As Robert Johnson writes:

> The most important event of one's inner life is portrayed in the story of the Grail castle. Every youth blunders his or her way into the Grail castle sometime around age 15 or 16 and has a vision that shapes much of the rest of their life. Like Parsifal, they are unprepared for this and do not have the possession to ask the question that would make the experience conscious and stable within them. (Johnson, 1989: 47)

In the ancient legend, the boy fails to ask the crucial question, 'Whom does the Grail serve?', this is the question which will not only heal the boy but the whole court, including the Grail guardian himself – the Fisher King – said to have been wounded as a young man when he first encountered the Grail. This 'Fisher King Wound' is a Holy or Sacred Wound and is so easily inflicted if our first encounter with the transcendental is botched or disrupted.[7] If not handled correctly the wound can last for decades afterwards, curdling someone's appreciation of religion – and ultimately life itself. Perceval himself will spend 20 years after his botched encounter with the Grail, struggling and wandering – trying to find the Castle again but never finding it. Then, all of a sudden, when least expecting it, the Castle appears again in mid life. This may be another opportunity for a Grail encounter but one beyond my brief in this chapter.[8]

Our encounter with the transcendent world as young people is unexpected, unbidden and overwhelming. Nothing can prepare us for it and very little can hold the experience. However, in this respect, we conclude with:

Eighth and last lesson for the discernment of vocation

The key task of the Vocation Guide is to hold, recognize and validate the young person's encounter with the Transcendent Other.

The Guide must be there to make the young person's Transcendent Encounter conscious and stable and help the young person articulate its significance for them. Often this will take the form of helping them form the question: *Whom does the Encounter serve?* (which is the real meaning of the Grail Encounter).

When we look back at our own journeys in our vocations how many of us, I wonder, owe where we are and who we are today to the wise and benevolent guidance of our own 'Gurnemanz'. Therefore, I think it is important for each of us to ask ourselves the question: 'What helped us at this stage in our quest? How did this person inspire me? In what way were they my role model? And, how did they nurture and stabilize the vocation that God was speaking in my life at that time?'

---

[7] I have spoken more about this in the context of the theology of St John of the Cross in Tyler 2010.
[8] For more on this, see my article in the *Pastoral Review* 'Becoming Adult' Tyler, 2008.

If we ask these questions then I think we will go a long way to helping the confused seekers under our charge who have inadvertently stumbled into the Realm of the Grail.

Conclusion

I would like to conclude by summarizing the eight lessons for the Discernment of Vocation discussed in this chapter:

1   Vocation is 'about living life to the full' and finding our place in the 'Mystical Body of Christ'.

2   Vocation evolves through interaction with Positive Role Models.

3   The process of discerning vocation is about discovering our name.

4   The source of vocation is close to the sources and education of desire.

5   Vocation guides are 'archetypal' in that they represent the wider transcendent realm.

6   The interaction of the Guide and Seeker will evoke many levels of psychological transference and countertransference.

7   Humility, and learning to serve God, is at the heart of the discernment of vocation.

8   Discovering vocation is about articulating and stabilizing our fleeting, and earth-shattering, encounter with the Transcendent.

I would like to end with one final aspect of the Legend that I have mentioned. Namely, that the keeper of the Grail Castle himself is sick and wounded. We are the keepers of the Grail Castle and, like the Fisher King, we are sick and wounded. The churches of the developed world lie in crisis: the child abuse scandal, growing materialism, disillusionment. All of them have contributed to a malaise in the Grail realm. In the legend it is from an unexpected source that the healing will come. The renewal comes 'from Wales', the neglected part of the realm, where we least expect – the realm of the Pure Fool. We await this healing source, knowing in faith that it will surely come.

Bibliography

Apostolicam Actuositatem, is accessible on www.vatican.va/archive/hist_councils/ ii_vatican_council/documents/vat-ii_decree_19651118_apostolicam-actuositatem_en.html.

Chrétien de Troyes, 'The Story of the Grail (Perceval)', in *Arthurian Romances* (trans. W. Kibler; London: Penguin, 2004).

Grof, S. and C., *Spiritual Emergency: When Personal Transformation Becomes a Crisis* (New York, NY: Tarcher, 1989).

Johnson, R., *He: Understanding Masculine Psychology* (New York, NY: Harper, 1989).

Otto, R., *The Idea of the Holy* (Oxford: Oxford University Press, 1923 [1917]).

Rohr, Richard, *Quest for the Grail* (New York, NY: Crossroad, 1994).

—*Adam's Return* (New York, NY: Crossroad, 2004), pp. 338–46.

—'Men and Spirituality', in *The Bloomsbury Guide to Christian Spirituality* (eds P. Tyler and R. Woods; London: Bloomsbury, 2012).

Rolheiser, R., *Forgotten Among the Lilies – Learning to Love Beyond our Fears* (New York, NY: Galilee/Doubleday, 2005).

Rule of St Benedict, (trans. T. Fry; Collegeville, MI: The Liturgical Press, RB 1980).

Smith, Cyprian O.S.B, *The Way of Paradox: Spiritual Life as Taught by Meister Eckhart* (New York, NY: Paulist Press, 1987).

Tyler, P. M., 'Thomas Merton: Ikon of Commitment for the Postmodern Generation', *The Way Supplement: The Postmodern Generation*, 98, 2000.

—'Becoming Adult: Reflections on the English and Welsh Catholic Bishops' Document 'The Priority of Adult Formation', *The Pastoral Review*, vol 4:2, March/April 2008.

—*St John of the Cross* (London: Continuum, 2010).

—*The Return to the Mystical: Ludwig Wittgenstein, Teresa of Avila and the Christian Mystical Tradition* (London: Continuum, 2011).

Ward, B., 'The Spirituality of the Desert Fathers and Mothers', in *The Bloomsbury Guide to Christian Spirituality* (eds P. Tyler and R. Woods; London: Bloomsbury, 2012).

Winnicott, D., *Deprivation and Delinquency* (Hove: Brunner-Routledge, 2000).

Wittgenstein, L., *Tractatus Logico-Philosophicus* (trans. D. Pears and B. McGuinness; London: Routledge, 1921 [2001]).

—*Lectures and Conversations on Aesthetics, Psychology and Religious Belief* (ed. C. Barrett; Oxford: Blackwell, 1989).

12

A culture of vocation

Fr Christopher Jamison

Catholic culture in twentieth-century Britain

In a not wholly mythic golden era, every Catholic boy and every Catholic girl
would at some stage of their education consider becoming a priest or a nun.
Such thoughts emerged as part of what could be called the totally Catholic
culture. In the totally Catholic culture, a young person's life was often completely defined by the life of the Church: born into a Catholic family, everything from school during the week, to the sports team on Saturday and the
youth club in the evenings could be a Church run institution, culminating
in Mass on Sunday. In Britain, the 1944 Education Act greatly strengthened
Catholic culture by providing state funding for religious schools, so enabling
every Catholic child to attend a Catholic school free of charge. Within such
a rich cultural experience, many boys and girls would experience the call of
Christ as a call to ministry within this great tradition. If they did not enter a
seminary or a religious house, then, in the language of the time, they didn't
have a vocation and usually proceeded towards marriage. The dominant
theology of vocation was Thomist, with the Ignatian tradition less widely
expressed.

While many elements of this Catholic culture continue to flourish, they no
longer interlock in the same way and they have ceased to constitute a Catholic

young person's whole world; the all embracing nature of the totally Catholic culture has disappeared along with many other all embracing cultures. The general disappearance of all such total cultures will be the starting point for the second part of this paper. For the moment, however, let's simply note that the totally Catholic culture began to disappear in Britain in the 1960s and had disappeared in most places by the end of the 1980s. Mass attendance figures for England and Wales are only available from 1989 onwards but in 1980 it was estimated that 2 million attended Catholic Sunday Mass; by 1990 it was 1.5 million and by 2000 attendance had declined to 1 million. So one outward sign of the disappearance of the totally Catholic culture was the halving of the number of those attending Sunday Mass between 1980 and 2000. During that period of declining Mass attendance, the population of England and Wales rose from 49 million in 1980 to 52 million in 2000 (source: Office for National Statistics) so a shrinking population was not the reason for declining numbers on Sunday. Since 2000, the national population has continued to grow while in that same period Mass attendance figures have remained steady at around 1 million.

In the totally Catholic culture, priesthood and religious life were the only real vocations. In essence, the totally Catholic culture contained a sub-culture of recruitment to priesthood and the religious life. This sub-culture recruited the best of Catholic youth to the best vocations. As Catholic culture declined so did vocations, because the sub-culture of recruitment relied on the totally Catholic culture. Each required the other. To illustrate this, let's take seminary entrants as a barometer. The number of those entering English seminaries declined from approximately 150 a year in 1980 to fewer than 100 by 1990 and fell below 50 in 2000, hitting just 22 entrants in 2001 (source: National Office for Vocation). So in the 20 years when Sunday Mass attendance halved (1980–2000), seminary entrants declined by two-thirds. The sub-culture of recruitment had died along with the totally Catholic culture.

Then in the twenty-first century the statistics showed an unexpected change. Between 2001 and 2010, while Mass attendance remained steady in the midst of a rising population, the number of men entering seminary rose from 22 to 56. A new approach to vocation had begun to emerge, one that took seriously the challenge of creating a culture of vocation.

What is a culture of vocation?

The phrase 'a culture of vocation' is a modern one and it first appeared in Blessed John Paul II's message for Vocations Sunday in April 1993. It received a more considered treatment with the Congress on Vocations to the Priesthood and to Consecrated Life in Europe that the Pope summoned in 1997. The final document of the Congress, entitled *NEW VOCATIONS FOR A NEW EUROPE: In Verbo tuo* (hereafter IVT) is focussed around the culture of vocation.

The vocational culture of which the document speaks is something new. Blessed John Paul asked the Congress to promote a '*new vocational culture in young people and families*'. What is new about this vocational culture is precisely that it exists in a Europe that no longer shares the Christian faith as normative, a Europe where the totally Catholic culture no longer exists. The effects of this cultural situation as it affects young people are described as follows in one of the concluding propositions of the Congress:

> A pluralistic and complex culture tends to produce young people possessing an incomplete and weak identity with consequent chronic indecision in the face of vocational choices. In addition, many young people do not possess the "elementary grammar" of existence, they are nomads: they move around without stopping either at the geographical, affective, cultural, or religious level; they are "trying out"! In the midst of such a great quantity and diversity of information, but with so little formation, they appear lost, with few points of reference.[1] Given this confusing situation, IVT recognises that 'the ability even to plan one's life is weakened.[2]

This is the context in which the culture of vocation comes into being. So *In Verbo Tuo* constantly affirms the task not of recruitment but of spreading the belief that life is vocation: 'there exists a specific vocation for every living

---

[1]IVT 10c.
[2]IVT 11a.

person . . . connected to the simple fact of existing.[3] For this reason the culture of vocation 'is a component of the new evangelisation.'[4] Each person's specific vocation is an expression of the general vocation of humanity described as follows by Blessed John Paul: 'Creating the human race in his own image and continually keeping it in being, God inscribed in the humanity of man and woman the vocation . . . of love and communion. Love is the fundamental and innate vocation of every human being.'[5] So to create a culture of vocation is to evangelize with the message that life has a purpose and that this purpose is to love.

The setting of the culture of vocation is therefore the polar opposite of the totally Catholic culture. While the totally Catholic culture reinforced Catholic teachings daily, the setting of the culture of vocation is one where basic Christian truths are rarely expressed. The primary task of the culture of vocation is simply to tell people that, as Pope Benedict put it, 'we were made for love.'[6] So the first element of the culture of vocation can be described as follows: the culture of vocation is the process by which the Church communicates the truth that all people are made by God for the purpose of expressing love in a specific way.

The second element of the definition is related to this, namely, that everybody has a vocation. This simple statement is now taken for granted but it demands careful consideration. While the basic Christian calling has always been the call to baptism and the Christian life, nevertheless, the word 'vocation' came to be used exclusively to refer to the call to the religious life and the priesthood. The process of undoing this use of 'vocation' as referring only to ecclesiastical callings was originally a work of the Protestant Reformation. The Reformers objected to the religious life per se and they changed the theology of the priesthood, as described by David Hoyle's essay[7]; however, having deconstructed the medieval language of vocation, the Reformers still wanted to speak about vocation but to what could they now attach the label 'vocation?' Many of them identified a person's vocation with their work. Calvin, for example, wrote

---

[3]IVT 13a.
[4]IVT 13b.
[5]*Familiaris consortio.* quoted in IVT 16c.
[6]Message to the Youth of Britain September 2010.
[7]See p. 99.

'men were created for the express purpose of being employed in labour of various kinds and . . . no sacrifice is more pleasing to God than when every man applies himself diligently to his own calling.'[8] Calling here clearly means labour and so, in the opinion of some commentators, this shift in vocational theology is the basis of the Protestant work ethic. In Britain, this attitude still influences the secular use of the term vocation as seen in the expression 'vocational qualifications' meaning those courses of study that lead directly into work in contrast to 'academic qualifications'. Confusingly, vocational qualifications is a term applied only to lower paid jobs such as carpentry or catering (both of which incidentally have the example of Our Lord's own work as paradigms) but not to higher paid jobs; nobody refers to the qualifications needed to become a lawyer as 'vocational'. Having said that, the word 'vocation' on its own is often applied to certain jobs such as teaching or medicine both of which require academic qualifications. These jobs are seen as rendering a particularly direct service to humanity and, in a former era, for less reward than those with academic qualifications might expect in the commercial world. So a latent Protestant attitude to vocation dominates the use of the terms vocation and vocational in Britain today but in a very confused and unhelpful way.

So if the Catholic Church today affirms the belief that everybody has a vocation, has it simply bought into the Protestant theology that sees a person's work as their vocation? The answer is an emphatic no. Perhaps the most important point to remember about vocation is that it is a metaphor for how God changes a person's understanding of their place in the world. A job, for example, is usually a necessity not a vocation; it becomes a vocation if it is seen as part of God calling a person to life in Christ. So some saints have made cleaning floors part of their vocation while some teachers have never discovered how teaching can become a vocation. As Bl John Paul II puts it in *Laborem Exercens* 'By enduring the toil of work in union with Christ crucified for us, man in a way collaborates with the Son of God for the redemption of humanity. He shows himself a true disciple of Christ by carrying the cross in his turn every day in the activity that he is called upon to perform.'[9] When life in Christ is seen the

---

[8]From *A Commentary on the Harmony of the Evangelists* (trans. McNeill, 1960, p. 142).
[9]*Laborem Exercens*, p. 27.

ultimate goal, a person's whole life becomes a response to a vocation. So the Catholic theology of vocation includes work as part of somebody's vocation but work in itself is not a vocation.

The Catholic tradition has evolved a theology of states of life as more fundamental to vocation than work. The four states of life are: priesthood, religious life, marriage and dedicated single life. The Catholic Reform took up the Protestant challenge in two ways: not only by affirming the superiority of the religious life at the Council of Trent[10] but also by affirming the dignity of different clerical and lay states of life in writings such as those quoted in Geoffrey Scott's note.[11]

In contemporary Catholic theology, the Dogmatic Constitution on the Church *Lumen Gentium* expresses this dogmatically: 'the laity, by their very vocation (*vocatione propria*) seek the kingdom of God by engaging in temporal affairs and by ordering them according to the plan of God'.[12] In that simple Latin phrase *vocatione propria* is a whole theology of the vocation of the lay person.

So the statement that 'everybody has a vocation' can be interpreted in two distinct ways: both ways agree that all share in the basic baptismal call to holiness in the Christian life but beyond that, the Reformed tradition sees just one further step, namely work, while the Catholic tradition sees several states of life as well as work. It's worth noting that work here has a broad interpretation. *In verbo tuo* has this description of the new work needed in the new Europe to express what it calls 'new models of holiness'; we need 'people *capable of cultural dialogue and of "cultural charity"*, for the transmission of the Christian message by means of the languages of our society; *professionals and simple people* who are capable of imprinting on their civil life and on their working relationships and friendships the transparency of the truth and the intensity of Christian charity'.[13]

So the second element in the Catholic definition of the culture of vocation is that those whom God calls to baptism are called to holiness in the Christian life as expressed in a state of life and in work.

---

[10]*Doctrina de Sacramento Matrimonii* canon 10 1563.
[11]See p. 112.
[12]*Lumen Gentium*, p. 31.
[13]IVT 12 b.

The third and final element in the definition is the recognition that vocational ministry is integral to the Church's life and not an additional extra. 'All pastoral work, and especially that with young people, is intrinsically vocational . . . pastoral work, from its beginnings and by its very nature, is orientated towards vocational discernment. This is a service offered to every person, so that they might discover the way towards the realisation of a life project as God wants it, according to the needs of the Church and the world of today'.[14]

Putting together the three elements, we have a working definition of the culture of vocation as follows: the Catholic Church affirms that God has made every individual with a purpose and seeks to accompany all people to help them express their fundamental human vocation to love. Those Christ invites to baptism are each called to holiness in a distinctive way, through their state of life and their work. Each Christian community has a duty to help people find their vocation and to live it out, so creating a culture of vocation at the service of the Church and society.

How can a culture of vocation find expression today? A case study of England and Wales

a) Youth culture

The development of the culture of vocation in England and Wales today takes as its starting point the current reality of both nations, especially the youth culture. So this section will concentrate on the culture of the group known as Generation Y, those born in the last 20 years of the twentieth century, now in their teens and twenties. The most impressive analysis of their culture from a Christian perspective is based on two research projects commissioned by the Church of England, 'Making Sense of Generation Y'[15] and 'The Faith of Generation Y'.[16] This research notes that in the post-modern world, no single

---

[14]IVT 26a.
[15]'Making Sense of Generation Y' (2006) by Savage et al.
[16]'The Faith of Generation Y' (2010) by Mayo-Collins et al.

cultural narrative holds the attention of the young. We see that it was not only the totally Catholic or Christian culture that collapsed. This generation's upbringing has been marked by two key events: by the death of one destructive global ideal, the collapse of Soviet Communism in 1989 and by the birth of another deadly global ideal, 9/11's terrorism in the name of God. This generation is suspicious of all big narratives be they political, economic or religious. But this lack of a big narrative can mislead an older generation into thinking that Gen Y is just egocentric and has no vision beyond the small one of fulfilling their own needs. The research suggests that Gen Y has created a narrative that is neither big nor small, a 'midi narrative' as the researchers call it. This narrative is focussed around the friendship group, a group that may also include some family members (siblings, for example). In itself, a group of friends is clearly a part of every generation's experience. It is the surrounding narrative that makes the current youth version of it both distinctive and potentially destructive. Or rather, it's the absence of any wider narrative that is the problem. The small group of close friends and immediate family now bears the whole weight of a young person's meaning; no other groups have any continuing role. The individual only has a duty to their friends and family; the wider picture of life is celebrated on the weekends when groups of friends meet up in large crowds with similar but anonymous groups at clubs and festivals. The clubbing culture can be described as the 'High Mass' of youth culture, the new weekend ritual. The world of my friends (and the celebration of our world in larger cultural events) is meaningful just as it is and there is no need to imagine any deep or ultimate significance. This midi narrative consciously excludes political, philosophical or religious visions, seeing in them sources of global misery, with such catch phrases as: politicians are in it for themselves, religions cause wars etc. However, it's worth noting that the global rock music industry and international sport provide some universal points of reference.

Alongside this social narrative is a scientific narrative that leads to what the American writer Marilynne Robinson calls the 'absence of mind'.[17] People today tend to think that human beings are genetically programmed, psychologically disposed and economically required to behave in certain ways. On

---

[17] *Absence of Mind* by Marilynne Robinson (2010).

this view, people are selfish genes in pursuit of a mate who work only for personal gain. Such half-understood pseudo-science convinces many people that they are not truly free. When combined with a commitment to the all embracing power of the friendship group, this is a closed and determinist narrative that is hard to penetrate.

Yet there is also a paradox within Gen Y's narrative. While superficial readings of evolutionary science and psychology can lead the young to doubt whether they are really free, day to day, young people insist on being left free to make up their own minds and resist coercion. Robinson's 'absence of mind' does not have the last word. Gen Y values freedom above all else. So a good place to begin building the culture of vocation is young people's desire to make free choices about the conduct of their lives.

b) Vocational culture

The recruitment sub-culture described earlier threatens a young person's freedom by putting pressure on people to sign up; there is evidence that the young with some sense of religious vocation still fear being press ganged by vocations directors. For example, Br Robert Verrill OP explains his vocational quest in 2005 as follows: 'Although my feelings on religious life were still fairly ambiguous . . . I felt I really needed to talk to someone, but I had no idea who to turn to. I didn't want to speak to my parish priest. I felt that if I spoke to him, the next thing I'd know, I'd be before the bishop being asked to sign on the dotted line'.[18]

So the culture of vocation that replaces the recruitment sub-culture must very explicitly respect a person's freedom. The culture of vocation must be about discernment not recruitment. Discernment is an offer of assistance to help people discover their path in life and so it's starting point recognizes a person's freedom. Some may ask at this point if this means abandoning the promotion of the specific vocations to the priesthood and religious life. The answer is definitely no; but this shift does mean abandoning vocations ministry as solely about recruitment of priests and religious in favour of the wider

---

[18]See www.compass-points.org.uk 'Experiences'.

work of discernment for all. IVT expresses this quite clearly: 'In fact, the short-age of specific vocations – vocations in the plural – is above all an absence of the vocational consciousness of life – vocation in the singular –, or rather the absence of a culture of vocation'.[19] To put it crudely, if you want more priests and religious nowadays, you have to help everybody find their vocation.

IVT explains the elements involved in discernment: 'vocational discern-ment happens in the course of precise communitarian journeys: liturgy and prayer; ecclesial communion; the service of charity; the experience of receiv-ing the love of God and offering it in witness. Thanks to these, in the com-munity described in Acts, "the number of the disciples multiplied greatly in Jerusalem"'.[20] These elements are all communitarian and yet they 'promote and accompany the vocational journey of each believer. A personal and commu-nitarian experience, systematic and committed in these directions, could and should help the individual believer to discover the vocational call'.

These four elements of prayer, communion, charity and witness provide a valuable template for those wishing to build a ministry of discernment. 'In synthesis, we can say that, in the dimensions of liturgy, ecclesial communion, service of charity and witness to the Gospel, the existential condition of every believer is condensed. This is his dignity and his fundamental vocation, but it is also the condition that allows each one to discover his own particular identity'.[21] This connection between community and individual discernment lies at the heart of the culture of vocation. Without the proactive support of the local community, young people today will find it hard to discover their particular identity. This is not communal discernment but it is personal dis-cernment made possible by the community of the Church.

Of course, any young person can participate in these elements of church life, but in order for this participation to be part of a vocational culture, the elements need to be brought together in the person's life by an explicitly voca-tional agenda. The four elements become vocational when the local church offers to help the young person to use them as vocational tools. Research

---

[19] IVT 13 B.
[20] *Acts* 6:7 quoted in IVT 27.
[21] IVT 28.

commissioned by the Catholic Youth Ministry Federation (CYMFed) in 2009[22] shows that only a small number of those who self-identify as Catholic are actively engaged in all four elements that make up the vocational journey. When this reality is fully understood, then vocations ministry is seen to be part of the New Evangelization, awakening the fullness of faith in culturally Catholic communities. The CYMFed research maps out the terrain that the culture of vocation needs to cover in order to do this.

c) Vocational culture in practice

The culture of vocation has already begun to take root in this country and there are several different types of community based discernment currently offered by the Catholic community in England. The common elements are, more or less, those four described by IVT with the explicitly vocational agenda is added by leadership from experienced priests and religious.

There are two distinguishing criteria. First, the amount of basic catechesis in a group will vary as many young people today seek a deeper understanding of Catholic identity, the essential prelude to discerning a vocation. The other differentiating element is the geography and timescale of the different discernment opportunities. The location and time involved varies on a spectrum from a city based occasional evening drop in to a year long process in a residential retreat centre in the countryside. Let's now consider examples along this spectrum.

TYPE 1: DROP IN GROUP. Example: In some dioceses, the diocesan vocations director and a religious sister welcome people to drop in one evening a month for a talk and prayer around the theme of vocation. Participants are free to come and go as they wish.

TYPE 2: LOCAL GROUP (catechesis): Example: In some parishes, there is a vocations group for young people who are still in full-time college or university education. The group meets about once a month for the celebration of Mass followed by a talk and a meal together. There is an emphasis on catechesis and spiritual formation of members as the basis for vocational discernment.

---

[22]See www.cymfed.org *Mapping the Terrain* in Resources section.

TYPE 3: LOCAL GROUP (lectio divina): Example: Cardinal Martini began Samuel Groups in Milan in 1989. Participants take time to listen to God and to His Word speaking to their life. They commit to attending monthly meetings with the group for a year and to meeting individually with a spiritual guide. There is now a network of English/Welsh Samuel Groups.

TYPE 4: RESIDENTIAL GROUP. Example: A group of religious congregations run a programme that involves staying at a retreat centre for one weekend a month for nine months and for Holy Week. The programme involves communal living, the Prayer of the Church and catechesis on poverty, chastity and obedience.

To this list can be added groups for men considering the priesthood, of which there are a growing number. For some men they fulfil the same role as the above groups and they are now paralleled by groups for women explicitly discerning the religious life. In addition, experience shows that certain kinds of pastoral activity are a fruitful field of vocational discernment; for example, gap year schemes of work in Church sponsored youth centres and missions at home and abroad. This typology of discernment is not claiming to describe the only kinds of vocational ministry but rather the main outlines of new initiatives that have grown up in the twenty-first century. Any such typology is never watertight and there are variations around these four types but they are a helpful guide to what has been happening in this country in the last ten years. Their emergence has not been coordinated and shows a spontaneous response to the call for a new culture of vocation that began in the pontificate of Blessed John Paul II.

d) The national vocations framework

In April 2012, the Bishops' Conference of England and Wales endorsed the National Vocations Framework, sub-titled 'Helping People Discover Discipleship'. This Framework seeks to take to a new level the culture of vocation that has been developing in recent years. The purpose of this project is to help people answer the question that Pope Benedict posed to the young people of this country at Twickenham in September 2010: 'what kind of person would you really like to be?' It's striking that the Pope posed this question in such humane terms. He could have said: what kind of person is Christ calling you to be? Chalcedonian faith tells us that the two questions are two sides of the same coin. To ask young people this question in this way, what kind of person would you really like to be?, is to situate the vocational question as both part of the New Evangelization. To un-churched young people, the question is a challenge to believe that there is a God who has created them with a purpose. This is the culture of vocation as evangelization; through this deep shift in vocations ministry, 'vocation lies at the heart of the new evangelisation'.[23] To the young who are more or less active in the Church, this question is a challenge to enter more deeply into the four elements of the Church's life outlined above, believing that in this way they will find their vocation.

To enable the Church to help people answer Pope Benedict's question, the Framework proposes three aims. Local church communities are invited to understand vocation, to communicate vocation and to discern vocation, with a series of specific objectives as ways of achieving these aims. Within these broad aims, the objective of proposing by word and example the specific vocations of priesthood and religious life finds a natural place. Creating the wider vocational context is the challenge.

Returning to the analysis of contemporary youth culture, young people's concern for freedom is the starting point for a culture of vocation and *discernment* enhances that freedom. The expression of discernment through discernment *groups* plays into that other key aspect of youth culture, the friendship group. Discernment groups provide friendship groups that break open the midi narrative of contemporary culture and offer a wider, deeper vision of life. In this way, discernment groups offer evangelization, catechesis and discernment, the particular emphasis of each group being determined by the starting point of the participants.

e) The future

Looking ahead, the emerging culture of vocation in this country faces several challenges. First, this essay has emphasized the communitarian dimension of

---

[23]Archbishop Rino Fisichella, President of the Pontifical Council for the New Evangelisation, address to European Vocations Service, Horn, Austria, June 2011.

both contemporary culture and vocational culture. However, alongside this there is a need for individual guidance; some discernment groups ask the participants to meet regularly with a spiritual director. Importantly, the spiritual director should not be the leader of the group, to avoid the personality of the leader dominating the participant and to avoid conflicts regarding confidentiality. There is a shortage of people able to undertake this role and, as part of the National Framework, steps are being taken to create a network of trained vocation guides.

Another challenge is to avoid one or other of the four elements of the communitarian process being emphasized to the exclusion of the others. Different groups within the Church can tend towards this, almost without realizing what they are doing. For example, service of the poor on its own does not enable vocational discernment nor does Eucharistic adoration on its own. Rather such elements are necessary parts of a wider vocational process.

The next challenge is facing Catholic schools in this country. The challenge they face is to make the mainstream curriculum, not just RE and assemblies, part of the culture of vocation. The whole curriculum needs to be a response to the question: what kind of person would you really like to be. This is a separate topic in its own right and is currently the subject of much research.[24] The school curriculum raises the question of readiness to enter the labour market and so the future of work is the final challenge facing the culture of vocation.

In this age of austerity that began in Europe several years ago and that shows little sign of abating, the work dimension of a person's vocation takes on a new urgency. Without falling into a Calvinist identification of work and vocation, the Catholic community has to recognize that finding work is a high priority for both Catholics and other fellow citizens; if work is part of a person's vocation, what will the vocational culture look like in an age of austerity? If I look over the horizon into unknown vocational territory, I see the culture of vocation having two strands. The first strand offers people support to deepen their baptismal calling and to discover how to express that in the fundamental choice of a state of life. The second strand helps people find work that suits

---

[24]See *International Studies in Catholic Education* March 2013 for a full treatment, including my essay on vocation at the centre of a Catholic curriculum.

their state of life and continues to help them discern how their work can be part of their Christian vocation. Youth unemployment is a terrible scourge for any society and is at disturbingly high levels in Britain and throughout Europe. Somehow, the culture of vocation needs to recognize this context. Vocation already lies at the heart of the New Evangelization and perhaps in time it will come to redefine the church's work for justice, expressing justice as helping the unemployed and the poor to live out their vocation.

Conclusion

The focus of this essay is vocation work with the young because to grow a culture of vocation today involves making a preferential option for the young. To achieve this the Church needs inter-generational witnesses, older people, married and celibate, ordained and lay, who will consciously seek to hand on their vocation to younger people. They will hand it on not only by word but above all by example. In turn, they will recognize that the next generation will make vocations their own in ways that may perplex their elders. Just as the needs of the Church and the world change, so too do people's religious aspirations. The culture of vocation which the Church is called upon to create is a Christ centred meeting place for the world's deepest needs and people's deepest desires.

Index

Note: Locators followed by 'n' denotes notes.